SEXUAL ASSAULT AND ABUSE

SEXUAL ASSAULT AND ABUSE

A Handbook for Clergy and Religious Professionals

Edited by

Mary D. Pellauer
Barbara Chester
Jane A. Boyajian

1817

Harper & Row, Publishers, San Francisco

Cambridge, Hagerstown, New York, Philadelphia, Washington
London, Mexico City, São Paulo, Singapore, Sydney

Grateful acknowledgement is made to the following publishers and authors for permission to reprint: Gail Burress, Amelie Ratliff, and Liz Schellberg, "Psalm 137: An Interpretation," first appeared in *Theological Perspectives on Violence against Women* by the participants in Seminary Quarter at Grailville, Summer, 1978, The Grail, Loveland, Ohio. Also available in *Image-Breaking, Image-Building*, edited by Linda Clark, Marian Ronan, and Eleanor Walker, Pilgrim Press, 1981. Reprinted with permission of Pilgrim Press and The Grail. Marie Fortune, "Confidentiality and Mandatory Reporting: A Clergy Dilemma," first appeared in *Working Together to Prevent Sexual and Domestic Violence*. With Judith Hertze, "A Commentary on Religious Issues in Family Violence," from *Family Violence: A Workshop Manual for Clergy and Other Services Providers*, by Marie Fortune and Denise Hormann. Reprinted with permission of Marie M. Fortune. Ellen Goodman, "If She Says No, It's Rape." Copyright ©, 1984, Washington Post Writer's Group, reprinted with permission. Martha Janssen, "Don't Tell Mother," first appeared in *The Lutheran*, November 3, 1982. Copyright © 1982, *The Lutheran*. Used by permission of *The Lutheran* and Martha Janssen. "Litany of Confession" and "Psalm" first appeared in *Woman-Soul Flowing* (available for $5.00 from the Ecumenical Women's Center, 5253 North Kenmore, Chicago, Illinois 60640). Reprinted with permission of the Ecumenical Women's Center. Mary Pellauer, "Violence against Women: The Theological Dimension," reprinted with permission, *Christianity and Crisis*, vol. 43, no. 9, May 30, 1983. "A Theological Perspective on Sexual Assault," reprinted with permission, *Christianity and Crisis*, vol. 44, no. 11, June 25, 1984. Ntozake Shange, "with no immediate cause," from *Nappy Edges*, St. Martin's Press, Inc., New York. Copyright © 1972, 1974, 1975, 1976, 1977, 1978, by Ntozake Shange. Used by permission. Daniel Silverman, "Sharing the Crisis of Rape: Counseling the Mates and Families of Victims," reprinted from *The American Journal of Orthopsychiatry*, January, 1978. Copyright © 1978, The American Journal of Orthopsychiatry. Permission from The American Journal of Orthopsychiatry and Daniel Silverman. Roland Summit, "Beyond Belief: The Reluctant Discovery of Incest," first appeared in *Women's Sexual Experience: Explorations of the Dark Continent*, Martha Kirkpatrick, ed. Copyright © 1982 Plenum Press. Printed with permission from Plenum Press and Roland Summit.

FIRST EDITION

Library of Congress Cataloging-in-Publication Data

Sexual assault and abuse.

Bibliography: p.
Includes index.
1. Pastoral counseling.   2. Sex crimes.   3. Family violence.   I. Pellauer, Mary D.   II. Chester, Barbara.
III. Boyajian, Jane A.
BV4012.2.S44   1987   261.8'33153   86-45825
ISBN 0-06-254810-7

---

87 88 89 90 91 HC 10 9 8 7 6 5 4 3 2 1

Contents

Invitations to the Reader

MARY PELLAUER

The young woman weeping in the chair had been raped on a Saturday evening. All day the following Sunday, she said, it kept running through her mind that she was supposed to forgive him not just seven times but "seventy times seven times."

The young woman sitting on the couch was the daughter of a preacher. She had been sexually and physically abused by a brother for ten years while she lived at home. "Why didn't they believe me? Why didn't they hear me? Why didn't they do something about it?"

A woman in her late thirties told her story. Sexually abused as a child, she had felt for decades that she was bad, unworthy, "rotten inside even if it didn't show on the outside." At age thirty-five she met some religious women, sisters, who were so accepting and understanding that her faith, renewed and transformed, helped her to heal. "I was truly liberated," she said, her eyes glowing.

A young professional woman gazed out the window of the counseling room. Recently assaulted, she found it hard to keep up with her demanding responsibilities at work and was afraid that she was going crazy. "When it gets really bad," she said, "I sit under the trees. They help me somehow. They tell me that I'm loved no matter what. It's weird, but they give me strength. Spiritual strength, I mean."

Countless stories like these can be heard daily around the country in rape crisis centers and pastoral offices. These stories are stories of sexual violence, of the sexual assaults and sexual abuses of adults and children in our culture. They are also stories of the ways in which victims struggle to become survivors, to affirm their healing and coping skills, to live beyond the crisis into resolution and health. They are often stories of how other people entered into the survivor's struggle to enhance healing or to revictimize. So many stories to hear—so painful, so beautiful, filled with hurt, and suffused with grace.

In the recent past, stories like these have been told and heard in a way that had never before happened in Western history. We have learned more about sexual assault and sexual abuse in the last two decades than in millenia before. In the process we have had to unlearn many old tales, stereotypes, and myths about rape. This has often been difficult and confusing. It has also been an adventure and a challenge. It is painful but deeply satisfying to participate in the personal struggles for healing that victims experience, and in the social and institutional changes being made.

The theological—or religious, or spiritual—aspects of these struggles are less well known than some other aspects of this work. In the early years of my learnings about sexual violence, it seemed that no one in the rape crisis movement wanted to have anything to do with religion, and no one in the churches or theological schools wanted to have anything to do with rape. As a theological student shuttling back and forth between the ends of this contradiction, I and women like me often felt stretched over a chasm. We felt perilously close to splitting up the middle or to falling into an abyss.

Many kinds of growing have been necessary to enable us to hear such stories. At first, we all had to grow past the cultural stereotypes and misunderstandings of these topics. The first rape story I ever heard was told in 1970 in a consciousness-raising group. One evening a woman, a graduate student, told us that she had been assaulted the year before. She was grabbed from behind in the lobby of her apartment building, held with a knife in her throat, and raped. I wish that I could say that I immediately responded with comfort, understanding, and sensitivity. I did not. I felt embarrassment and shame for her that she would tell us this awful thing about herself. I felt impatient; perhaps it was her own fault, perhaps this was not really relevant or important for the rest of us. It is important to remember this chapter in my story, to remember the seriously mistaken reactions I once had. Remembering this first encounter with a rape victim, like remembering that I didn't spring from my mother's womb a feminist, beckons me to remember how much I've changed. That memory teaches me that change *is* possible, for my own life bears witness to it. The memory restores some of the broken fabric of my hopes.

Those changes are occurring on every side. People working in this field often hear of clergy who say, "I preached on the topic right after your workshop, and several victims approached me in the next week." Similarly, at a workshop a clergyperson sometimes says, "I just realized that I did all the wrong things in an incest situation I dealt with last year." Such utter honesty and openness warm my heart. The ability to admit we have a long way to grow speaks of an emerging willingness to change and move in our religious communities. Sometimes great risks are taken in doing so. The same minister said, "I'm going to go back to that family and admit my mistakes. I've got to see if we can rebuild trust and start again."

No sooner had we changed enough to hear the victims' stories from the inside out than new threads appeared, new themes that asked us to grow some more, elements weaving in and out of victims' stories speaking about religion—like those I have highlighted above. Many of these stories tell of the ways in which religious faith intertwined with the suffering and the healing of sexual assault and sexual abuse. What to do with these?

Some stories tell of ways in which a traditional religion or its representatives added to the hurt. These are hard to hear. We may not want to accept that parts of a faith we cherish have caused harm. We may assume that the story is not really representative of the church or its leaders. We may not know what to do with these religious themes, and so we ignore them. But these stories have much to teach us.

Some stories tell of ways in which traditional religion or its representatives graciously held out understanding, hope, acceptance, and healing. In these stories, the pains of victims are received, embraced with sympathy and understanding. Growth is nourished. That these stories exist is a sign of great hope, of changes and transformations alive in our religious communities. These stories also provide important learnings.

Other stories are like the story of the woman and the trees. They are not traditional at all. Some don't even mention God or spiritual strength. But they are religious stories too. From these stories as well we have much to learn.

Ten years ago we didn't know how to deal with these themes and stories. No books or articles or classes in theological schools helped us to see and connect and respond. Sometimes it was scary to allow ourselves to hear these parts of victims' stories. Sometimes hearing meant we had to feel the anger and pain—not just about the assault but about the church. Sometimes hearing meant that we had to be challenged by a gracious faithfulness beyond our own. Often hearing meant that we had to confront the unknown or find a center of gravity in our own authority. It makes sense to me today that we often find such themes hard to hear. When a victim of childhood abuse says that her experience makes it impossible for her to tolerate God the Father, I am asked to unravel and reweave many central portions of the faith we have received. No sooner have I rewoven this God-language than another victim of a similar abuse says that she hates her mother and wants nothing to do with God the Mother. The newly rewoven portion of my theology is ripped up the center. This is very hard. It may be easier not to hear.

But we must hear. So much depends upon our having the ears to hear and having the courage and creativity to respond. We do need to change. We *can* change. We *are* changing. Over the last decade, rape crisis centers and hotlines have sprung up around the nation; support groups for victims of child sexual abuse and incest have blossomed; shelters blanket the nation. Many pastors and seminarians, knowing that these issues surface in ministry, have come to such centers to be advised and trained. More need to do so. Laypeople are responding, telling their stories, volunteering at crisis centers, consoling one another, pressuring for change. Centers, committees, commissions, and task forces related to such violence and violation are springing up around the country.

This book invites us in religious communities to hear with new ears the stories told by victims. It invites us to change so that more stories will be stories of healing and liberation for the victims of sexual violence.

ABOUT THIS BOOK

This handbook grew from a series of workshops on sexual violence for clergy in 1984 in the Twin Cities, thanks to a grant from the Episcopal diocese. Together with several other counselors, activists, and religious leaders, the three editors of this volume planned and facilitated these sessions. At the time, Marie Fortune's *Sexual Violence, The Unmentionable Sin* was virtually the only published material available in book form. It seemed to us that a handbook would be helpful for similar workshops, for seminary classrooms, and for anyone in religious communities seeking guidance for dealing with victims. We also hope that crisis centers will find more religious and theological material helpful.

Thus our aims are very practical. The longest section of this work is devoted to responding to victims. Its essays are loaded with information about how victims may react to their crises and with practical guidelines for enhancing their healing. This practical aim has guided us in other ways as well. The essays are as readable, clear, and understandable as any combination of editors and authors can made them. We've added a selected reading list at the end of the book. Together with the endnotes in the articles that use them, these lists may guide readers to other printed material. But practical resources are more than publications. While we cannot provide addresses and phone numbers for all the agencies and organizations in the nation, the appendix offers a brief guide to some of these, including regional services for dealing with sexual assault and sexual abuse.

These practical aims should not obscure the importance of some large theoretical issues about sexual assault and sexual abuse. First, we editors believe that theory and practice always go together. But especially in the area of religion and sexual violence, theological questions and practical responses are thoroughly intertwined. Solid theology is always in movement between the concrete and the abstract, between action, thought, and passion. Anyone who takes seriously the practical guidance in the third section of this book can respond with compassion and understanding.

Our new practice in the area of sexual violence must deepen and grow. It must become more consistently effective. These changes on behalf of victims demand reevaluation of many theological issues. Good pastoral care of victims requires theological reconstruction. It requires that we look with grave seriousness at victim blaming, at our premises and prejudices about violence and about sexuality, at our life experience and deepest feelings about women and men, at our beliefs about parents and children and family life. It requires us to look at understandings of God, at worship practices, at the meaning of ministry. This new practice asks us to eradicate every vestige of patriarchy from our theologies. No one can do this overnight or with a calm and detached logic. It is a slow process. It may be filled with turmoil, personal pain, uneasiness, resistance—and also excitement, challenge, new growth, and joy. It is not an individual process but a collective one in which we may stumble over the angry protests or gentle chiding of others, a process in which we learn and grow from one another.

But we must be involved in the processes of theological change that go hand in hand with practical changes. We invite you to let this book become an important ingredient in the mix of your theological reflection and pastoral practice.

RECOGNIZING THE PATTERNS

In Part One of this book, we lay out some of our new knowledge. "Myths and Facts about Sexual Assault and Child Sexual Abuse" are commonly circulated by crisis centers as a quick means of dispelling old misunderstandings. We hope that you will read these carefully and honestly, identifying for yourself the myths you accept and resolving to work on them in some way. It is normal for people just beginning to work in this area to accept some myths about these subjects, just as I did the first time I heard a victim's story.

Both new information and new perspectives are available today about sexual violence. As information about these subjects expands and explodes, we need to become sophisticated and critical readers of the data and the theoretical frameworks that create and organize the facts. Barbara Chester, formerly Executive Director of the Sexual Violence Center of Hennepin County, Minnesota, has had extensive experience in this field and is well equipped to guide us through the numbers. Her essay, "The Statistics of Sexual Violence," offers both critical questions to ask of any empirical study, as well as the most reliable data presently available.

In a different vein, columnist Ellen Goodman succinctly points out, "If She Says No, Then It's Rape." This simple statement expresses a truth that, upon reflection, is not simple at all. But it is a truth that is becoming increasingly accepted in our legal system and in the ordinary practices of our individual lives.

Neither these articles nor these changing understandings of rape are sufficient to help us understand the human realities of sexual assault and sexual abuse. We must also see the patterns of human experience, including patterns that make victims afraid to disclose their wounds, even sometimes unwilling or unable to admit them to themselves. It is helpful therefore to recognize the behavioral and experiential signs of sexual violence. Chester's second essay, "Recognizing the Symptoms and Consequences of Sexual Assault and Abuse," provides a basic guide to the patterns of reactions victims in different stages of life may display. She discusses the stories of several persons who did not receive immediate help for their traumas. She urges us all to ask direct questions about sexual violence when we observe such patterned reactions. This essay is a concrete and practical guide for the initial stages of pastoral counseling.

Jane Boyajian's research, described in "Elder Abuse: The View from the Chancel," reminds us that not only children and adults are at risk. Sexual and physical abuse reaches across the entire life span. She informs us of recent facts and provides a much-needed framework for understanding the hidden pains of elder abuse. She offers specific practical guidelines for the ministry of churches as we struggle toward intervention and change. Like Chester, who lists the symptoms of sexual abuse, Boyajian includes many behavioral or physical signs of elder abuse at the conclusion of her essay. Once again, religious leaders are alerted to watch for patterns and to ask questions.

UNDERSTANDING THE ISSUES

The second section of this book is more exploratory. We believe firmly that the issues raised by the experiences of victims and by our culture's transmission of distorted messages about sexual violence are theological issues. No single theological theme or perspective or even genre of work can be expected to do full justice to the array of our new emerging knowledge. This section therefore includes a variety of resources—a poem, a firsthand account of a victim's experience, and essays that meditate upon aspects of sexual violence in the light of the theological tradition.

Ntozake Shange's poem, "With No Immediate Cause," immerses us powerfully and directly into a full range of the issues and insights. Shange's passions and perceptions were the impetus for my essay "Violence against Women: The Theological Dimension." The essay begins with Shange's poem, moves to my personal life and to the changes in our society and churches, then suggests general guidelines for ministry and the beginnings of some new God-talk. Like many others in this field, I have had to learn that recovering my own experience is an essential and central part of my theological and ethical work. I remain convinced that we must reach widely and broadly across the whole scope of human experience and effort in order to do theology about violence against women.

"Don't Tell Mother" by Martha Janssen is a poignant account of the experience of a survivor of incest in a good churchgoing family. She conveys her story in a clear, simple, and moving fashion. Her perspective is shaped by many solid concepts about victimization, offenders, compassion, healing, and theology. She describes from the inside out the effects of incestuous abuse upon her religious life. Such firsthand accounts are the substance of newly emerging theological perspectives.

"A Commentary on Religious Themes in Family Violence," the collaborative effort of Marie Fortune and Judith Hertze, speaks from both Jewish and Christian traditions. Marie Fortune has pioneered in teaching many of us to hear theological questions asked by victims. This theological language can either be a roadblock or a resource for the healing process. The essay alerts us to explicit religious themes in the lives of victims, especially the meaning of suffering and the meaning of marriage and family in Christian and Jewish theological traditions. These authors invite us to reinterpret theological material so that we participate in liberation rather than perpetuate victimization.

Note also that Fortune and Hertze focus on family violence more than on sexual assault. The two issues overlap to a great extent, so it is appropriate to treat them together. Marital rape and the sexual abuse of children by family members result when family violence and sexual violence intersect. Some raped women are also beaten or threatened with weapons; some are not. Some battered wives are sexually abused by their assailants; some are not. Some children are both beaten and sexually abused; some experience one or the other. Many crisis centers deal with both battered women and sexual assault victims. Furthermore, the theological issues treated in this essay parallel and resemble many questions asked by rape victims. The theological comments by Fortune and Hertze often apply to victims of sexual assault and sexual abuse as well as to victims of family violence. While this book focuses on sexual assault and sexual abuse, it is clear that anyone dealing with such issues needs more than a nodding acquaintance with domestic violence.

However, we must beware of overemphasizing the resemblances between domestic violence and sexual assault. Sometimes the issues raised by victims of family violence are *not* the same as those raised by victims of sexual violence. All adult rape victims, for instance, do not have to confront questions about the meaning of family, although those assaulted by husbands or intimates might do so. Often battered women's shelters and rape crisis centers work with a strong division of labor. More work is necessary so that we can respond with insight and effectiveness to the similarities and differences between such abuses.

My second essay, "A Theological Perspective on Sexual Assault," relies upon the work of Fortune and Hertze while following a different pathway. It suggests that whether or not victims directly use theological language in traditional ways, there are still theological or spiritual issues inherent in the crises of sexual violence, especially the life-threatening quality of the experience, trust and betrayal, dirt and cleansing, and the healing process itself. It remains to be seen how such themes (and others like them) may be more fully developed.

Patricia Wilson-Kastner, in "Theological Perspectives on Sexual Violence," pursues yet another set of strands. She reminds us that any theology about sexual violence must be critical, confronting the mixed messages our theological tradition gives us on the issue. Yet she finds sources of hope in the tradition as well—in its explicit treatment of evil, in the cross and resurrection, in the image of God. Wilson-Kastner also briefly explores theological issues for assailants, particularly the importance of freedom and responsibility. She calls us all, as members of an interdependent community, to action.

Many voices, speaking in different accents and rhythms, will be needed for theological and religious work in this field. We hope that these essays invite and challenge readers to do your own theological reflection on these topics, in your own voices and by your own methods.

RESPONDING WITH COMPASSION

Our new knowledge about responding with compassion and understanding, helping victims heal and grow, is the subject of the third section of this book. It may be helpful for religious leaders to understand that victims do not necessarily require psychotherapy, esoteric techniques, or the expertise gained in long years of training. Rape trauma syndrome is not an illness or a personality disorder. It is a normal response to abnormally traumatic events. The vast majority of those who work with victims do not have graduate degrees in this subject (indeed there are none available); they are volunteers from a wide variety of backgrounds. Long-term studies of rape victims done by Ann Burgess and Lynda Holmstrom, whose work we praise and rely upon often in this work, indicate that the single most important factor leading to a relatively speedy recovery is that the victim has some social support, people with whom she can share her story. Indeed, if victims have respectful social support from family, friends, or other intimates, they may not necessarily need professional intervention.

However, some victims may indeed need therapy with a trained counselor. For instance, those who have previously existing emotional or mental difficulties exacerbated by the present trauma or those whose survival mechanisms for coping with earlier trauma have become dysfunctional in later life may benefit from such concentrated skills. However, all therapists and counselors do not have experience with sexual violence. When referring, it may be essential to inquire about the counselor's experience and understanding of this field. Several essays in this section provide guidelines for referral.

The essays collected here provide a solid introduction for anyone desiring to bring healing aid to victims. It may still be helpful to seek out sources of practical training available from local crisis centers and women's shelters. There is no substitute for specific guidance in individual cases and the careful supervision by experienced workers.

The first four essays of this section focus on responding to sexual assault, especially the assault of an adult victim. The first and fourth are by ordained ministers, the second and third by secular counselors. Empowering victims is a primary theme in all these essays.

"Standing by Victims of Sexual Violence: Pastoral Issues," by Jane Boyajian, begins squarely within an understanding of the role and function of the ordained minister. Calling for several changes in our practice as religious leaders with regard to sexual violence, the author identifies these changes within some classical understandings of ministry.

Chris Servaty provides basic information on typical reactions by victims, the phases of the recovery process, and lucid, clear, practical guidelines for counseling victims. Thus her essay, "Support Counseling with Victims of Sexual Assault," is the linchpin of this section. It is basic to any grasp of the healing and empowering processes that can lead to restoring a victim's sense of health and well-being. For quick reference Servaty has summarized guidelines for support counseling at the end of her essay.

We must also see that sexual assault affects the family and friends of the primary victim. In "Sharing the Crisis of Rape: Counseling with the Mates and Families of Victims," Daniel Silverman sketches typical responses of these "secondary victims" and provides effective means for counselors working with those who know and love a rape survivor. Religious communities and their leaders have long emphasized working with the whole family. Religious leaders may well have unique opportunities for ministry with these concerned persons.

The vast majority of ordained religious leaders are men. Many victims may not feel comfortable disclosing an assault to a male, however caring. Yet it is realistic to understand that female clergy are available in small numbers, and that male religious leaders too must be involved in such work. In "The Male Minister and the Female Victim," Cooper Wiggen reflects with honesty and insight on his role as an ordained man when he counsels victims. He suggests that male anxiety may decrease the male pastor's effectiveness with victims. Sensitively handled, however, such anxiety may become an asset for increased gentleness and concern.

The sexual assault of an adult, however, is only one portion of sexual violence. Sexual harassment, child sexual abuse and incest, and sexual exploitation by other professionals all call for new responses on the part of religious communities. As with sexual assault and battering, there are both similarities and differences in the dynamics of these abuses and in recovery processes for survivors. Several essays in this section explore these issues in more detail.

Sexual harassment is just beginning to be acknowledged by religious communities as a significant issue. The Commission on Women and the Church of the United Presbyterian Church in the U.S.A. has pioneered in creating resources for church people—policies and procedures for the church, a film strip and pamphlet, "Naming the Unnamed" which describe sexual harassment in the church. Whether victimized in the church or in some other place of work or schooling, victims deserve compassionate and understanding responses by religious leaders. Barbara Chester has done concentrated work with victims of sexual harassment in the workplace. Her essay "Sexual Harassment: Victim Responses" shares information about typical patterns and case studies of this abuse. She supplies specific guidance for counseling interventions with victims of sexual harassment.

In some ways child sexual abuse and incest are the most painful and difficult areas of sexual violence. Extremely damaging for victims, often deeply confusing and upsetting to those who would intervene, sexual abuse of children by family members and relatives calls for an in-depth treatment such as that provided by Roland Summit's essay, "Beyond Belief: The Reluctant Discovery of Incest." His careful and sensitive description of the normal responses of children to sexual abuse and incest, so different from our adult projections, is essential for anyone who would intervene. Summit further spells out implications for treatment and prevention.

Some words of caution are in order. We strongly encourage religious leaders to be supportive of child victims in appropriate ways—to ask about sexual abuse if you see patterns of symptoms, to believe child victims' stories. But working directly in a therapeutic way with children requires special skills. Thus we encourage religious leaders to understand that therapy with child victims is best pursued by a trained child psychologist with experience in sexual abuse issues. Most victims of child sexual abuse and incest reach adulthood without disclosing the abuse they have experienced. Your supportive understanding, especially as a religious leader, can be a deeply important ingredient in the healing process. However, be realistic in assessing the victim's needs and your own skill level. The damage such victims sustain may reach into many areas of life beyond your abilities; they may require long-term counseling.

Child sexual abuse can also be painful and controversial for ordained religious leaders. Professionals with knowledge or suspicions of child sexual abuse are required by law to report to police or child protective agencies. We believe that mandatory reporting is not only appropriate but crucial. It is most often the only means of securing protection and safety, let alone counseling, for victims. In some states, clergy are specifically exempt from this mandatory reporting. (Check the situation in your own area.) Confusion and conflicts can arise for ordained persons in such cases. In "Confidentiality and Mandatory Reporting: A Clergy Dilemma?" Marie Fortune addresses some concerns clergy may have on this subject. We believe this deeply serious issue needs to compel the attention and thought of theologians and ethicists throughout religious communities. We have supplied information and guidelines about reporting child abuse at the end of Fortune's essay.

Even more recent have been regular news reports of sexual abuse perpetrated by ordained persons themselves. For many years at the Walk-In Counseling Center, Minneapolis, Minnesota, Jeanette Milgrom and Gary Schoener have seen clients victimized by other professionals, including clergy. Their essay, "Responding to Clients Who Have Been Sexually Exploited by Counselors, Therapists, and Clergy," emphasizes issues in the recovery process that may be faced by such victims.

Under the impact of new laws making sexual exploitation by such professionals in the course of their professional duties a crime, many counseling centers have produced new statements of ethics. We include here one sample, "A Client Bill of Rights," from the Sexual Violence Center of Hennepin County, Minnesota. We encourage pastoral counselors to adapt this or similar statements to their own practices and to display such a statement prominently in their offices.

Religious communities are more than ordained leaders, and ministry is more than counseling. Our final selections point to other programs and efforts in which people of faith need to be involved.

From the office of Ministries with Women in Crisis of the United Methodist Church, Peggy Halsey appeals to the whole community of faith to be involved in combating sexual violence at the local level. For a local congregation seeking to respond to new knowledge about sexual assault and sexual abuse, her essay, "What the Church Can Do," makes specific suggestions about a range of possible programs.

Finally, we could not complete this anthology without offering some resources that are less linear and more poetic. All three of us who edited this volume find rituals, images, symbols, stories, and song important ways to refresh ourselves and to drink from the wells that nourish us. Victims need these deep sources of recreation, both individually and collectively. Furthermore, we believe it is crucially important for caregivers working in these areas to nourish themselves as well. In "Resources for Ritual and Recuperation," we offer only the barest smattering of possible resources—for litanies, prayers, devotions, symbolic occasions. We invite you to create others and to share them.

ABOUT THE FUTURE

There are some gaps in this handbook. There is, for instance, nothing here about pornography, although pornographic materials are a matter of increasing concern to activists and church leaders dealing with sexual violence. None of these essays deals with male victims of sexual violence in an extended way. (What we have learned so far indicates that understanding the responses of female victims is helpful for dealing with male survivors as well.) Prevention questions have not been addressed. There are special needs of minority populations, both in straightforward counseling and in religious aspects of these questions; the best source of information is your local crisis center or women's shelter. Several authors mention the importance of group work with victims, but we have not found a useful way to present such a perspective.

Many readers will notice that some essays mention assailants. Since many assailants, especially those abusing family members, may be members of churches, how to deal with offenders may be an important concern to religious leaders. Since we have not provided an in-depth treatment of such questions, this gap in our handbook requires some explanation.

We believe firmly that ministers and religious leaders are *not* appropriate counselors for assailants, whether rapists, batterers, or child sexual abusers. The special skills and expertise required are simply beyond the reach of the ordinary parish pastor. There are several reasons why this is so. The truth is that *no one knows* what makes up a reliable treatment model for offenders. Professionals who work with offenders readily admit the difficulties of this new and complicated field. There are special risks of working with this group of persons. It is extremely easy to be drawn into colluding with the offender's world view and distorted processes. Offenders minimize their behavior so typically that it is essential for a counselor to have the court record of the victim's story (or some other record) available in order to maintain a grasp of reality. This alone requires the coordination of many kinds of information and resources not available to the pastor.

Indeed, special risks and dangers exist for the parish pastor in dealing with offenders. Without the institutional connections for working as a team with other professionals, clergy may work at cross-purposes with them and so sidetrack the best therapy available. One measure of this difficulty, for instance, is the increasing concern of mental health practitioners whose clients have significant contact with churches. Such practitioners often find offenders appealing to pastors for confession and absolution as a substitute for rehabilitative therapy. This is extremely dangerous. Furthermore, if the victim is also a member of the religious community, the victim may view you as allying yourself with the offender. Thus, the victim may not view you as a place to get support in the victim's crisis.

The gaps in this handbook are symptomatic of the gaps in our theology and practice in religious communities. There is much room for the growth and development of the topics named—and many more. I cannot recall a time in my long graduate theological education when a simple topic like safety was ever addressed in a significant way. Yet safety is fundamental and essential to the concerns of victims as well as to issues of prevention. Similarly, concentrated historical work upon the tradition's views of these abuses remains to be done.

An important recent development is the discovery and conceptualization of "post-traumatic stress syndrome." It now appears that there are significant parallels between the experiences of victims of sexual assault and those of Vietnam veterans, of persons in police work or firefighting, of hijacking victims, of those who have lived through mudslides, earthquakes, and other natural disasters. These may be extremely important leads for the development of ministry and theology in the next decades.

We invite our readers to be alert to the development of new resources in these areas and others. We invite you to be active participants in creating them.

The pains and perplexities, the growth and healing around sexual assault and sexual abuse are radical. Transformations of a deep and fundamental sort are both urgently necessary and occurring daily. Anyone who counsels victims in any way knows the double-edged truth of such statements. The healing that victims experience can be rapid and dramatic. The agonies and torments that make such healing necessary propel counselors to rage and despair, to gentle patience, and to creative, committed action.

Confronting any radical issue finally requires us to account for the faith that is in us. In the face of such a demand, there is no substitute for speaking personally. Through the vagaries of my personal life, through my experience counseling with victims in schools and crisis centers, through years of struggling to understand and to care for such questions, my life and many of the deepest parameters of my faith have changed.

I believe today that God is active in the movements against sexual and physical violence. God is present in the healing of victims, in the courage and desperation that impels victims to disclose their pains and reach out for help, in the affirmation that it does not need to be this way, in the struggle for fundamental change. It has been hard to learn that I believe these things. It has often felt as though I cannot believe such things and remain a member of the Christian tradition.

I am both heartened and impelled to make new affirmations, however, by many strands of new activity in recent years. The courage and sensitivity of those who work in crisis centers and the growing networks across the nation provide hope for the future. New directions in theology, especially liberation theology and feminist theology, are refreshing breezes of renewal flowing through religious communities. Resources such as those we present in this book enliven and encourage me. But especially working with survivors of sexual assault and sexual abuse moves me in the deepest places of my being and calls me to theological movement. I am not always sure how to speak about this or where it leads.

The closest I can come appears in portions of the ministry of Jesus. One of the stories he told rings and echoes with special meaning as I work on sexual assault and sexual abuse. Matthew 25 pictures Jesus pausing on the headlong course toward his crucifixion to share final words with his friends and followers. The last of those sayings, as Matthew relates them, was about the final judgment, the great last accounting that divides the virtuous from the wicked. One of the most powerful insights of the Christian tradition is embodied in Jesus' words:

> I was hungry and you gave me bread,
> I was thirsty and you gave me drink,
> I was a stranger and you welcomed me,
> I was naked and you clothed me,
> I was sick and you visited me,
> I was in prison and you came to me.

To those who ask, "When, Lord, did we see you like this?" Jesus provided a simple reply: "In so far as you did this to one of the least of these, you did it to me" (Matt. 25:31–46).

These lines are not directly about sexual assault and sexual abuse. They are about neediness of several kinds. But as I form my ears anew to hear the stories told by the victims of sexual assault and sexual abuse, I hear Jesus' lines whispering and echoing insistently with new meanings. I hear these lines saying:

> I was raped and you stood by me,
> I was battered and you sheltered me,
> I was abused and you intervened.

Clearly, Jesus' story invites us to minister to the least of these. Indeed, he tells us that we will go down to perdition if we do not. But that strenuous and important call to act on behalf of the oppressed, essential as it is, does not exhaust the importance of such a text for this subject.

For there is an image of God in the lines of this parable. It is an image of God who knows full well the pains and anguish and torment and craziness and fear and neediness of victims. It is not solely the image of God as the supremely all-powerful One who has the power and the right to dominate. It is the image of God who is present with us in the person of the least. This is what I glimpse as I gaze into the eyes of victims of sexual assault and sexual abuse, as I hear the stories told: God peeping back at me, shimmering in the glitter of tears shed and unshed, shining in the human riches reclaimed and newly discovered.

Some women may object here. They may point out that the king who presides at the judgment saying these words is male and the Jesus who tells the story is male. Most victims after all are female —not all, but most. These women may agree that it is deity who gazes back from victim's eyes, that it is the Goddess who reveals herself in the neediness and the healing of victims. But they may object to identifying this experience with the Christian tradition and Jesus. For, these women might say, that tradition is utterly and essentially patriarchal.

They may be right. It may be that the full expansion and flourishing of that experience I have with victims, with all the religious changes it may require of us, can never be at home within Christianity. The stories told by victims in which Christianity added to their suffering are an eloquent witness to this possibility. I take this challenge and this objection with great seriousness; I respect the integrity of those who choose other religious options available to us today.

But it is my wager that the Jewish and Christian traditions can be reconstructed in an antipatriarchal direction (not merely a nonpatriarchal one, as though being neutral were enough). This is a faith, if you will—not a certainty, in the way many people use the word faith, as though it were a kind of sureness of knowledge beyond science or other experiences. It is a risk. I might be quite wrong, spending the remaining decades of my life in a futile pursuit. On the other hand, it is not a blind risk. I have some experiences and some other views that encourage me in this wager, views that go well beyond the space of these pages. For instance, the full parable tells us that the king is also the least, that the dichotomy between the most high and the lowliest is overcome in this moment of final judgment. It may be for us in our time to hear other dichotomies, like that between male and female, also overcome in such a story, just as it has taken until the twentieth century for us to hear Gal. 3:28.

Finally, however, such a wager, such a faith as this, is not only a theoretical matter. It cannot be decided by a wave of the theological hand, or by discussions on paper. It is to be decided by the quality of our actions—the changes we make in ourselves, in our dealings with victims, in our institutions, in the world. This too, I learned from Jesus, telling us "by their fruits you will know them." If Jesus' words, "I was hungry and you gave me bread," mean anything at all, they must also mean, "I was raped and you stood by me." We must carry this meaning into the fullness of our lives, into the ordinary actions we take on a daily basis.

Perhaps the question of whether we pursue such courses of justice and mercy and healing inside or outside Judaism or Christianity is also finally irrelevant. The parable, after all, did not say that the orthodoxy of our theological positions was the criterion. My faith is not in the church, but in the God that the church proclaims —a God who calls us to love justice and mercy, to love God fervently with our whole selves and our neighbor as our selves, not only to refrain from harm but to be active in goodness toward the other persons with whom we share this planet. In a sense, I refuse to put the church before this God. And I do not believe that God seeks of us a sterile theological uniformity, but that we praise and bless this God as we speak and act the truth as we know it out of the centers of our whole selves in community. God loves and learns from our differences as much as we do. We are not called to agree theologically any more than we are all called to the same vocations.

But we are called to respond to the needs of victims, to be responsible to the new knowledge we are acquiring about sexual assault and abuse. We are invited, each in our different ways, to account for the faith that is in us, in the light of sexual assault and sexual abuse.

1. RECOGNIZING THE PATTERNS

The new information about sexual assault and abuse developed over the last two decades invites us to reconstruct our pictures of the world.

"Myths and Facts" about sexual assault and abuse are a quick way of dispelling old misunderstandings.

"The Statistics about Sexual Violence" provides a summary of recent empirical evidence about the various forms of sexual violence in the United States today.

"If She Says No, Then It's Rape" points to one of the basic changes we will need to make in our values in order to deal seriously with sexual assault.

"Recognizing the Symptoms and Consequences of Sexual Assault and Abuse" provides a basic guide to patterns of reactions victims are likely to display. We encourage you to study these patterns and to ask direct questions when you observe these reactions.

"Elder Abuse: The View from the Chancel" provides recent information about elder abuse and practical guidelines for the ministry of churches. Signs of elder abuse are listed at the end.

We invite you to study this new information closely and to allow it to inform your framework for ministry.

1. Myths and Facts about Sexual Assault and Child Sexual Abuse

Stereotypes and misunderstandings about sexual violence are so widespread in our culture that everyone is likely to have some distorted views. To correct these mistaken ideas is essential. We cannot do effective ministry or insightful theology without accurate information about victims, assailants, and the nature of these abuses.

SEXUAL ASSAULT

Myth: Rape is a minor crime affecting only a few people. Its significance is overexaggerated.

Fact: In one random sample, 44 percent of the women interviewed had experienced either an attempted or a completed rape. Two women in five may have a sexual assault experience in her lifetime. Between one in five and one in three girls are sexually abused by an adult before they are eighteen years old. Men and boys may also be victims. In one study 8% of boys had experienced sexual abuse as children.

Myth: Like Potiphar's wife accusing Joseph, women frequently "cry rape." There is a high rate of false reporting.

Fact: Studies show that only 2 percent of rape reports are false, the same rate that is usual for other kinds of felonies.

Myth: Rape is provoked by the victim. Any woman could prevent it if she really wanted to.

Fact: Studies indicate that most rapes (60 to 70 percent) are at least partially planned in advance; the victim is usually threatened with death or bodily harm if she resists. Rape is not a spontaneous act of sexual passion. It is a violent attack on an individual using sex as a weapon. For the victim it is a humiliating, life-threatening situation.

Myth: Only certain kinds of women get raped. "Nice" women do not get raped, only "bad" women. Good Christians would not get sexually assaulted.

Fact: Rapists choose their victims without regard to whether they are "good" or "bad." Victims are of every type, race, socioeconomic class. Ages of victims range from six months to ninety years. Victims may be religious people or secular, Protestant, Catholic, Jewish, Buddhist, of every faith, or of no faith.

Myth: Rape does not occur in the religious community. "It can't happen in my congregation."

Fact: Rape occurs everywhere. Both perpetrators and victims come from all faiths and denominations.

Myth: Rape occurs only in large cities.

Fact: Sexual assault occurs in every environment: the city, suburbs, small towns, and rural areas. It may be less likely to be reported in small towns because of the lack of anonymity for the victim.

Myth: Sexual assault occurs only among strangers.

Fact: In one random sample study, only 15 percent of assailants were unknown to the victim. In Minnesota studies of reported rapes, up to 65 percent of victims had encountered or been acquainted with the assailant in some way. Marital rape involves not strangers but intimates. In one study, one in seven (14 percent) of the women who had ever been married had been raped one or more times by a husband or exhusband. A majority of the children who are sexually abused are victimized by family members, family friends, or people in positions of authority over children.

Myth: Rapists are abnormal perverts or men with an unsatisfied sex drive. Only "sick" or "insane" men rape women. The primary motive for rape is sexual.

Fact: Rapists have normal sex drives, may be married or have available and willing sexual partners with whom they are sexually active, and exhibit "normal" behavior. On a statistical average, rapists have normal personalities. They may differ from nonoffenders only in being more violent. The motives for rape are related to power and anger. Sex is the weapon of rape, not the reason. Some authorities suggest that rapists "overconform" to masculine stereotypes rather than deviate from them.

Myth: Most rapes involve black men and white women.

Fact: FBI statistics indicate that most commonly the assailant and the victim are of the same socioeconomic and racial group. Of reported rapes, 93 percent are intraracial rather than interracial. Racist attitudes are widespread in our culture. When racist attitudes affect thinking about rape, women of all cultures are encouraged to fear black men, and the rapes of minority women may not be taken seriously due to mistaken views of nonwhite women. We must struggle against racism at the same time that we struggle against rape.

CHILD SEXUAL ABUSE

Myth: It is strangers and weirdos who represent the greatest potential threat to the child.

Fact: The most common offender is an adult male who is known to the child. Repeatedly, studies find that 75 percent to 95 percent of offenders are known to the child.

Myth: Children lie or fantasize about sexual activities with adults.

Fact: Developmentally, children cannot make up sexual information unless they have been exposed to it. They speak from their own experiences.

Myth: The sexual abuse of a child is usually an isolated, one-time incident.

Fact: Especially within the family, child sexual abuse is usually a situation that develops gradually over a period of time and the sexual abuse occurs repeatedly. Without intervention, child sexual abuse continues, often for years.

Myth: Child sexual abuse is so rare that we need not talk about it with our kids.

Fact: Repeatedly, studies have found that child sexual abuse is much more common than we would like to think. Between one in three and one in five young girls may be at risk; some studies find that one in eleven young boys may be victimized as a child. Prevention programs like Illusion Theater in Minneapolis find that when children are adequately informed about child sexual abuse, boys report more frequently, bringing the proportions of boys and girls into rough equality.

Myth: It is not important for children to have information about sexual assault. Talking to children about it will only scare them.

Fact: It is just as important for children to have information about sexual assault for their own safety as it is for them to have information about fires, crossing the street, or swimming. Inaccurate information is more frightening to children.

Myth: Nonviolent sexual abuse is not emotionally traumatic.

Fact: Although child sexual abuse may involve subtle manipulation rather than extreme force, it is invariably damaging psychologically to the victim and to family members.

Myth: Child molesters are dirty old men.

Fact: In a recent study of convicted child molesters, most were found to have committed their first offense before the age of forty, eighty percent before the age of thirty.

Myth: Just as many adult women abuse young boys as adult men exploit young girls.

Fact: Most reported cases of child sexual abuse involve adult men and young girls. When young boys are exploited, they are usually the victims of adult men.

Myth: The lower the family income and social status, the higher the likelihood of the sexual abuse of children.

Fact: There is no data to support this conclusion. It is safe to assume, however, that the lower the income and social status, the higher the likelihood of the abuse coming to the attention of a public agency.

Myth: Multiple sexual abuse (such as a father abusing two or more daughters) is extremely rare.

Fact: If there are two or more daughters in the home, without discovery or intervention, a sexually abusive father will usually be involved with each of them. It is rare for a father to sexually abuse only one daughter if there are several in the family. Sons may also be victimized.

Myth: Any parent who would sexually abuse his or her own child has to be mentally ill.

Fact: The vast majority of abusers are not mentally ill. Most hold jobs, function well in the community, and are well respected by their peers. Most abusers deny the events, and some claim seduction by the child.

Myth: Family sexual abuse is easy to treat once it becomes known.

Fact: Sexual abuse of children is extremely difficult to treat because it involves three people moving at different speeds (father, mother, child). Often none of the three is ready for treatment.

Myth: Most people realize that the child is just a victim and don't put any blame on the child.

Fact: Most often the child is more likely to suffer as a result of the abuse and its disclosure than any adult. Often the child and not the abuser is removed from the home, making the child believe that she or he did something wrong.

2. The Statistics about Sexual Violence

BARBARA CHESTER

Not so long ago, most of us believed that rape was a rare and dramatic event in our society and that the sexual abuse of children was even more unusual. Early estimates of the incidence of incest were as low as one case per million persons,[1] and our information about perpetrators was restricted to incarcerated offenders. During the last decade, the presence of rape crisis centers, the women's movement, and more adequate empirical research have challenged our previous understandings. Presently we are bombarded with news stories about sexual assault and sexual abuse. We watch sensationalized made-for-television movies depicting rape, incest, and abuse. More responsible documentaries and articles report demographics and precise numbers.

These statistics can be confusing and often overwhelming if we are not sophisticated about reading them. They can be misleading, used to prove almost any point—as well as its opposite. If read correctly and used responsibly, however, statistical evidence can be used to answer some necessary questions and to aid in planning services.

It may help to remember that no statistic in itself is a pure, absolute, objective truth. All numbers come from somewhere, and they require interpretation by somebody. These suspicions are especially apt when the subject is sexual violence. In most of our communities sexual violence of any kind is still a matter of shame and embarrassment to the victim. Furthermore, many kinds of sexual violence are crimes. This criminal dimension has a large impact on the gathering of numbers. Many victims do not report to the police; some definitions leave many other victims out of their tallies. The following points should be kept in mind when you encounter another study or news story or hear a lecture on these topics. Ask yourself:

1. *How representative is the population from which the numbers are taken?*

A report on criminal victimization in Lake Wobegon, Minnesota, does not apply to Detroit, Miami, or even Minneapolis—and vice versa. College students are an accessible research pool; they may be the most intensively studied group in the nation. But findings from studies using college freshmen cannot be directly translated to the larger population.

2. *For what purpose are these statistics gathered? What agency do they come from? Who is collecting the data?*

Figures collected by police vary tremendously from court data or data from social service agencies. This does not make this police data useless, but you must decide if what you are seeing is an underestimate or an overestimate of the true picture. Since much crime is underreported and unsolved, police data are usually an underestimate of the true crime picture.

The extent of this underreporting to police may be disputed. For many years the FBI used a ratio of nine unreported rapes for every one reported; in the last decade, law enforcement agencies have shifted this figure downward, claiming that one in five rapes is reported. But at least one recent ground-breaking study found a report rate in a randomly generated sample closer to the traditional figure (9.5 percent).[2]

In addition, we must ask how representative reported cases are to the majority of actual rapes or to the unreported cases. We know, for instance, that rapes by strangers are more likely to be reported than those by friends, dates, acquaintances, or family members.

It is also important to remember that statistics are often used for political and fundraising purposes, and while objectivity is rare in research, it is almost nonexistent in the realm of politics.

3. *What data is left out?*

Many states, for example, do not consider marital rape a crime and so do not include it for reporting purposes. In some cases, data is only collected on adults over the age of sixteen, or only on female victims. In many instances the issue of assault is overlooked or not considered, especially where evidence exists for a more recognizable or easily proven crime (for instance, burglary).

4. *What definitions of sexual violence have been used?*

For many years, rape laws relied on English common law definitions, which required "carnal knowledge" and evidence of resistance. Many forms of sexually assaultive behavior were therefore not in statutes, despite the fact that the offender's motives and behaviors, as well as the consequences for victims, were as traumatic.

Similarly, if we concentrate on incest rather than child sexual abuse, we may miss situations in which offenders are not related by blood ties to the victim though they do stand in a relationship of power, authority, intimacy, and "family."[3]

Given these healthy suspicions and realistic limitations, there is still a vast amount of relatively recent evidence about sexual assault and sexual abuse. We can only provide samples from the many studies available, which today compose a large bibliography in themselves. The most reliable, the most respected, or the most recent of these findings follow.

RAPE AND SEXUAL ASSAULT

The *Uniform Crime Report,* compiled regularly by the Federal Bureau of Investigation, is often taken as an indicator of the national picture with regard to crime. In 1976 it indicated 56,000 cases of reported rape in the U.S., a number that had risen to 81,500 five years later in 1981. If we use the 1/10 ratio of reported and unreported rapes, we can see that in 1981, more than three-quarters of a million completed or attempted rapes occurred in the country, by the *legal* definitions of rape alone. Even using these official figures, one researcher compiling lifetime probabilities for women to be raped concluded that "a *conservative* estimate is that, under current conditions 20 to 30 percent of girls now twelve years old will suffer a violent sexual attack during the remainder of their lives."[4]

A random sample of nearly a thousand women in San Francisco found that *44 percent* had been subjected to a rape or attempted rape at least once in their lives. Only 11 percent of these victims were assaulted by strangers; adjusted for multiple attacks, only 6 percent of the total numbers of assaults were perpetrated by strangers. The majority of assailants were husbands or exhusbands, friends, dates, boyfriends, acquaintances, lovers or exlovers, or authority figures.

Using a fairly conservative definition of rape, this study found that one in every seven women who had ever been married (14 percent) had been raped by their husbands or exhusbands. These figures on wife rape are remarkably consistent with studies done in western Europe and Australia. Furthermore, this study found that many victims of marital rape were also battered. Though the study did not specifically ask about battering, some women also described battering without wife rape. When we add together the number of women experiencing rape, battering, or both, in the home, one in four of the women who had ever been married had been victimized by sexual and/or physical violence at the hands of her husband.[5]

Furthermore, by factoring this sample into age cohorts, this random sample research validated a reality that rape crisis center workers have intuitively known for years: The rape rate *is* increasing in the United States.

Even reported rapes are rarely brought to justice. Of every hundred rapes of adult women, twenty are solved by arrest, twelve are charged, eight plead or are found guilty, one to two receive prison terms.[6]

Though sexual abuse is viewed as an issue predominantly affecting women and girls, men and boys are also at risk. Although most adult men presently seen by rape centers have been victimized in prison and military settings, the pressures against reporting in this population makes an accurate picture impossible. Research in progress indicates that, at least in terms of stranger rape, as many boys as girls may be at risk. It is incumbent upon all of us to enable and facilitate the reporting of sexual abuse by males by dispelling the myth that the only victims of sex offenses are women.

CHILD SEXUAL ABUSE

The sexual abuse of children is far more widespread than early reports indicated. Much work, often done even before the recent wave of interest and research but ignored at the time, found that between one in five and one in three girls, and between one in ten and one in five boys, are at risk for sexual abuse.[7] In the random sample study mentioned earlier, 38 percent of the women interviewed reported one or more experiences of sexual abuse before the age of eighteen; 16 percent reported one or more experiences of sexual abuse *within the family* before that age. Of these women, 12 percent had been sexually abused by a relative before age fourteen.[8] Very few of these cases of sexual abuse were disclosed while they were occurring. (Only 2 percent of those intrafamilial cases and 6 percent of the extrafamilial cases were reported.) In some studies, the average age of such children when intrafamilial sexual abuse begins seems to be around age nine; on the average, such abuse continues about three and one-half years.[9]

The cyclic nature of childhood sexual abuse is both clear and frightening. Over one-third of incarcerated sex offenders were themselves victimized as children.[10] Although early studies reported a preponderance of low social class and minority perpetrators of childhood sexual abuse, these studies were biased because they looked only at men in prison. Sexual abuse of children occurs among every social and economic group. Most rapists are male, married, Caucasian, and between sixteen and thirty years of age.[11]

OTHER ABUSES

Surveys related to sexual harassment on the job report between 45 percent and 90 percent of women respondents experience this kind of abuse.[12] Approximately 42 percent of women working for the federal government reported some form of sexual harassment during the two-year period under study.[13] Sexual harassment also occurs in schools. From 20 to 30 percent of women students in colleges and universities across the nation report sexual harassment by male faculty.[14]

Testimony given at the joint congressional hearings on the needs of the aged estimated that 10 percent of all dependent elderly are abused by their families.

Sexual exploitation by counselors and therapists is an abuse recently coming to public attention. Studies of sexual contact between therapist and client have been occurring since the early 1970s. They indicate that 5 percent of therapists *admit* to having sexual intercourse with clients, and another five percent to other sexual contact. Half or more of all therapists have seen clients sexually victimized by other members of the profession. Both secular therapists and pastoral counselors engage in sexual contact with clients. Explicit policies related to the ethics of professional behavior in this area and serious attention to treatment programs and preventative measures are needed.

These are general national figures. They indicate that there is a range of certainty and a range of the unknown about our factual knowledge. But even given the limits and the specifics of these figures, one thing ought to be clear: *Sexual violence is not uncommon in our society.* It is *not* a rare and unusual occurrence. We ought *not* to take it for granted, in the sense of accepting its occurrence. Rather, in this stage of our society's development, we ought to be aware that we all know someone who has been sexually assaulted as an adult or a child. We certainly ought to assume that if we address such issues in public, our audiences will include numbers of victims.

These general and national figures must also be made more specific. Every reader of this manual needs to inquire and investigate the situation in your home state and in your home city, and perhaps even in your neighborhood. In Minnesota where the editors of this volume have lived and worked, we know that:

- The Department of Corrections of the State of Minnesota collects data from the state's twenty-seven rape crisis centers. In 1984 services were provided to 4,633 victims of sexual assault or sexual abuse. (An increase of nearly 50 percent from 1982, when Minnesota's rape centers served over 3,000 victims.) Nearly half of these victims (47 percent) were under the age of eighteen. Of this total, 27 percent were victims of sexual abuse by family members. Most victims using rape center resources were female (89 percent), but a growing number were male (11 percent).
- A specific rape center's figures, however, may cast a different light on those same facts. For instance, though Minnesota as a whole reported over 3,000 victims in 1982, a single rape center in the state's metropolitan area logged 7,564 total contacts from victims and secondary victims. Victimization is not a one-time event, nor are its effects limited solely to the primary victim. Of those victims served by this center in 1983, 38

percent reported the assault to the police. Given this state's progressive services, it is possible that the ratio of reported and unreported rapes is different from those at national levels. It is also possible that people who contact rape centers are also more likely to report to other agencies as well (i.e. law enforcement).

The women who call or come to a local rape crisis center are no longer simply numbers. They are faces, they are stories. They are real persons who have experienced the loss of personal power and the extreme grief inherent in the shattering of one's world view. To people who work in rape crisis centers or who counsel victims, the numbers, however uncertain, are no longer dry and distant indicators of a problem "out there." The rise of those numbers means more stories, more damage, more resources needed to heal and transform.

Check the statistics in *your* community. Find out who collects the statewide numbers, what they are this year and over the past ten years. Ask the police and social workers and the nearest rape crisis center what the statistical picture is like from their vantage point. If you live in an urban area, find out if there are breakdowns by neighborhood. Learn what the crime picture is where you live and where your church or synagogue is located. Even a simple questionnaire, allowing respondents to remain nameless, may surprise you and make these issues come alive for you in your work. These specific figures will give you a better feeling for the risks women and children run in your own community. The answers may challenge you to question your own world view. And to take some action.

3. If She Says No, Then It's Rape

ELLEN GOODMAN

There are a few times when you can actually see a change of public mind. This is one of those times.

For as long as I can remember, a conviction for rape depended as much on the character of the woman involved as on the action of the man. Most often, the job of the defense lawyer was to prove that the woman had provoked or consented to the act—that it was sex, not assault.

In the normal course of events, the smallest blemish, misjudgment, misstep by the woman—Did she wear a tight sweater? Was she a "loose" woman? Was she in the wrong part of town at the wrong hour?—became proof that she had invited the man's attentions. A woman could waive her right to say no in an astonishing number of ways.

But in the spring of 1984, in Massachusetts, three cases of multiple rape came into court and three sets of convictions came out of juries. These verdicts point to a change in attitudes. A simple definition seems to have seeped into the public consciousness. If she says no, it's rape.

The most famous of these cases is the New Bedford barroom rape. There, two separate juries cut through complicated testimony to decide the central issue within hours. Had the woman been drinking? Had she lied about that in testimony? Had she kissed one of the men? In the end, none of these points was relevant. What mattered to the juries that found four of these six men guilty was that they had forced her. If she said no, it was rape.

The second of these cases involved a young woman soldier from Ft. Devens who accepted a ride with members of a local rock band, the Grand Slamm. She was raped in the bus and left in a field hours later. Had she flirted with the band members? Had she told a friend that she intended to seduce one of the men? Had she gone on the bus willingly? The judge sentencing three of the men to jail said, "No longer will society accept the fact that a woman, even if she may initially act in a seductive or compromising manner, has waived her right to say no at any further time." If she said no, it was rape.

The third of these cases was in some ways the most notable. An Abington, Massachusetts, woman was driven from a bar to a parking lot where she was raped by four men, scratched by a knife, had her hair singed by a cigarette lighter, and then was left half-naked in the snow. The testimony at the trial showed that the woman had previously had sex with three of the men, and with two of them in a group setting. Still, the jury was able to agree with the district attorney: "Sexual consent between a woman and a man on one occasion does not mean the man has access to her whenever it strikes his fancy." If she said no, it was rape.

Not every community, courtroom, or jury today accepts this simple standard of justice. But ten years ago, five years ago, even three years ago, these women might not have even dared press charges.

It was the change of climate that enabled, even encouraged, the women to come forward. It was the change of attitude that framed the arguments in the courtroom. It was the change of consciousness that infiltrated the jury chambers.

The question now is whether that change of consciousness has become part of our own day-to-day lives. It isn't just rapists who refuse to take no for an answer. It isn't just rapists who believe that a woman says one thing and means another.

In the confusion of adolescence, in the chase of young adulthood, the sexes were often set up to persist and to resist. Many young men were taught that "no" means "try again." Many young women were allowed to excuse their sexuality only when they were "swept away."

The confused messages, the yes-no-maybes, the overpowered heroines and overwhelming heroes, are still common to supermarket gothic novels and *Hustler* magazine. It isn't just X-rated movies that star a resistant woman who falls in love with her sexual aggressor. It isn't just pornographic cable TV that features the woman who really "wanted it." In as spritely a sitcom as "Cheers," Sam blithely locked a coyly ambivalent Diane into his apartment.

I know how many steps it is from that hint of sexual pressure to the brutality of rape. I know how far it is from lessons of sexual power plays to the violence of rape. But it's time the verdict of those juries was fully transmitted to the culture from which violence emerges. If she says no, it means no.

4. Recognizing the Symptoms and Consequences of Sexual Assault and Abuse

BARBARA CHESTER

Unlike many other life-threatening traumas, evidence regarding the occurrence of sexual assault and abuse is not always readily discernible. This is especially true for children and elders, but also for a large number of cases in which the coercion involved did not leave physical scars. For these groups in particular, outward evidence of assault or abuse will be, to a large extent, behavioral in nature. It is especially important for people in helping professions to be attuned to patterns of characteristics, since a large majority of reports of abuse of children and elders are made by third parties.

Sexual assault and abuse are acts that have profound and life-long consequences for victims, families, and communities. If left undisclosed and unprocessed, survivors of these experiences may be shunted through various systems on the basis of overt symptoms without the root cause of the problem ever being addressed. It is therefore imperative that the issue and possibility of abuse, as well as protocols for organized and consistent caring responses to this abuse, be an integral part of training for mental health, criminal justice, human service, medical, clergy, and educational personnel.

Victims of sexual abuse may be first encountered by the criminal justice system, the social service or mental health system, by schools, or medical professionals. They may come to the attention of the criminal authorities for running away, for status offenses, shoplifting, chemical dependency, burglary or auto theft, or for rage acted out in homicide, sex offenses, or other violent crimes. In social service or mental health agencies, professionals may see regression, low self-esteem, eating disorders, multiple victimization, depression, self-mutilation, suicide. In the educational system, victims may surface for truancy, hyperactivity, learning disabilities, behavior problems, a drop in academic performance. Medical and public health practitioners may see children with various physical disorders including stomach problems, rashes, or venereal disease. Treating these effects without treating their causes is rarely effective.

This essay will provide some basic information about the range of behaviors which have been observed among victims. I will also offer some case histories to indicate ways in which these clues may be best utilized to determine whether sexual violence has occurred. For further information about counseling, see Chris Servaty's essay, pp. 124–139.

SYMPTOMS AND CONSEQUENCES

Reactions to trauma will differ according to many things, including the nature of the assault, age, and life experiences of the victim, as well as upon the victim's relationship to the perpetrator (for instance, stranger, family member, boss, coworker, acquaintance). This is no less true for victims of sexual violence than for victims of other crises. There are, however, some characteristic patterns of reactions to abuse within broad developmental categories.

CHILDREN

Most children do not understand what has happened or is happening in abuse, nor are they able to explain verbally the nature of their discomfort. Symptoms may include:

- physical trauma to genital area
- venereal disease
- fear of a particular adult
- withdrawal
- clinging behavior
- refusal to leave home or unwillingness to return home (in cases of incest)
- eating disorders, including loss of appetite, compulsive eating, or food hoarding

- change in sleep patterns
- nightmares
- bed wetting and encopresis (night soiling)
- excessive masturbation
- regression
- frequent genital infections
- agitation
- hyperactivity
- unexplained gagging
- sexually suggestive behavior or explicit knowledge of sexual acts beyond the developmental stage of the child
- somatic complaints such as nausea and vomiting

Children react strongly to the distress of an adult, believing that they are at fault for causing this distress. It is therefore important to remain calm and to phrase questions in age-appropriate language. For example, a child can be asked if anyone has touched her, or forced her to touch them, in ways that make them feel bad or ashamed. It is also important not to blame or judge the perpetrator to the child, because there is often love and loyalty involved. Many children do not want the perpetrator harmed but do want the abuse to end.

ADOLESCENTS

Although able to verbalize the nature and circumstances of the assault, adolescents often keep information about victimization to themselves, due in part to the nature of the feelings around their developing sexuality, independence, and sense of self. Symptoms may include:

- depression
- somatic complaints such as severe headaches, infections, muscle cramping, and dizziness
- eating disorders, including anorexia and bulimia
- fear of pregnancy
- overly seductive or attention-getting behavior
- multiple runaway
- overly restricted by parents or heavy household responsibilities (in cases of incest)
- withdrawal and isolation
- suicide attempts

- self-mutilation such as cutting, burning, or tattooing the self
- chemical abuse
- truancy
- drop in academic performance
- poor self-image as evidenced by dress, lack of cleanliness and grooming
- prostitution

Questions should avoid implications of "good" or "bad," especially as it relates to sexuality. Thus questions such as "I am surprised at your behavior considering the nice family you come from" should be avoided at all costs. One can say instead, "Sometimes a change in grades like this means that a person has some stressful things going on in their life. Is there anything distressing going on with you right now? Is anyone hurting or threatening to hurt you?"

Male victims in particular tend to believe that rape by an older woman should be seen as seduction rather than as a violation, regardless of their real feelings of anger, helplessness, and loss of control. Assault by an older person of the same sex often causes painful and anxiety-provoking questions of sexual identity that must be handled calmly and without judgment.

ADULTS

Although we tend to think of victimization as a discrete act, it is actually a process that precedes overt acts of abuse or assault by shaping and reinforcing a link between sex and violence. This process gives rise to many myths and stereotypes about sexual assault. One consequence of these myths is to blame the victim. Although assault and abuse of adults are reported with increasing frequency, older adults, women of color, physically and developmentally handicapped adults, and male victims are still extremely hesitant about reporting to authorities or seeking help from social service agencies. Although responses to rape vary, people do describe certain feelings and behaviors consistently. The symptoms of what has been termed rape trauma syndrome[7] include physical, emotional, and behavioral reactions, such as:

- shock and disbelief
- fear
- disorganization

- disorientation
- denial
- suppression
- guilt
- self-blame and low self-esteem
- avoidance of the opposite sex
- phobic symptoms (for instance, acrophobia)
- depression
- suicide attempts
- compulsive and/or eating disorders
- nightmares and other sleep disorders
- changes in life style

Because many victims of childhood abuse reach adulthood without healing interventions, they too may exhibit various behavior patterns and symptoms, which may include:

- a history of abusive relationships
- multiple hospitalizations (physical and/or mental)
- chronic depression
- complete repression of entire portions of earlier life
- amnesia
- homicidal or suicidal tendencies
- multiple personality disorder
- a pattern of multiple victimizations
- compulsive and/or eating disorders
- self-mutilation

It must be emphasized that it is a *pattern* of characteristics in a child, adult, or family that can alert us to the likelihood of assault or abuse. Simply relying on a single behavior is of little value in most cases. It is also important to remember that sexual assault takes on specific meaning to victims depending on their stage of development in the life cycle.

When several indicators are present, action needs to be taken. If the victim is a child, reports must be made to the police, sheriff and/or child protective services. Most states also mandate reporting of abuse involving vulnerable adults, which may include the frail elderly as well as the physically, emotionally, and developmentally handicapped. For more information regarding elder abuse, including signs and symptoms of its occurrence, see Jane Boyajian's essay on pp. 31–49.

SOME CASE HISTORIES

In order to make the range of potential symptoms more understandable and immediate, let us look briefly at several case histories. They illustrate how various symptoms may interact in the experience of victims. They may help professionals in recognizing possible responses that may alert them to the possibility of sexual violence.

CASE HISTORY 1

The following case history is a retrospective account. At each point in this woman's developmental history, indicators were present that could have resulted in some healing intervention. Although this story is both painful and poignant, it is by no means atypical.

J, a twenty-nine-year-old woman, came to a sexual violence center in extreme distress. Watching a television movie about incest released a host of repressed memories of her own physical and sexual abuse at the hands of both parents.

J and her five brothers and sisters grew up in the rural Midwest. Her earliest memories of abuse dated back to age four, when she was raped by her father in the family barn. From that point on, abuse was a constant fact of life. Crying or showing hurt or anger were swiftly punished by both parents; punishment could include beating, verbal abuse, or being locked outside the house in midwinter. By age eight, J had developed an atypical eating disorder that included gagging, severe stomach pains, and an aversion toward food. As an adolescent, she was withdrawn and socially isolated. She became pregnant at age fourteen and went to live with her daughter at an older sister's house. This sister reported the abuse to the authorities, resulting in their father's imprisonment.

At the initiation of her therapy, J functioned at a preadolescent level, both socially and emotionally. She weighed a scant eighty-seven pounds and was extremely anxious and depressed. Entire years of her life had been totally repressed, resulting in partial amnesia. During the course of therapy, she was hospitalized twice as a high suicide risk.

J was married and the mother of two children, one of whom was in therapy for acting-out behavior. Her husband, a former alcoholic, was physically and emotionally abusive.

A story such as this one can seem overwhelming. The primary issue, of course, must be the client's present physical safety. Also, because the client is often feeling great shame and trepidation over what she feels is a disgusting and horrifying revelation, referrals must be handled with great care and not be made to seem a rejection.

Throughout the course of her life, J had had significant interaction with both formal and informal care systems, including medicine, education, welfare, family, church, and neighbors. No questions were ever asked, in spite of the myriad symptoms she displayed as a child, an adolescent, and an adult. Once a doctor, treating J for severe abdominal pains, inquired *of the mother* about the possibility of sexual abuse. (The mother had participated in J's abuse.) After her mother's denial, the topic was never broached again, despite J's fear and anxiety when forced to leave the hospital. Threats of death, liberally laced with messages of shame, insured J's silence on the issue until her father's trial. The silence continued until a media event much later in her life forced the floodgates to open on a seemingly endless and overwhelming deluge of pain.

In this case, we are dealing with a person who has lived all her life without any place that could be called safe. Imagine the kinds of behaviors, emotions, and affect that would be displayed by a child or adolescent in such a situation, and you can easily see how logical and consistent are the symptoms listed. The child, feeling trapped and totally powerless, suffers physical symptoms, anxiety, or in rare cases might retreat into another personality. The adolescent often retreats into suicidal or self-destructive behavior. By adulthood, a powerful set of patterns and messages have developed that will not easily be surrendered. For the adult victim of childhood abuse, these patterns have meant survival in a very hostile world. To be without them is a terrifying prospect.

CASE HISTORY 2

S is a twenty-five-year-old woman who came to a sexual violence center out of concern for her two-year-old daughter. She feared the possibility that her daughter was being abused and felt that she might be overreacting to publicity about the issue. After we learned that the child had been asked about abusive touch and that the child displayed no other symptoms, we concluded that the child did not seem to be at risk of sexual abuse. But the mother's concerns were real. It became clear that her concern stemmed, at least in part, from a sexual assault that S had undergone a number of years ago. The assailant was the husband of a close friend, leaving S with feelings of betrayal and confusion. In addition, after she finally spoke to her friend about the assault, S was told that it was her fault; the long-standing friendship was ended. S developed a fear and distrust of men in general and was unable to have a meaningful sexual relationship with her husband. She also experienced violent nightmares on a regular basis.

The issues involved in this case are typical of acquaintance rape, by far a more common occurrence than rape by a stranger. S had a problem even defining the assault as a rape, although it fit every existing legal criteria. Her difficulty calling the assault rape stemmed from the fact that the assailant was a trusted friend. After an agonizing decision to tell someone, she was blamed and rebuffed. It is hardly any wonder, then, that her distress came out either indirectly (nightmares) or was not recognized by her as stemming from the assault (lack of ability to enjoy a sexual relationship). It is interesting to note that in the course of some marital counseling, the issues of sexual assault as a possible cause for the marital unhappiness were never explored by the counselor.

During the course of counseling, S was able to define the assault as rape and to undergo a natural grieving process for the loss of a friendship. Ultimately, S was able to separate her fears for her daughter from her own, finally acknowledging fears for her own safety.

Case History 3

As S did, often a person will come to a counselor, pastor, or even a rape center with a presenting issue that ostensibly has nothing to do with sexual assault. This can occur because the client, overwhelmed with shame, fear, and guilt, is testing the counselor's reactions and trustworthiness. It can also occur because the client herself is uneasy, anxious, or frightened but has repressed the source of these feelings. It is always essential to deal with the client's presenting issue; not to do so is discounting as well as disrespectful. However, it is also incumbent upon us to use gentle probing when and where appropriate, and above all to be aware of the possibility of sexual assault and abuse regardless of the nature of the presenting issue. The following examples may prove useful.

C, a sixty-two-year-old woman, came to a rape center with multiple physical ailments, developing agoraphobia, and an acute anxiety reaction. Her presenting issue was a mugging that she had experienced two months prior to calling us.

I suggested that many of the feelings she was experiencing (guilt, self-blame, shame, fear, anxiety, poor self-image, nightmares) were similar to feelings experienced by people who have been sexually abused. She then admitted to being sexually abused as a child by a neighbor and family member.

V was sent to her pastor after several incidents of kleptomania. Viewing this as typical adolescent rebellion, the man delivered a lengthy, shaming lecture on the commandment "Thou shalt not steal." At that time V, age fourteen, was a multiple runaway. She had been suffering sexual abuse at the hands of her father for almost three years.

In this case, it might have been helpful to examine the cause of V's behavior, rather than assuming that her goal was to steal. V did not receive counseling about the sexual abuse until she was twenty-eight years old.

J, a schoolteacher, came to a rape crisis center seeking information about parenting. She was extremely anxious, fearful, and had been suffering severe headaches for the three-year duration of her marriage. She asked some very basic questions about sex and sexuality that revealed an almost complete ignorance of the topic. She also exhibited bruises at times on her face and arms, which she explained as symptoms of a vitamin deficiency. After several sessions, she was questioned about possible abuse by her spouse. She then revealed a horror story of what amounted to sexual torture and humiliation at the hands of her husband. As a woman who had been raised in a very strict fundamentalist family in which sexuality was never discussed, she was unaware that these behaviors were not a part of a normal marital relationship.

The counselor involved with J wisely allowed her to speak about her presenting issue (parenting), recognizing that the real problem was far too frightening to discuss immediately with a stranger. Again, it was imperative in this case to assess the physical safety of the woman and her child and to counter the minimization and denial with a validation of the seriousness of the situation. For example, one could say, "I appreciate your concern about your ability to parent your child. It sounds like we immediately need to look at Susan's safety and your own as well. What you have described to me is serious and life-threatening. I would like to give you some options right now that will help you protect yourself and your daughter."

Of course, the questions you ask and the language you use will vary with your own style and the facts of the story.

SOME PRACTICAL GUIDELINES

With increased awareness of the symptoms and consequences of sexual assault and sexual abuse, keep in mind the following factors:

1. Be aware of your own comfort level with the issues of sexual assault, abuse, and sexuality. We all have our own biases and prejudices, and certain types of people with whom we do not work well. *Do not hesitate to refer* people with whom you can't work so that they may get help from a colleague.
2. We are often reluctant to ask about things like abuse, suicidal feelings, or rape, fearing that we are being impolite. We may feel that we should somehow know these things instinctively. Shame, fear, and embarrassment often inhibit us from asking directly for the information we need to help us help our clients. *When you observe symptoms or suspect abuse, ask.*
3. Make a habit of routinely including questions about possible experiences of sexual violence in your intake interviews for pastoral counseling or on other appropriate occasions as you get to know the members of your community. Premarital counseling offers a ready-made occasion to inquire about ways the couple deals with conflict. Personal interviews with confirmands or other occasions to speak with teenagers in private can be important. Should a victim share her story with you, ask if she has been to a rape crisis center or other source of aid; if she has not, find out if she wishes to contact someone or to talk with you further about it. Respect her decision if she

is not ready but let her know that you, or other resources, are available.

4. Ask your questions in a matter-of-fact, normal, respectful tone of voice. Your calmness and professional attitude can ease the feelings of shame and secrecy and may make disclosure possible at some future time. Some examples: "A lot of people have experienced a situation in which someone has abused or assaulted them. Has that happened to you?" "People troubled with anorexia (or some other symptom) have sometimes been sexually assaulted. I'm wondering if that's the case with you."

5. If there are no counseling centers nearby or readily accessible to members of your community, consider going yourself to take some in-depth training. If people in your area are unwilling or unable to drive long distances to a specialized center, you may provide greatly needed resources. You can call a center to ask for counseling advice when you are stumped or need consultation and guidance.

5. Elder Abuse: The View from the Chancel

JANE A. BOYAJIAN

Looking out at the faces of our parishioners, it is hard to believe that there are abused elders sitting in the pews.[1] But consider these elders:

- An eighty-five-year-old woman is sexually assaulted in her home. No one believes she is a rape victim, neither family nor police, until her daughter discovers physical evidence that a stranger has been there.
- A seventy-six-year-old woman lies awake at night fearing for her life. Her son, newly discharged from a state hospital, is visiting. He has hit her and threatened to kill her in the past.
- An elderly man, dependent on his son's family for care, is taunted by having his walker hidden.
- A nursing home employee regularly abused female nursing home residents. He was discovered and discharged but quickly found a new job at another facility, where he resumed his sexually abusive behavior. Again, after discovery, he was discharged without public reprimand. When a third nursing home discovered his abuse, he was finally prosecuted and jailed, three years after being fired by the first facility.

Most people believe that elder abuse does not happen to people they know. Many professionals are misinformed about the kinds of elder abuse they are likely to see. Thus we may not be alert for signs of abuse and neglect in home visits, for we believe that such problems occur mostly in institutions. Others may believe that sexual abuse cannot happen in nursing homes "since there is no privacy." In our own congregations, we may expect love and charity and believe that elder abuse may possibly happen—elsewhere.

So we cannot reach out to victims. Indeed, *we do not even see them.*

It matters that clergy recognize the realities. Once alerted, clergy can become important resources in identifying elder abuse when it occurs. Clergy have ongoing access to the homes of elders and to the care facilities in which they reside. More than many formal care providers, clergy are in a position to identify, assess, and intervene in abusive situations. They see elders in their own context, over time. Religious communities are vital links in an area's informal service delivery system, providing volunteer respite care, home visitation, transportation, and chore services.

The vast majority of families provide loving care for their elderly relatives, often at great sacrifice. Most elders are loved. Most institutional care givers and families offer respectful care to their elders. They often do so without adequate support, time, or resources. Some elders are not lovable, having developed attitudes, habits, or illnesses that do not promote intimacy. Others are dependent for so long that their families are worn down over time. Yet most families manage even these difficult and arduous situations.

These positive realities should not blind us to the extent of the problem where it exists nor to the actions we in the churches can take to remedy these problems. In this essay we will first look at some of the emerging facts about elder abuse and the patterns it may assume. Second, we will look at some of the practical steps churches and synagogues may take to act on such mistreatment and injustice.

PATTERNS OF ELDER ABUSE

Almost all of the present awareness of elder abuse comes from the last short decade. One national estimate suggests that some 4 percent of the nation's elderly may be victims of some sort of abuse, from moderate to severe. In other words, one out of every twenty-five elder Americans may be victims of such abuse each year. The Select Committee on Aging of the House of Representatives estimates that only one in five or six cases of elder abuse comes to our attention.[2] In three-quarters of the reported cases, the abuser lives with the victim; in 86 percent of the cases the abuser is a relative—a spouse, a son, or daughter (in that order of frequency).[3] The average victim is eighty to eighty-four years old and has at least one major disability. Women are sixty-eight percent of the victims. Most have lived with their families for over ten years. And thirty-six percent of the time, their abusers are themselves elders.[4]

Elders themselves may not report abuse for a variety of reasons. They may be reluctant to speak of family matters or sexual issues. They may have been threatened or coerced into remaining silent. They may be ill, isolated, incompetent, or ignorant of their rights and potential remedies. They may fear the alternatives, such as being removed from their homes or being placed in a family care facility. Like many victims, they may not speak up because they believe they are at fault and caused the abuse to happen. Others may take abusive behavior for granted. As one elder commented about an abused friend, "She didn't know that what her husband has been doing all these years is abuse; she thinks that's the way marriage is." Furthermore, "a large proportion of family violence is committed by people who do not see their acts as crimes against victims."[5]

Elder abuse can take a number of forms. It may include physical abuse (as overmedication, rape or sexual abuse, enforced nudity, use of restraints, rough handling, beating), negligence (withholding medication or nutrition, poor hygiene, unnecessary pain), psychological abuse (verbal abuse, infantilizing, threats, isolation), financial abuse (stealing, scams and con games, overcharging for services, unauthorized use of social security checks). Some abuses violate the constitutional rights of the victim, including: usurping decision-making powers without a court hearing; disrupting rights to privacy or self-determination; presuming incompetence because the elder is judged to be upset, depressed, or sick; moving an elder from the home into an institution against their will; seeking guardianship of an elder without due process. Such abuses may be committed by family members or by professionals, including counselors, therapists, physicians, clergy, and attorneys.

Mistreatment of elders may take different forms in different settings. The abuses of an elder who lives alone and independently require different preventive strategies and interventions than an elder who resides in an institution or a family setting. Let us look briefly at these patterns.

ELDERS LIVING INDEPENDENTLY

Many elders live independently. We think of them with pleasure; they are symbols of hope for our own coming later years. But for many others reality is quite different.

Many residents in public housing are financially or sexually exploited by employees and then coerced into silence. While formal complaints may be filed and investigations conducted, their assailants are still allowed to work and continue their harassment.

The independence of other elders may be profoundly shaken by a violent act. When assaults or robberies occur in the elder's place of residence, funds and physical mobility required to move and begin anew are often lacking. The confidence and well-being of such persons are destroyed, and they may require institutionalization.

Fear of crime and concerns for personal security are life-altering. These fears may in fact cause life-threatening behavior. Consider the fearful elders who become recluses; when ill, their presence may not be missed by neighbors or trash collectors. There are many elders who sleep by day and watch television all night; they live with their blinds drawn because they are afraid. Such fear distorts reality and affects their sense of self-sufficiency.

While the perceptions of danger may be greater than the actual incidence, crime does occur against elders who live independently.[6] Elders often live in large, older homes or apartments in deteriorating neighborhoods where they are vulnerable to crime. The myth of hoarded valuables entices breaking and entering. Where there is a high concentration of such elderly persons (in public housing and apartment buildings), criminals are attracted by the large number of potential victims. Evidence indicates that because of their more frail physical condition, elders are likely to be injured when criminal acts do occur.

As a society working towards self-sufficiency for elders ("aging in place"), we emphasize ensuring adequate housing, clothing, and nutrition. But attention also must go toward teaching elders self-protection and crime prevention strategies if that later independence is to include freedom from fear. Caring communities have advocacy roles here. Elders do need meals on wheels, transportation, chore services, respite care. But they need far more.

Well-being is profoundly diminished when one lives in an atmosphere of fear. A well-clothed elder who eats balanced meals can hardly be said to live well when fearing for life and property. When an elder withdraws from the community because she or he fears walking to the market or waiting at the bus stop, then the quality of life is deeply affected.[7]

ELDERS IN INSTITUTIONS

We should neither ignore nor exaggerate the sexual or physical abuse of elders by employees of nursing homes. The spectrum of abusive behavior may range from rough handling and disrespectful language, on the one hand, to battering and sexual violence on the other. Some behavior that was once permitted in care facilities is now recognized as abusive.

Institutional abuse may continue because other staff do not report violations; fear of liability and a reluctance to become involved contribute to collegial silence. In addition, most institutions do not have standard, clearly stated operating procedures to follow when abuse is discovered. Patients may not know their rights or may take certain abusive behaviors for granted.

Attitudes about professional accountability and improved understanding about patient rights are changing the institutional environment. For example, the use of restraints, which was once routine, may make managing a patient easier for the staff. With the recognition that people are entitled to the least restrictive alternative, we now look upon the casual use of restraints as a civil liberties violation. Management problems for staff do occur when elders are frightened, upset, or have chemical dependency problems or degenerative diseases. But it is too easy to dismiss the complaints of residents as paranoid, senile, hysterical, or controlling. Some jurisdictions have a bill of rights for nursing home patients mandated by statute. Nursing home residents councils and family councils (for the families of residents) are important new vehicles for promoting autonomy among institutional residents. They are legitimate on-site groups to whom complaints can be referred.

ELDER ABUSE BY FAMILY CAREGIVERS

Some family caregivers intentionally hurt their elders. In many families, abuse is a learned response. Some families and some cultures do not value elders. In some families, violence is a dominant theme, a way to express rage, handle stress, or make proprietary claims on other family members. In other families, elder abuse becomes a means of repaying past grievances. Thus one pattern "is that in which the aggressor suffered real or perceived mistreatment by his [*sic*] parents or caregivers earlier in life and who now reverses the behavior."[8] And of course, abuse can be affected by the mental impairment of the abuser or by chemical dependency problems.

Such abuses are not usually a single lapse in behavior, evidence of a momentary blindness. Most often they are established patterns of interaction within the family. A spouse who batters does not usually begin late in life; more likely the battering pattern began earlier.

Some abuse by family care givers is unintentional—bad effects from good intentions. The realities in a specific care-giving context may promote the environment in which abuse occurs. Often family members have unrealistic expectations about the care they can provide. When they are unable to live up to these visions, they feel frustrated and guilty. Many care givers in the family are drained of energy, with physical or economic resources pushed beyond the breaking point. Having begun to care for an elder with the best of intentions, they themselves are now also in crisis, without perceived options. Unprepared for the task and unsupported in it, they may feel overwhelmed by the long years of care which lie ahead. Caretakers may find their own lifetime plans suddenly changed as the return of a parent ends cherished visions for freedom from dependents. Others may see siblings who are not sharing the burdens of the caretaking, who are free to travel or to spend their money on discretionary items. In anger and hopelessness, such persons may turn on a vulnerable elder.

Economic issues seriously complicate these emotional dynamics. Professionals report that economic factors affect abuse in two-thirds of the cases.[9] Some families may have the financial resources but are reluctant to spend their money on outside help. But more often, the financial resources are simply not available. Both coping skills and financial resources are drained. Furthermore, many such care givers are middle-generation women, "caught between the care needs and financial liabilities of their children and their parents . . . at the very time they should be preparing for their own retirement."[10]

These situational factors in elder abuse are not a justification for abuse, of course. But recognizing these factors helps us see what interventions the church can offer care-giving families. Churches can play important roles in identifying families who are at risk and supporting care givers whose emotional resources are being drained away. Furthermore, understanding the factors that contribute to elder abuse can help us identify and prevent crises before they occur.

Recent trends in our society make it likely that elder abuse will increase in the future. Changes in family structure, the deteriorating economy, increases in poverty and in single-person households, increased life expectancy for the aged, cost-cutting measures in health care delivery systems, and trends toward deinstitutionalization of elders are not causes for optimism about the future of our elders.[11] Given the trend in the public sector to rely more and more on the informal service delivery system, religious communities are likely to have the opportunity to intervene in ways that promote well-being.

WHAT RELIGIOUS LEADERS CAN DO

The religious community can play an essential role in intervening in situations of elder abuse, helping to bring more humane treatment. It can also be a significant force in helping to prevent elder abuse before it occurs.

BE AWARE

As representatives of a caring community, religious leaders need to educate ourselves about the facts of elder abuse. Be aware of the patterns of stress that can lead to elder abuse. Be sensitive and alert on home or institutional visits. (See the list of possible signs of elder abuse at the end of this chapter.)

Many states have recently enacted mandatory reporting statutes, making the identification and reporting of abuse of dependent and vulnerable people a nondiscretionary issue for professionals. Find out the situation in your state. One study indicates that over 70 percent of all reports of elder abuse are made by third parties. In another, 60 percent of reported cases were discovered by routine home visits.[12] Recognizing symptoms and assuring appropriate and timely responses are critical first steps that home visitors—both clergy and lay—can readily provide. In suburban and rural settings, the importance of church involvement may be even greater because formal support services are often less available than in metropolitan areas. Intervention and referral to those skilled in family violence or to public authorities offers hope for those suffering in the present and the possibility of breaking cycles of abuse for future family members.

Identify the community resources available before crises comes to your attention. Seek out the personnel of your community's adult protective services, women's shelter, or sexual violence center. Become familiar with the processes followed once formal complaints have been filed. Be sure that someone from the caring community follows the family and the elder through the process. While the recommendations of many authorities (including the Attorney General's Task Force on Family Violence) is to remove the abuser from the home rather than the vulnerable victim, in many instances it is the victim who is torn from familiar surroundings. In such cases, the active presence of the religious community can be vital.

Pastoral care courses in theological schools and continuing education programs should utilize the growing expertise of adult protective services, ombudspersons, sexual violence centers, and women's shelters. This training must also include deepened understanding of civil liberties issues of autonomy, respect for persons, informed consent, the right to the least restrictive alternatives. In addition, pastoral care programs should consider such complex problems as the borderline cases in which an elder seems competent at times and incompetent at others, or the implications of degenerative diseases.

BREAK THE SILENCE

The educational ministry of the church can be effective in highlighting the facts of elder abuse as we presently know them. Preaching and teaching on such topics can spread such information more widely in our communities. It can also validate the reality of those victims who now live in isolation. We must alert elders to the dangers and necessary precautions without frightening them irresponsibly. Promote community-building activities in your area, such as neighborhood watch and block events, to cut through the isolation elders may feel as neighborhoods change. Make sure that safety and crime prevention strategies are taught to elders in ways that take into account the physiological changes of aging and are realistic about their fears.

It is helpful to assist elders and their families to evaluate options for care before they are needed and to alert people to their rights and remedies when abuses do happen. Encourage elders to name formal and informal advocates who are aware of their values before a crisis occurs so that such persons will have standing in legal, medical, and family settings. Caretaking families can be helped to plan more realistically the care they can provide, to assess their own limitations, and to identify community resources before they reach a crisis point.

In addition, we in the churches need to examine our own religious source materials. Do our sacred writings and hymns exhort victims to remain suffering victims? Do we blame victims?

Undo Ageism

Ageism in our society feeds and perpetuates the abuse of elders. Our stereotypes about older people close our eyes to the realities in which they live. So we may not believe that an eighty-two-year-old woman has been raped. We forget that sexual assault is a crime against a vulnerable person, not restricted by age.[13] We may believe that a complaining elder is hysterical, paranoid, or forgetful of facts. We may, in keeping with trends, label behavior we do not understand as related to Alzheimer's disease.

We should presume that elders are competent when they tell us they are being threatened or harmed. The bottom line is: Believe the elder. Few people are more isolated than elders whom no one believes and who are without advocates.

Respect Persons

Trivializing elders and their concerns is abusive and sometimes life-threatening. Respect for persons means empowering them to live fully, promoting the conditions in which they can thrive. We should review programs we offer to the elderly. The bright minds who did not play bingo at thirty-five can hardly be expected at seventy to look upon it as the pivotal moment of their week.

Growing old often means becoming increasingly dependent on others. It carries with it the curse of the disrespectful attitudes on the part of those who give care. But dependence is a state of being, not a state of mind. In some societies this dependency is labeled normal rather than pathological, and it is the right of both the old and the young. When we respect persons, we respect their right to explore, to continue to grow, and to exercise their freedom, whatever their age. Being free means being able to choose even that which others might not want for us. It means being free to make mistakes.

PROMOTE AND PROTECT AUTONOMY

One study shows that elders consistently seem optimistic about their ability to provide for their own needs while caregivers are consistently pessimistic about their ability to do so. Family and staff are inclined to think protectively about elders. We should push hard against that inclination and towards the freedom that is the right of all persons.

Three tricky labels are often applied to elders: noncomplaint, self-neglectful, self-abusive. Care givers may inadvertently develop a proprietary attitude toward those in their care, believing that "we know better" what dependent elders need than they do themselves. We cannot presume incompetence when an elder's choices differ from our own. Personal eccentric lifestyles and unwillingness to accept a specific treatment are not *prima facie* evidence of incompetence.

Serious ethical issues of informed consent may easily arise. Consent is informed only when we have full information about the diagnosis, prognosis, treatment options, and likely outcomes. Consent is only voluntary when the patient makes a free, uncoerced choice. Competence means being able to understand the immediate situation and likely consequences of a decision. Religious leaders are often called to assist the decision-making process when an elder is acutely ill or when chronic long-term care is needed. We have a responsibility to remind those who would choose for an elder, even from deep love and concern, that care decisions rest with that elder; that patients have the right to choose or refuse unless they are truly incompetent. If the elder is no longer truly competent, we need to help families remember that elder's values. What would she tell us to do if she could? How would he describe a life worth living?

Refusing or agreeing to treatment is a decision that emerges from an individual's views of life, death, and responsibility to others. Many elders fear the final abuse of the body and spirit through medical interventions that only prolong death. Many fear a dying process that is emotionally and financially destructive to their loved ones. Religious leaders have a unique role in such situations. Just as we would stand against intentionally inflicting harm on elders, so we should affirm respect for their decisions. We can remind others that death is not the worst that can happen to an elder. We can state that choices and refusals flow out of the elder's value system, which is religiously rooted.

We can urge all parishioners to think about these issues in advance of an illness or crisis. How do I wish to be cared for in specific situations? Do I have a doctor who understands my views and will respect them? Have I selected an advocate who understands my values and will monitor my care? Have I documented my plans through such vehicles as living wills and entries in my physician's records?

Support Public Policy Changes

The prophetic ministry of the church can make important statements where public policy is developed. In nursing homes in your area or under the sponsorship of your denomination, encourage the formation of standard, clearly stated policies and operating procedures that residents and employees are expected to follow when abuse is discovered. Encourage the legislature of your home state to enact a bill of rights for nursing home patients if it has not already done so. Be concerned about declining community revenues and potential reductions in human services. Many of the strategies that could have an impact on elder abuse depend upon major government funding, new priorities among service providers, and enlightened administrative and legislative policies.

CELEBRATE CREATION

Whatever their age and circumstances, elders are a part of our community. Their lives and their places in the world need to be acknowledged, lifted up, celebrated as matters of rejoicing. We need to provide affirmation of their many pasts, the opportunity to hope realistically, and the right to thrive as fully as their conditions permit. Being in community means knowing that one matters; knowing that we matter has an effect on our well-being. This is participating in creation, the work of the church.

INDICATORS OF ABUSE, NEGLECT, AND EXPLOITATION OF THE ELDERLY[14]

The importance of educating service and care providers about indicators of abuse cannot be overemphasized. These can include:

PHYSICAL APPEARANCE

Burns, especially located in unusual sites
Bilateral bruises on upper arms (from shaking)
Clustered bruises on trunk (from repeated striking)
Bruises resembling an object
Old and new bruises (injury repeated)
Bone fractures or signs of fracture
Lacerations, welts, black eye
Bedsores
Unhealed sores, untreated injuries
Tremors
Broken glasses or frames
Lack of prosthetic devices
Clothing inappropriate for weather, filthy, torn, too big, rags
Lack of clothing
Same clothing all the time
Shoes on wrong feet
Odorous
Fleas, lice
Rash, impetigo, eczema
Malnutrition

Wheezing, persistent cough
Unintentionally noncommunicative
Untreated medical conditions
Swollen ankles (heart, kidney ailment)
Decayed teeth
Swollen eyes
Severe or constant pain
Swelling of legs
Coldness in parts of body
Red, painful eyes (glaucoma)
Coma
Swelling of joints accompanied by weakness or fever
Blue feet (vascular problem)
Vomiting
Shortness of breath
Chest pains
Sudden weight loss or gain
Blood in excretions
Lumps
Loss of sight or hearing
Heat exhaustion
Incontinence
Dehydration
Intentional or unintentional overmedication by caregiver
Hair thin as though pulled out
Scars
Dilated pupils
Narcolepsy
Nails need clipping

Behavior

Recent or sudden changes in behavior
Unjustified fear or unwarranted suspicion
Refusal to discuss situation or communicate need for help
Unwillingness to talk
Unreasonable excuses
Denial of problems
Unaware of how much money they receive and regular monthly
 expenses

Changes in will or in representative payee or in power of attorney
Payment of exorbitant prices for services, repairs, rent
Depleted bank account with nothing to show for it
Large amount of purchases on time payment plan
Chronic failure to pay bills
Frequent requests at end of month for supplemental income

ENVIRONMENT

Hazardous condition, such as poor wiring, rotten porch, unventilated gas, broken glass, no locks, roof leaks
Many outdated medications from different doctors
Medicines not clearly marked
Fecal/urine smell
Soiled bedding or furniture
Urine-soaked bed
Evidence of restraints
Food is not present, inadequate, or spoiled
Empty bottles of liquor
Lack of electricity, water, heat, toilet, cooking facilities, refrigeration
House infested with fleas, lice, roaches, rats
Burst water pipes
Frequent moving
Disappearance of personal property or household items
Home too cold or too hot
Overcrowding

BEHAVIOR OF FAMILY OR CAREGIVER

Marital or family discord
Continuous friction
Striking, shoving, beating, name calling, scapegoating
Conflicts with others in community
Hostile, secretive, frustrated, shows little concern, poor self-control, blaming elderly client
Denial of problems
Arguments within extended family on care provided to client
Manipulates client into paying bills, loaning money
Recent family crisis

Alcohol or drug use by family
Family has other ill members
Resentment by caregiver
Caregiver lacks knowledge of client's condition and needed care
History of mental illness in the family
Client left alone for extended periods of time
Excessive payment for care
Unusual household composition
Caregiver does not provide needed personal care
Withholds food, medication
Overly frugal
Client locked away
Caregiver does not allow visitors
Family does not interact with client
Resentment, jealousy
Unrealistic expectations of client
Someone other than caregiver brings client for treatment
Prolonged interval between injury and treatment
Doctor-hopping
Explanation of injury not feasible or consistent
Other unreported injuries found
Sudden appearance of previously uncaring relatives
Transfer of property, savings, insurance, wills
Unexplained cash flow

2. UNDERSTANDING THE ISSUES

Sexual assault and abuse raise serious theological issues. We cannot respond adequately to victims without dealing with these theological dimensions. The essays in this section remind us that we in religious communities will not understand these topics until we see their spiritual and religious dimensions, which are especially the responsibility of religious communities.

The poem, "with no immediate cause," is the impetus for an introduction to these theological dimensions in the following essay, "Violence against Women: The Theological Dimension."

"Don't Tell Mother" is the firsthand account of the experience of a survivor of incest in a good churchgoing family.

"A Commentary on Religious Themes in Family Violence" alerts us to several themes that may emerge in the lives of victims such as the meaning of suffering and the meaning of marriage and family in the Jewish and Christian traditions. We are invited to interpret these themes carefully so that we may participate in healing and liberating victims rather than revictimizing them.

"A Theological Perspective on Sexual Assault" points to still other religious dimensions of the experiences of victims—the life-threatening quality of the experience, issues of trust, feeling dirty, and the healing process.

"Theological Perspectives on Sexual Violence" explores the tradition's treatment of women, evil, the cross and resurrection, the image of God, and some issues for assailants.

This array of theological elements of sexual assault and abuse is only a beginning. We invite you to pursue your own theological reflection on these topics from your own experiences and perspectives.

WITH NO IMMEDIATE CAUSE

every 3 minutes a woman is beaten
every five minutes a
woman is raped/every ten minutes
a little girl is molested
yet I rode the subway today
I sat next to an old man who
may have beaten his old wife
3 minutes ago or 3 days/30 years ago
he might have sodomized his
daughter but I sat there
cuz the men on the train
might beat some young women
later in the day or tomorrow
I might not shut my door fast
enough push hard enough
every 3 minutes it happens
some woman's innocence
rushes to her cheeks/pours from her
  mouth
like the betsy wetsy dolls have been
  torn
apart/their mouths
menses red split/every
three minutes a shoulder
is jammed through plaster and the
  oven door/
chairs push thru the rib cage/hot
  water or
boiling sperm decorate her body
I rode the subway today
and bought a paper from an
east Indian man who might
have held his old lady onto
a hot pressing iron/ I didn't know
maybe he catches little girls in the
parks and rips open their behinds
with steel rods/ I can not decide
what he might have done I only
know every 3 minutes
every 5 minutes every 10 minutes
I bought the paper
looking for the announcement
there has to be an announcement
of the women's bodies found
yesterday the missing little girl
I sat in a restaurant with my
paper looking for the announcement
a young man served me coffee
I wondered did he pour the boiling
coffee on the woman because she was
  stupid
did he put the infant girl in

the coffee pot because she cried too
  much
what exactly did he do with hot coffee
I looked for the announcement
the discovery of the dismembered
woman's body
victims have not all been
identified today they are
naked and dead/some refuse to
testify one girl out of 10's not
coherent/ I took the coffee
and spit it up I found an
announcement/ not the woman's
bloated body in the river floating
not the child bleeding in the
59th street corridor/ not the baby
broken on the floor/

> "there is some concern
> that alleged battered women
> might start to murder their
> husbands and lovers with no
> immediate cause"

I spit up I vomit I am screaming
we all have immediate cause
every 3 minutes
every 5 minutes
every 10 minutes
every day
women's bodies are found
in alleys and bedrooms/at the top of
  the stairs
before I ride the subway/buy a paper
  or drink
coffee from your hands I must know
have you hurt a woman today
did you beat a woman today
throw a child cross a room are the
  little girl's pants in your pocket
did you hurt a woman today
I have to ask these obscene questions
I must know you see
the authorities require us to
establish
immediate cause
every three minutes
every five minutes
every ten minutes
every day

—Ntozake Shange

6. Violence Against Women: The Theological Dimension

MARY D. PELLAUER

To anyone whose life has been touched by the many forms of violence against women, Ntozake Shange's poem is a powerful statement. It expresses the anger, pain, and fury of those who have been working in the last decade to combat sexual and domestic violence. It evokes the fear and suspicion, some might say paranoia, of those who have looked steadily at the abuse of women and found it an abyss. There are no exterior signs, no marks of Cain, to distinguish the batterer or the rapist.

Shange's poem speaks directly out of such experiences in other ways, too. Despite the valiant efforts of feminists to establish and maintain rape crisis centers and battered-women's shelters, and the occasional responsiveness of funding centers, law enforcement agencies, government officials, and the general public, there still remains a distance between the perspectives of activists and those of the "authorities" or the media—a chilling, killing distance.

Furthermore, the rhythmic repetitions in Shange's language express all too well the seemingly endless stream of women and girls who are victimized. A stream? No, a flood. Dreadful as is Shange's refrain, the poem perhaps underestimates the extent of violence against women. All such calculations are risky, given the uncertainties of estimating unreported crimes and the political interests of those doing the arithmetic. To the best of my knowledge, Shange's figures are accurate and representative of the data base up to 1976. (I checked, for example, with the Office of Statistics of the Department of Justice, the FBI Uniform Crime Report, and the National Center for Child Abuse and Neglect of the Department of Health and Human Services.) More recent estimates by feminists who take into account the vagaries and complexities of reporting procedures (for example, *battering* is not a term used by law enforcement agencies), and by sociologists who study domestic violence, run higher: Every *two* minutes a woman is raped. Every *eighteen seconds* a woman is beaten by the man she lives with. Every *five* minutes a child is molested. Every *thirty* minutes a daughter is molested by her father.

However, we should not lose ourselves in overly nice calculations. No more than the announcement read by Shange in the newspaper do such statistics convey the horrors of sexual and domestic violence. They are as terrible as Shange's poem recreates them to be.

Those realities insistently call us who are Christian people to meditate once again upon our experiences and tradition and to act and reflect theologically in new and more humane ways. These realities especially summon us to reflect from our base in ministry —that is, from the wholeness of our religious lives in ongoing traditions. Ministry is the task of all Christians, lay and ordained, at every level of the church from our smallest local parishes through denominational and ecumenical structures. The task of that ministry is to bring the healing and wholeness and liberation promised by God's grace to every facet of human life, from personal woundedness to social and institutional structures.

The pervasiveness of sexual and domestic violence challenges us to a significant, if not fundamental, reconstruction of our Christian heritage in thought, feeling, and action, ranging from our institutional forms to our piety and worship. So comprehensive a demand cannot be fully justified here; nor can the full range of that reconstruction be sketched. Guidelines for that task, however, need to be proposed and widely discussed among religious persons. To begin the process, I suggest three such guidelines. By way of introduction, I share some vignettes from my own life. As a feminist theologian, I claim that the extent to which any theology obscures its experiential base is the extent to which it participates in patriarchy.

I became interested in women's history about ten years ago. Reading about the women's suffrage movement, that piece of American life which nobody had ever told me about before, I felt both empowerment and despair. Empowerment, because these women were my feminist foremothers; here, at last, was *my* tradition. Despair, because the struggles, arguments, and claims of the last women's movement were astonishingly like our more recent ones. I became haunted by a sense that we were repeating ourselves.

One day I stumbled across early feminist attacks on the "rule of thumb"—the judicial precedent, based on English common law, that a husband might beat his wife provided that the rod used was no thicker than his thumb. I was devastated to find the origins of this piece of our language. But I also remember thinking: Here at last is some *progress.* Here, surely, is a relic of a barbarian past left behind as we became more "modern."

My complacency was shattered when the women's movement discovered battered women. Over the past years, the growing literature regarding violence against women circled what became a familiar theme, virtually a litany: No one had ever studied this material or asked these questions before. No one asked, for example, whether the women Freud saw might genuinely have been victims of incest. No one asked the women in primitive cultures what they thought about the ritual rape male anthropologists shrugged off so easily. No one asked whether being beaten by one's husband was a private trouble or a public issue.

It took some months, nearly a year, in the earliest stages of my discovery of battered women, for me to *realize,* to *remember,* that as a child I had seen battering in my own home. I had seen my father lunge at my mother with a butcher knife. I had seen her pick up a big black frying pan to fend him off. I stood paralyzed in the door to the stairs watching this swift and passionate duel. I stood in the door to the living room. I sat on a kitchen chair: I had seen it more than once. I had seen him slap and hit, seen him after her with a baseball bat, heard the endless reams of abusive language that spilled from my father's lips.

I had taken it for granted—just as had the police, the school system, the newspapers we read, the books in the public library, the social workers. I believed that this was just the way it was for women. While I had a hard time dealing with those memories, I had an even harder time dealing with the fact that I had *forgotten,* forgotten so effectively that I never connected my own personal experiences of those stark and terrifying tussles in my home with the women's history I had read, or even with the testimony of contemporary battered women.

I recall too that when our pastor came to call, we all sat about properly on our chairs, smiled stiffly, and said: "Yes, everything is fine, fine, just fine."

In those same early 1970s, while in graduate school, I began teaching in several Chicago-area seminaries. Once at a Christmas party, a male faculty friend wandered over, a glass of Scandinavian glogg in his hand, to mention that he was counseling a seminarian who was beating his wife. I was thunderstruck, shaken to the core of my confidence in Christianity. I looked around at the seminarians I taught with eyes even more suspicious and wary than a stiff dose of Mary Daly's *Beyond God the Father* had previously made them. And I found connections. Even the friends I admired and trusted knew almost nothing about rape and battering. Worse, they took these abuses for granted in the same casual way our culture as a whole did. Those who became concerned often acted as though it were a problem "out there," somewhere beyond the churches. They did not believe that these were issues that they would find, starkly, in their own parishes. Such things do not happen to "Christian women."

This combination of personal experience and perceived need led me to develop and coteach with Lois Gehr Livezey a course on "Violence and Violation." We were glad for each other's company, for neither of us was very sure that these were *really* theological issues. More than once we scared ourselves with the novelty of what we were saying. Nowhere in any traditional theological books could we find guidance on such topics. In the following ten years I *never* taught this course without finding among my students women who were prey to these forms of abuse.

Over the past decade, some things *have* changed. There are now rape crisis centers and hotlines, as well as a sizable battered-women's movement, with a national coalition to share information and strategy. Attention has focused on other forms of abuse— pornography, sexual harassment on the job, strip searches of women by police, sterilization abuse, to name but a few.

This movement, however, is just beginning to have an impact on Christian ministry and our churches. Thanks to ground-breaking work by the United Methodist Women in Crisis project, we now *know* that our local parishes include sizable numbers of victims of these forms of violence. But so far, church agencies and sociologists of religion have not been very interested in whether or how many victims turn to their clergy for support. Nor do we have anything beyond anecdotal evidence on how clergy treat abused women who do turn to them. Feminist grassroots groups may be wary of clergy because victims all too frequently report that their minister or priest exacerbated the victim's plight. ("This is a cross you must learn to bear" or "turn the other cheek" can be deadly dimensions of traditional Christian piety in this context.) Occasionally one does meet pastors who are aware, compassionate, and active in coalition building for structural change, but we don't know how typical they are.

As increasing numbers of women enter seminaries, consciousness of such abuse has increased among ministers. This may be due to the unspoken solidarity among women, since many of us will never be comfortable telling a man about these intimate wounds. It may be due to the fact that women in ministry are more aware of the threats and menaces against all women and hence willing to speak about them, to communicate understanding and openness. It may also be a function of the sheer novelty of women in ministry: Because the bonds of congregational expectations are not yet solidified, new roles are possible for women clergy.

But women in ministry are few and far between and overextended. For change to occur, therefore, clergymen also must hear and respond in new ways. They must become convinced that violence against women is literally a life-and-death issue; they must learn to respond from the new knowledge of such abuses rather than from old stereotypes and to engage in the social analysis that embeds our understandings of violence against women in larger understandings of sexism. Clergymen must be transformed, personally and theologically, as women have been. If men in the clergy learn nothing more than to refer to women's agencies, to support shelters and rape crisis lines, it will be a gain.

In order for us all to take serious and effective steps toward eradicating these abuses, I propose three broad guidelines for ministry.

1. Churches must break the dynamics of silence surrounding rape, batter-

ing, and sexual abuse of children. Taken most simply, this means information and education, tasks that have been integral to our churches' lives. We have Sunday schools, bulletins, books, devotional guides, memoranda, denominational statements, study guides. They must now be used to spread the word. This process has already begun: Thanks to its Commission on Women and the Churches, the United Presbyterian Church in the U.S.A. has submitted materials regarding sexual violence to its General Assembly. The United Methodist Office of Women in Crisis has become an important center for collecting and distributing information. Magazines such as *The Lutheran* have published articles on rape, incest, battering, and pornography.

But most essential is our communication at the *local parish* level, for that is where U.S. churches and the Christian faith live and move and have their being, to paraphrase the liturgy. There human interaction is crucial. And it is here, I fear, that we most frequently fall short.

Like my family, many victims may never take these wounds to their ministers. This may be realistic, especially when so few clergy know how to deal with these evils. But I do not believe that there is a parish anywhere in this nation that does not include victims of domestic and sexual violence. The parish clergy may or may not know who they are, particularly in the "last taboo" of father-daughter sexual abuse. Even should the clergy know, the congregation may not. Obviously, it is fundamental to guard the privacy of each victim, whose right alone it is to decide with whom to share their story. But it is nonetheless important for a congregation to understand that it is *likely* to include such people. Our silence reinforces and perpetuates the inhibitions and taboos that contribute to the suffering of the victim; it allows many myths and stereotypes regarding such victimization to undermine each woman's movement toward health. Furthermore, our silence contributes to the sense that churches are places where people go when all is well, when we have on our best clothes, where we smile at each other and say, "things are fine, fine, just fine," where we act out the pretense that we are in control of our lives.

Such dynamics may vary among social classes, ethnic groups, and denominations. Perhaps the glazed smile is most in evidence in those circles where keeping up appearances is most prized. But among other groups different dynamics may function to the same end, such as in my lower-class family who perceived the pastor as a primary authority figure.

Other dynamics also undermine our ministry to the victims of abuse. The notion that anger is not a Christian virtue, for example, or the fear of conflict. I would add also the suspicion that both the less happy and the more extravagant emotions do not belong in church—melancholy, tears, fear, anxiety, panic, urgency, deep need, insecurity.

Once when I was speaking on these topics to a middle-class congregation, a member said to me, "Why do you dwell on these matters? It will just make you unhappy." This reaction may not be unusual, though that person was unusually honest in saying aloud what many seem to believe. I have some sympathy with this reaction. But I am not just "unhappy" about rape and battering and child sexual abuse; I am furious, agonized—and determined. What the women's movement has made us see, however, is not simply the massive pain of sexual and domestic violence. It has made us see that these conditions are not the will of God or the inevitable workings of nature, but that they can and must be changed. It has made us see that our pain and anger are legitimate and that they can become sources of energy to change the world.

Averting our eyes from the agonizing realities does more than guard our individual "peace" of mind. It *ensures* that we will not participate in the struggles of social transformation that are required. Ministry occurs when the skin of the soul is rubbed raw. If we turn our eyes from the pain of such issues, we turn away from the deepest work of our Christian calling to ministry and away from the real locus of its power and beauty.

What can churches begin to do? The presence of congregations in every corner of the nation suggests that they would be an ideal network of safe homes. Seminaries need courses to help students deal with such issues. We need more organizations such as the Center for the Prevention of Sexual and Domestic violence under the pioneering leadership of the Reverend Marie Fortune, who first made us aware of the theological questions asked by rape victims. Synodical bodies need to take some steps such as that of the Minnesota Council of Churches, which between 1977 and 1985 employed the Reverend Joy Bussert to provide clergy continuing education regarding rape, battering, and child sexual abuse. Sunday schools and women's groups can provide basic self-defense classes for women. More, we might consider prayerfully whether, in Shange's words, "we all have immediate cause" for striking back at our assailants or whether there are more appropriate and effective ways to transform the cycles of violence. We need to generate liturgical resources, songs and prayers, sermons and rituals, for weeping and lamenting these pains and for celebrating true wholeness for abused women.

However, we barely begin to understand ministry regarding sexual and domestic violence when we consider such issues primarily as they relate to churches, congregations, and clergy.

2. *Adequate ministry on sexual and domestic violence requires moving toward full-scale social justice.* Many rape victims, battered women, and sexually abused children have no contact with a church. Our responsibilities do not end with those with whom we come face to face. Nor is humane and informed counseling of victims, however necessary, enough. We must address ourselves to structural changes in the institutions of the social order so that we can prevent abuse.

Adequate ministry to women who are already victimized itself requires sweeping changes in our institutions. Until recently, hospitals, police, court systems, laws, schools, and churches were virtually united in what I can only call organized thoughtlessness and *organized mercilessness* toward abused women. Over the last few years, some have changed; others have not. Government budget cuts and inflation endanger even the few programs in existence. To ensure their permanence, such changes need to reach into the medical school, the law school, the police academy, the graduate department of psychology or education, the theological seminary, where images of women are distorted. All these institutions need to be scrutinized, to be called and pressured to offer victims compassionate treatment that enhances the healing of their physical, psychic, and spiritual wounds, and to ensure that offenders are treated with a moral seriousness that demands their transformation.

Such changes will require thoughtful and strategic coalition with feminists rather than the defensiveness that often characterizes our behavior as churches. Here I fear that it is we who are churchpeople who will need to prove our credentials and our seriousness, rather than the other way around. We in the churches have not been the pioneers of the movement against violence against women.

Prevention is even harder. Sexual and domestic violence does not have a single, tidy "cause" that can be readily isolated in one set of practices, beliefs, or institutions. Rather, it is part of a massive social pattern of our common life: sexism. These dramatic abuses are related to the less dramatic dimensions of the patriarchal order: to an advertising industry that sells products with pictures of women chained astraddle chairs or with precocious hip-bumping gyrations of preadolescent girls; to a clothing industry that produces and markets garments reinforcing images of women as sexual objects and actively encouraging our physical helplessness; to segregated labor markets that price women's work at 59 percent of men's; to structures in which so many of us learn to accept or to inflict violence; to movies and television that portray male violence as attractive and desirable.

Precisely because violence against women is so deeply embedded in this patriarchal whole, many feminists believe talk of prevention to be a utopian dream. Indeed, if we could get reliable and institutionalized guarantees of understanding, thoughtfulness, and mercy for victims, we might be a long way toward utopia. I for one find that I need to hold on to a small piece of that utopianism, that piece which lives in our longing for "justice that flows like living water," not intermittent justice, but a continuous flow, a mighty flood.

3. Adequate ministry on sexual and domestic violence requires a theological reconstruction in a feminist vein. The last ten years have witnessed a deepening and widening of the streams of feminist theology. There is more than one theological reconstruction required of us if we are to come seriously and critically to terms with sexual and domestic violence. Historical theology and biblical criticism, for example, must grapple with those traditional stories and comments which explicitly portray or perpetuate abuse against women. Pastoral care courses in seminary after seminary must rework their psychological and spiritual perspectives so that they can both cease perpetuating notions that take such abuses for granted and also reconstruct their perspectives toward healing and health of the victims.

We need both new words and new actions, new concepts and

new institutions, as integral parts of this theological reconstruction. It is our theological creativity in thought and feeling and action that is at stake for me here. This creativity both depends upon and enhances our creativity in ministry—just as the misogynous neglect of abused women in our tradition perversely reinforces itself in theology and ministry.

We need, for example, to listen with new ears for the ringing sounds of God's voice rippling through the voices of women as they come up against rape, battering, and child sexual abuse. When women who are raped speak of it as a life-threatening experience, we need new words—words surely that can replace the silly, brutalizing old words that said implicitly that rape was barely important, if they did not say explicitly that nobody should kick about being given a good time.

We need new words that can express the ultimate dimension that can be a part of rape as women come face to face with an evil meant to them. We need to listen to the rape victim who goes home in a daze to wash herself, and we need to wonder whether she is expressing a spontaneous theology, a theology that asserts that the violation of the body is a fundamental, perhaps an *ontological* violation. (One of the meanings of "violate" suggests this: "to profane, to desecrate.") In short, we need to learn to do theology *from the body.* This may be difficult for a tradition with body-mind dualisms as deeply embedded as ours. But a theology that takes rape, battering, and child sexual abuse seriously will be a fresh one, fed by new insights into the victim's perspective, enhancing our abilities to do justice and love mercy.

A feminist theology involves us directly with power and sisterhood, both central to theological movement in the midst of sexual and domestic violence. Like anger, these are not comfortable topics to address in the context of ministry. Many themes in our tradition imply that the abnegation of power is good, especially for women. With the separation of church and state and with massive industrialization power has largely departed for "secular" realms.

But it is power that keeps sexual violence in place. When we women stand up for ourselves, learning self-defense, rejecting passivity, affirming our own thinking, speaking, and feeling, fighting back in whatever way we can, remembering our own experience even when our tradition tells us it isn't so, then we undercut the cycles of sexism and its violence. A feminist theology that takes women's power and sisterhood as a theological resource is a small but luminous gift we may have yet to offer to the women's movement and to our churches.

Sisterhood is sisterhood wherever it occurs—within or outside the church. Where there is sisterhood, there is a women's movement. It is in sisterhood that empowerment of women happens: by the stroke of a hand on a back, by the ear listening at the other end of the telephone, by the voice saying exactly what I have felt but could not bring myself to admit, by the occasional confrontation that we can accept from one who knows our experience, by the anger gathering, the tears mingling. Slowly, we learn to think theologically about those tears. We learn to affirm that the tears we shed are God's tears. As our anger burns within us, it turns into determination. As our determined anger strikes sparks off others, we learn to affirm that a small fire is struck in God, God who has been waiting for that small flame. She begins to wake, to shake herself, to turn tears and anger into determination.

She comes to join us.

As we learn to work together, as we gather power, our voices converge in our own speech. As we speak our new words, she teaches us to learn to hope again, to be born in and to be borne on a slender hope, that in the end we may sing a new song.

We are not there yet, in that new epoch, singing that new song. But as we begin to understand the abuse of women—and understanding we begin to act, and acting we begin to understand—we gather strength and courage and the capabilities to transform our situation. As we gather in the resources of a whole ministry—resources of theology, of action, of institution-building—in cooperation with the women's movement, we may yet, God willing, live in that day.

And she *is* willing.

7. "Don't Tell Mother"

MARTHA JANSSEN

The pain, confusion, fear, and rage from my early childhood have passed now. I've taken the first steps toward reconciliation. But the negative effects of those formative years will never be "past." No amount of intellect or adult experience can ever erase them. My story begs to be told because it happened to Christians and it was survived because of Christian love. It is the story of a child.

People said of me, "She's a pretty child." To one I might resemble Daddy, to another Mother. We were a middle-class family, raised in the church. People in our house generally talked nicely to each other. Spankings were not common. I was the oldest of three children.

One thing missing in our home was freedom to express our feelings. Anger came out as irritation, but seldom loudly. People didn't talk about feeling discouraged or inadequate. Daddy wanted to look and act strong at all times. Even in his childhood pictures he always looked brave or stern, sometimes wearing a World War I uniform. Daddy was silent about feelings. Affection was cautious. But we looked like a handsome group! Everyone was friendly and generous.

I was only three when Daddy sat me on his knee—how much I liked to have him smile at me—and as we delicately say, he "handled" me. It wasn't anything I made judgments about. I was just a little girl, and I thought that was what fathers did to show their love. I didn't know that Dad was unable to manage his feelings. He hadn't learned to control his impulses, to deny his desires for the sake of his child. He wasn't a "bad" person. But he secretly acted out his desires on a person he was sure would not reject or question him. The price would be devastating.

To my knowledge, Mother never knew. Who would tell her? Not Dad. Not a little girl who viewed his behavior at bathtime or when we went for a walk as part of the fun of parent-child relationships.

By the time I reached the age of six Mother had taught me (more by the tone of her voice than her direct statements) that one did not do certain things. One wore clothes in public. One was nice to people. A little girl shouldn't talk to strangers and especially strange men.

I went to Sunday school every week. I knew the basic rules of right and wrong and I was good. But as I grew, I became less comfortable with Daddy's behavior.

I had the distinct feeling that other grownups didn't do the things he did. I didn't like his smile anymore. I was becoming more private about my body. I wasn't enjoying his attention as I once had. Besides, Daddy would often say to me, "Don't tell Mother" or "Don't tell anyone."

I had no choice. I did what I was told. I didn't tell anyone. I was ashamed because I thought I was misbehaving. I concluded what little girls in my situation conclude. The guilty person was me, not my father.

I was eight, then ten. I was caught between guilt and shame and the power of a misguided parent. When I resisted, I was brought into line with a too-firm grab of my arm. I was a victim.

Girls deal with such a dilemma in many ways. Some finally break down and tell the truth if someone allows them to be honest. They are in the minority. Some girls are afraid of most men, never trusting them to treat them properly. Some girls repress all memory of events of this nature. I was one of those. In fact, many girls do that because the conflict between behaving in a way that will please one parent but displease the other and disobey society is so intense that "forgetting" seems the only solution. Some girls grow up and become promiscuous, using their bodies to gain recognition and please men. I didn't do that, thank goodness. Rather, I married someone who would be less demanding and who would be a trustworthy father. I was lucky.

The word for this behavior hasn't yet been written in this article. That's because the word is so volatile and threatens our family ideals so much that people do not want to say it or think it. The word is *incest*. It is such a taboo behavior in our culture that people pretend it isn't happening.

The truth is it is happening all the time, in ordinary families, between men and girls, brothers and sisters, mothers and sons. Its greatest damage comes when it happens between a parent and child. As long as we refuse to discuss it, it will remain a problem. To say that it can happen is to defuse some of its likelihood. Who will speak the truth? I will.

Incest is not something that happens only with step-parents, poor families, or families greatly disturbed. Incest has its source, like many social diseases, in the individuals who need help but cannot admit the need and are afraid to admit the sin. It happens to churchgoers just like any other failing.

Incest is especially cruel because it is kept a secret. If a girl can know that it is all right to tell the truth to someone, her parent might get help or she might be rescued. As long as she is left to carry the burden of the secret alone she is powerless to change her situation. She buries her guilt and shame or goes through life confused (and likely to pass on her confusion to her own children). When parents and relatives overlook a suspicious situation because it makes them uncomfortable to consider the truth, the child becomes even more a helpless victim.

My dilemma was, I could stop him only if I told someone, but whom could I tell? It was a shameful admittance. I reasoned that I must have done things that caused my father to behave as he did. I pictured my mother's deep sadness if she were to know. I was afraid she would have to leave my father.

I was in intense conflict within myself. That conflict was magnified in the church because of a most common image—that of God, the Father. How could God be like a father? As far as I could tell, fathers did bad things. I grew up being unusually self-sufficient, for I dared not trust an earthly father, let alone one I could not see.

I asked myself about the fourth commandment. One should honor one's parents. I did what I was told. I couldn't turn to my pastor. He would not think well of me. I was too sinful. I couldn't leave home until I was at least eighteen. So I put it out of my mind. When I hinted the matter to an adviser, the person squirmed and changed the subject. No one wanted to know. It was clear from the silence of our culture that this topic was off limits.

Thank God I had a friend who heard my hints and gently suggested that child abuse was something I could talk about with a professional. I dared, on the basis of that Christian support, to "remember" the truth. I went to a skilled counselor, and after a long period of learning to trust that person, I admitted to myself and to him that I was an abused child. It was the beginning of healing.

A long period began of recalling many sordid and confusing incidents. Over and over the counselor told me that no matter what I had done, I was still a fine person. I was worthy of love and caring. I was not at fault.

I couldn't believe it! I didn't feel it for a long time. My early impressions continued to convince me that the little girl was to blame. But the counselor stayed with me. He reminded me that the little girl had only been small and in the complete power of her parent. Finally I realized as a mother myself that parents could indeed persuade their children to do whatever they wanted them to do. That is the awesome responsibility of parenting. I had not erred; I had only done what I was told.

Then I became angry. Only I couldn't admit it. I pretended that I felt mature, understanding my father's problem. Gradually I began to acknowledge that his behavior had caused me incredible pain—fear of men, fear of one I was supposed to be able to trust, self-degradation, a feeling that I was scum. I had been depressed during periods of my life. I had seldom confronted my husband with my opinions of his behavior because deep down I didn't trust that a man could be confronted without my being punished. I had back trouble, nightmares, an irrational phobia, and finally a terrible period of intense stomach pain. The pain was rage! I was furious that a beautiful little girl had been so used, so hurt. She would never be the person she could have been.

What would I do with the anger? First, I chose what many misguided Christians choose. I kept it to myself. But the pains and nightmares began to intensify. I had to do something. For a long time I couldn't face my father. I was still a little girl, scared to death of him, afraid to humiliate him or the family.

One day I realized, I want to live! I must not destroy myself because of someone else's mistake, not as long as it was possible to live a full life. God gave me life.

I resolved to talk to Dad. I was terrified. He might collapse and weep. I would feel sorry for him and guilty for hurting him. I was still genuinely afraid for my well-being. He might deny it and I'd feel like a fool. The family might desert me, unable to face the truth and humiliation. But I had to claim life. If forgiveness was possible, I had to try. I had long since left the great forgiveness up to God, the one who could handle it. But I felt that to forgive there had to be awareness of sin.

I first told my family, and they believed me. It wasn't a secret anymore.

Then I went to Dad. I told him how his behavior had affected my life. I did not scream or yell or blame. I simply said I was angry that I had been hurt by his unwillingness to be a good parent, to get help, to admit his weakness. He was, I knew, a broken man already. He did not admit to me his error, but his life had been distorted by his actions toward me. I didn't need to punish him. But I did not keep the awful secret and perpetuate the evil. I spoke the truth, because truth sets people free, even if it is uncomfortable or convicting.

Today I am free. I no longer let my past bother me daily, nor do I have nightmares or stomachaches. I tell potential counselors, especially pastors, that if they even slightly suspect this problem in a family, they should refer their counselees to skilled professionals. It is not an easy situation with which to deal.

I will not tell you that once the problem of incest is out in the open everything is happy ever after. Many families continue to deny it, which is painful for the victim. But I will tell you that unless we are willing to admit that incest happens, it will continue.

Life isn't fair. But God is present in loving people. The Holy Spirit moved me to want to live and to speak the truth. Jesus Christ insists, despite our fear of the terrible truth, that we are accepted no matter what we have done to others, if we will acknowledge our failings. You and I have the responsibility to see the truth and say it. Children are not to blame. In order to begin the process of forgiveness and healing, we adults must admit our frailty.

It can and does happen.

8. A Commentary on Religious Issues in Family Violence

MARIE M. FORTUNE AND JUDITH HERTZE

THE IMPORTANCE OF RELIGIOUS ISSUES: ROADBLOCKS OR RESOURCES?

The crisis of family violence affects people physically, psychologically, and spiritually. Each of these dimensions must be addressed, both for victims and for those in the family who abuse them. Approached from either a secular or religious perspective alone, certain needs and issues tend to be disregarded. This reflects a serious lack of understanding of the nature of family violence and its impact on people's lives. Treatment of families experiencing violence and abuse requires integrating the needs of the whole person. Thus the importance of developing a shared understanding and cooperation between secular and religious helpers to deal with family violence cannot be emphasized too strongly.

Occasionally a social worker, psychotherapist, or other secular service provider will wonder, "Why bother with religious concerns at all?" The answer is a very practical one: religious issues or concerns that surface for people in the midst of crisis are primary issues. If not addressed in some way, at some point, they will inevitably become roadblocks to the client's efforts to resolve the crisis and move on with her or his life. In addition, a person's religious beliefs and community of faith (church or synagogue) can provide a primary support system for an individual and her or his family in the midst of an experience of family violence.

For a pastor, priest, rabbi, lay counselor, or other person approaching family violence from a religious perspective, there is little question about the relevance of religious concerns; these are primary for any religious person. Rather, they may doubt the importance of dealing with concerns for shelter, safety, intervention, and treatment. "These people just need to get right with God and everything will be fine." This perspective overlooks the fact that these other issues are practical and important as well. Family violence is complex and potentially lethal: these seemingly mundane concerns represent immediate and critical needs.

When confronted with a personal experience of family violence, like any other crisis whether chronic or sudden, most people also experience a crisis of meaning in their lives. Very basic life questions arise and are usually expressed in religious or philosophical terms. Questions like, "Why is this happening to me and my family?" or "Why did God let this happen?" or "What meaning does this have for my life?" are all indications of people's efforts to understand, to make sense out of experiences of suffering, and to place the experiences in a context of meaning for their lives. These questions are to be seen as a healthy sign because they represent an effort to comprehend and contextualize the experience of family violence and thereby regain some control over their lives in the midst of crisis.

Thus for many individuals and families in crisis, the questions of meaning will be expressed in religious terms and, more specifically, in terms of the Jewish or Christian traditions, since the vast majority of people in the U.S. today grew up with some association with these traditions. Many continue as adults to be involved with a church or synagogue. In addition, Jewish and Christian values overlap with cultural values of the majority American culture, so most Americans carry a set of cultural values, consciously or unconsciously, that are primarily Jewish or Christian in nature.

Religious concerns can become roadblocks or resources for those dealing with experiences of family violence because these concerns are central to many people's lives. The outcome depends on how they are handled.

The misinterpretation and misuse of the Jewish and Christian traditions have often had a detrimental effect on families, particularly those dealing with family violence. Misinterpretation of the traditions can contribute substantially to the guilt, self-blame, and suffering that victims experience and to the rationalizations often used by those who abuse. "But the Bible says . . ." is frequently used to explain, excuse, or justify abuse between family members.

This need not be the case. Reexamining and analyzing those biblical references which have been misused can lead to reclaiming the traditions in a way that supports victims and those who abuse while clearly confronting and challenging abuse in the family.

A careful study of both Jewish and Christian scriptures makes it very clear that *it is not possible to use scriptures to justify abuse of persons in the family.* However, it is also clear that it is possible to misuse scripture and other traditional religious literature for this purpose. This is a frequent practice (see below). Attempting to teach that there are very simple answers to the very complex issues that people face in their lives is another potential roadblock within contemporary teachings of some Jewish or Christian groups. Thus, religious groups have often not adequately prepared people for the traumas they will face at some point in their lives: illness, death, abuse, divorce, and so forth.

"Keep the commandments and everything will be fine."
"Keep praying."
"Just accept Jesus Christ as your Lord and Savior and you will be healthy, prosperous, popular, and happy."
"Go to services each week."
"Pray harder."

While these teachings may be fundamental teachings of religious faith, alone they are inadequate to deal with the complexity of most experiences of human suffering like family violence. When offered as simple and complete answers to life's questions, they create in the hearer an illusion of simplicity that leaves the hearer vulnerable to becoming overwhelmed by an experience of suffering. In addition, the teachings set up a dynamic that blames the victims for their suffering

"If you are a good Christian or a good Jew, God will treat you kindly, or take care of you, or make you prosper as a reward for your goodness."
"If you suffer, it is a sign that you must not be a good Christian or a good Jew and God is displeased with you."

If one accepts this simple formula (which makes a theological assumption that God's love is conditional), then when one experiences any form of suffering, one feels punished or abandoned by God. The simple answer alone cannot hold up in the face of personal or familial suffering. When people attempt to utilize the simple answer and it is insufficient, they feel that their faith has failed them or that God has abandoned them. In fact, it may be that the teachings or actions of their particular congregation or denomination have been inadequate to their needs. Thus they may be feeling abandoned.

The religious teachings of the Jewish and Christian traditions are adequate to address the experiences of contemporary persons when the traditions acknowledge the complexity, the paradox, and sometimes the incomprehensible nature of those experiences. The most important resource that the church or synagogue can provide is to be available to support those who are suffering, to be a sign of God's presence, and to be willing to struggle with the questions that the experiences may raise. Offering sweet words of advice to "solve" life's problems reduces the experience of the one who suffers to a mere slogan and denies the depth of the pain and the potential for healing and new life.

COOPERATIVE ROLES FOR SECULAR COUNSELOR AND MINISTER/RABBI

Both the secular counselor and the minister or rabbi have important roles to play in response to family violence. Families in which there is abuse need the support and expertise of both in times of crisis. Sometimes the efforts of the two will come into conflict, as illustrated by the following situation:

We received a call at the center from a local shelter for abused women. The shelter worker indicated that she had a badly beaten woman there whose minister had told her to go back home to her husband. The worker asked us to call the minister and "straighten him out." Ten minutes later we received a call from the minister. He said that the shelter had one of his parishioners there and the shelter worker had told her to get a divorce. He asked us to call the shelter and "straighten them out."

In the above case, both the shelter worker and the minister had the best interests of the victim in mind. Yet they were clearly at odds with each other because they did not understand the other's concerns which related to the needs of the victim. The shelter worker did not understand the minister's concern for maintaining the family and the minister did not understand that the woman's life was in danger. We arranged for the minister and the shelter worker to talk directly with each other, sharing their concerns in order to seek a solution in the best interest of the victim. This was accomplished successfully.

The need for cooperation and communication between counselors and ministers or rabbis is clear so that the needs of parishioners/congregants/clients are best served and the resources of both religious and secular helpers are utilized effectively.

Role of the Secular Counselor

In the secular setting, a social worker or mental health provider may encounter a victim or abuser who raises religious questions or concerns. When this occurs, the following guidelines are helpful.

1. Pay attention to religious questions/comments/references.

2. Affirm these concerns as appropriate and check out their importance for the client.

3. Having identified and affirmed this area of concern, if you are uncomfortable with it yourself or feel unqualified to pursue it, refer to a pastor/priest/rabbi who is trained to help and whom you know and trust.

4. If you are comfortable and would like to pursue the concern, do so, emphasizing the ways in which the client's religious tradition can be a resource to her or him and can in no way be used to justify or allow abuse or violence to continue in the family. (See below.)

Role of Clergy

The minister/rabbi can most effectively help family abuse victims and offenders by cooperating with secular resources. Combined, these provide a balanced approach that deals with specific external, physical, and emotional needs while addressing the larger religious and philosophical issues.

When approached about family violence, the minister/rabbi can use the following guidelines.

1. Be aware of the dynamics of family violence and utilize this understanding in evaluating the situation.

2. Use your expertise as a religious authority and spiritual leader

to illuminate the positive value of religious traditions while clarifying that they do not justify or condone family abuse. (See below).

3. Identify the parishioner/congregant's immediate needs and REFER to a secular resource (if available) to deal with the specifics of abuse, intervention, and treatment.

4. If you are comfortable pursuing the matter, provide additional pastoral support and encouragement to help families dealing with violence to take full advantage of available resources.

SCRIPTURAL AND THEOLOGICAL ISSUES

SUFFERING

The experience of physical or psychological pain or deprivation can generally be referred to as "suffering." When a person experiences suffering, often the first question is, "Why am I suffering?" This is really two questions: "Why is there suffering?" and "Why me?" These are classical theological questions to which there are no totally satisfactory answers.

Sometimes a person will answer these questions in terms of very specific cause-and-effect relationships:

I am being abused by my husband as punishment from God for the fact that twenty years ago, when I was seventeen years old, I had sexual relations with a guy I wasn't married to.

In this case, the victim of abuse sees her suffering as just punishment for an event that happened long ago and for which she has since felt guilty. This explanation has an almost superstitious quality. It reflects an effort on the part of the woman to make sense out of her experience of abuse by her husband. Her explanation takes the "effect" (the abuse), looks for a probable "cause" (her teenage "sin"), and directly connects the two. This conclusion is based on a set of theological assumptions that support her view: God is a stern judge who seeks retribution for her sins and God causes suffering to be inflicted on her as punishment.

Unfortunately, the woman's explanation neither focuses on the real nature of her suffering (the abuse by her husband), nor does it place responsibility for her suffering where it lies: on her abusive husband.

Sometimes, people try to explain suffering by saying that it is "God's will" or "part of God's plan for my life" or "God's way of teaching me a lesson." These explanations assume God to be stern, harsh, even cruel and arbitrary. This image of God runs counter to a biblical image of a kind, merciful, and loving God. The God of this biblical teaching does not single out anyone to suffer for the sake of suffering, because suffering is not pleasing to God.

A distinction between voluntary and involuntary suffering is useful at this point. Someone may choose to suffer abuse or indignity in order to accomplish a greater good. For example, Dr. Martin Luther King, Jr. suffered greatly in order to change what he believed to be unjust, racist laws. Although the abuse he experienced was not justifiable, he chose voluntary suffering as a means to an end.

Involuntary suffering that occurs when a person is beaten, raped, or abused, especially in a family relationship, also cannot be justified but is never chosen. It may, on occasion, be endured by a victim for a number of reasons, including a belief that such endurance will eventually change the person who is being abusive. However, this belief is unrealistic and generally only reinforces the abuse.

Christian tradition teaches that suffering happens to people because there is evil and sinfulness in the world. Unfortunately, when someone behaves in a hurtful way, someone else usually bears the brunt of that act and suffers as a result. Striving to live a righteous life does not guarantee that one will be protected from the sinfulness of another. A person may find that she or he suffers from having made a poor decision (by marrying a spouse who is abusive). But this in no way means that the person either wants to suffer or deserves abuse from the spouse.

In Christian teaching, at no point does God promise that we will not suffer in this life. In scripture, God does promise to be present to us when we suffer. This is especially evident in the Psalms, which give vivid testimony to people's experience of God's faithfulness in the midst of suffering (see Ps. 22 and 55).

One's fear of abandonment by God is often strong when experiencing suffering and abuse. This fear is usually experienced by victims of abuse who often feel they have been abandoned by almost everyone: friends, other family members, clergy, doctors, police, lawyers, counselors. Perhaps none of these believed the family members or were able to help. It is therefore very easy for victims to conclude that God has also abandoned them. For Christians, the promise to victims from God is that even though all others abandon them, God will be faithful. This is the message found in Romans:

For I am sure that neither death, nor life, nor angels, nor principalities, nor things present, nor anything else in all creation, will be able to separate us from the love of God in Christ Jesus our Lord (Rom. 8:38–39, RSV).

Often this reassurance is very helpful to victims of violence or to those who abuse them.

Sometimes people who regard suffering as God's will for them believe that God is teaching them a lesson or that hardship builds character. Experiences of suffering can, in fact, be occasions for growth. People who suffer may realize in retrospect that they learned a great deal from the experience and grew more mature as a result. This often is the case, but only if the person who is suffering also receives support and affirmation throughout the experience. With the support of family, friends, and helpers, people who are confronted with violence in their family can end the abuse, possibly leave the situation, make major changes in their lives, and grow as mature adults. They will probably learn some difficult lessons: increased self-reliance; how to express anger; that they may survive better outside than inside abusive relationships; that they can be a whole person without being married; that they can exercise control over their actions with others; that family relationships need not be abusive and violent.

However, this awareness of suffering as the occasion for growth *must come from those who are suffering* and at a time when they are well on their way to renewal. It is hardly appropriate when someone is feeling great pain to point out that things really are not so bad and that someday she or he will be glad that all of this happened. These words of "comfort and reassurance" are usually for the benefit of the minister/rabbi or counselor, not the parishioner/congregant or client. At a later time, it may be useful to point out the new growth that has taken place, and very simply to affirm the reality that this person has survived an extremely difficult situation. Suffering may present an occasion for growth: whether this potential is actualized depends on how the experience of suffering is managed.

NATURE OF THE MARRIAGE RELATIONSHIP: A JEWISH PERSPECTIVE

The Jewish marriage ceremony is known as "Kiddushin" or sanctification. Through it a couple's relationship is sanctified or set apart before God. This sanctification reminds Jews to strive to express their holiness through marriage and the home in a covenantal relationship based on mutual love and respect.

Judaism views marriage as necessary for fulfillment. Marriage is part of God's plan. The first time God speaks to Adam, God says that it is not fitting that Adam should be alone. "Shalom Bayit," peace in the home, is a major family value in Judaism. "Shalom," which is simply translated as "peace," also signifies wholeness, completeness, fulfillment. Peace in the home, domestic harmony, encompasses the good and welfare of all the home's inhabitants.

The rabbis consider domestic tranquillity as one of the most important ideals because it is the essential forerunner to peace on earth. "Peace will remain a distant vision until we do the work of peace ourselves. If peace is to be brought into the world we must bring it first to our families and communities."[1]

The concept of Shalom Bayit should not be misinterpreted as encouraging the preservation of an abusive marriage. When domestic harmony is impossible because of physical abuse, the only way for peace may be dissolution of marriage. Although marriage is viewed as permanent, divorce has always been an option according to the Jewish tradition.

In Judaism conjugal rights are obligatory upon the husband who must be available for his wife:

A wife may restrict her husband in his business journey to nearby places only so that he would not otherwise deprive her of her conjugal rights. Hence he may not set out without her permission.[2]

While the husband is responsible for his wife's sexual fulfillment, the wife, in return, is expected to have sexual relations with her husband. Maimonides[3] teaches us about the relationship between husband and wife in a Jewish marriage. He asserts that if the wife refuses sexual relations with her husband,

> She should be questioned as to the reason. . . . If she says, "I have come to loathe him, and I cannot willingly submit to his intercourse," he must be compelled to divorce her immediately for she is not like a captive woman who must submit to a man that is hateful to her.[4]

This suggests that no wife is expected to submit to sexual activity with a husband she fears or hates. The arena of sexual sharing for Jewish couples is one of mutual responsibility and choice.

NATURE OF THE MARRIAGE RELATIONSHIP: A CHRISTIAN PERSPECTIVE

Christian teaching about the model of the marriage relationship has traditionally focused heavily on Paul's letters to the Ephesians, Corinthians, and Colossians. Misinterpretations of or misplaced emphasis on these texts create substantial problems for many married couples. Most commonly, directives on marriage based on scripture are given to women and not to men and state that wives must "submit" to their husbands. This often is interpreted to mean that the husband/father is the absolute head of the household and that the wife and children must obey him without question. Unfortunately, this idea has also been interpreted to mean that wives and children must submit to abuse from husbands and fathers. This rationalization is used by those who abuse, as well as by counselors, clergy, and the victims of the abuse themselves.

A closer look at the actual scriptural references reveals a different picture. For example, Ephesians 5:21:

> Be subject *to one another* out of reverence for Christ (RSV, emphasis added).

This is the first and most important verse in the Ephesians passage on marriage and also the one most often overlooked. It clearly indicates that all Christians—husbands and wives—are to be *mutually subject* to one another. The word translated "be subject to" can more appropriately be translated "defer" or "accommodate" to.

> Wives *accommodate* to your husbands as to the Lord (Eph. 5:22).

This teaching implies sensitivity, flexibility, and responsiveness to the husband. In no way can this verse be taken to mean that a wife must submit to abuse from her husband.

For the husband is the head of the wife as Christ is the head of the Church, his body, and is himself its savior. As the church is subject to Christ, so let wives also be subject in everything to their husbands (Eph. 5:23–24, RSV).

The model suggested here of husband-wife relationship is based on the Christ-church relationship. It is clear from Jesus' teaching and ministry that his relationship to his followers was not one of dominance or authoritarianism, but rather one of servanthood. For example, Jesus washed the feet of his disciples in an act of serving. He taught them that those who would be first must in fact be last. Therefore, a good husband will not dominate or control his wife but will serve and care for her, according to Ephesians.

Even so husbands should love their wives as their own bodies. He who loves his wife loves himself. For no man ever hates his own flesh, but nourishes it and cherishes it, as Christ does the Church because we are members of his body (Eph. 5:28–29, RSV).

This instruction to husbands is very clear and concrete. A husband is to nourish and cherish his own body *and* that of his wife. Physical battering that occurs between spouses is probably the most blatant violation of this teaching and a clear reflection of the self-hatred in the one who is abusive.

It is interesting that the passages quoted above from Ephesians (5:21–29), which are commonly used as instruction for marriage are instruction primarily for husbands: nine of the verses are directed toward husbands' responsibilities in marriage. Only three of the verses refer to wives' responsibilities, and one refers to both. Yet contemporary interpretation often focuses only on the wives and often misuses those passages to justify the abuse of the wives by their husbands. While spouse abuse may be a common pattern in marriage, it certainly cannot be legitimated by scripture.

In terms of sexuality in marriage, again this passage from Ephesians (see also Colossians 3:18–21) has been used to establish a relationship in which the husband has conjugal *rights* and the wife has conjugal *duties*. In fact, other scriptural passages are explicit on this issue:

The husband should give to his wife her conjugal rights, and likewise the wife to the husband. For the wife does not rule over her own body, but the husband does; likewise, the husband does not rule over his own body, but the wife does (1 Corinthians 7:3-4, RSV).

The rights and expectations between husband and wife in regard to sexual matters are explicitly equal and parallel and include the right to refuse sexual contact. The expectation of equality of conjugal rights and sexual access and the need for mutual consideration in sexual activity is clear. The suggestion that both wife and husband "rule over" the other's body and not their own refers to the need for joint, mutual decisions about sexual activity rather than arbitrary, independent decisions. A husband does not have the right to act out of his own sexual needs without agreement from the wife; likewise, the wife also. This particular passage directly challenges the incidents of sexual abuse (rape) in marriage frequently reported by physically abused wives.

THE MARRIAGE COVENANT AND DIVORCE

A strong belief in the permanence of the marriage vows may prevent an abused spouse from considering separation or divorce as options for dealing with family violence. For the Christian, the promise of faithfulness "for better or for worse . . . 'til death do us part" is commonly taken to mean "stay in the marriage no matter what," even though death of one or more family members is a real possibility in abusive families. Jews view marriage as permanent, but "til death do us part" is not part of the ceremony. The Jewish attitude embodies a very delicate balance. Marriage is taken very seriously. It is a primary religious obligation and should not be entered into or discarded flippantly. Nevertheless, since the days of Deuteronomy, Jewish tradition has recognized the unfortunate reality that some couples are hopelessly incompatible and divorce may be a necessary option.

For some Christians, their denomination's strong doctrinal position against divorce may inhibit them from exercising this means of dealing with family violence. For others, a position against divorce is a personal belief often supported by their family and church. In either case, there is a common assumption that any marriage is better than no marriage at all and, therefore, should be maintained at any cost. This assumption arises from a superficial view of marriage that is concerned only with appearances and not with substance. In other words, as long as marriage and family relationships maintain a facade of normalcy, there is a refusal by church and community to look any closer for fear of seeing abuse or violence in the home.

The covenant of Christian marriage is a lifelong, sacred commitment made between two persons and witnessed by other persons and by God. Jews also regard marriage as sacred and intend that it be permanent. A covenant between marriage partners has the following elements:

1. It is made in full knowledge of the relationship.
2. It involves a *mutual* giving of self to the other.
3. It is assumed to be lasting.
4. It values mutuality, respect, and equality between persons.

A marriage covenant can be violated by one or both partners. It is common thinking in both Jewish and Christian traditions that adultery violates the marriage covenant and results in brokenness in the relationship. Likewise, violence or abuse in a marriage violates the covenant and fractures a relationship. In both cases the trust that was assumed between partners is shattered. Neither partner should be expected to remain in an abusive situation. Often one marriage partner feels a heavy obligation to remain in the relationship and do everything possible to make it work. This is most often true for women. A covenant relationship only works if both partners are able and willing to work on it. In both traditions, it is clear that God does not expect anyone to stay in a situation that is abusive (i.e. to become a doormat). In the Christian tradition, just as Jesus did not expect his disciples to remain in a village that did not respect and care for them (Luke 9:1–6), neither does he expect persons to remain in a family relationship where they are abused and violated. In Jewish literature, the expectation is also clear:

If a man was found to be a wife-beater, he had to pay damages and provide her with separate maintenance. Failing that, the wife had valid grounds for compelling a divorce.[5]

If there is a genuine effort to change on the part of the one who is abusive, it is possible to renew the marriage covenant, including in it a clear commitment to nonviolence in the relationship. With treatment for the family members, it *may* be possible to salvage the relationship. If the one who is being abusive is not willing or able to change in the relationship, then the question of divorce arises. At this point in the marriage, divorce is really a matter of public statement: "Shall we make public the fact that our relationship has been broken by abuse?" The other option, of course, is to continue to pretend that the marriage is intact. (A woman reported that she divorced only a month ago but that her marriage ended ten years ago when the abuse began.)

 In violent homes, divorce is not breaking up families. Violence and abuse are breaking up families. Divorce is often the painful, public acknowledgment of an already accomplished fact. While divorce is never easy, it is, in the case of family violence, the lesser evil. In many cases divorce may be a necessary intervention to generate healing and new life from a devastating and deadly situation.

PARENTS AND CHILDREN

"Honor your father and your mother" is one of the ten commandments taught to all Jewish and Christian children. Unfortunately, some parents misuse this teaching in order to demand unquestioning obedience from their children. In a hierarchical, authoritarian household, a father may misuse his parental authority to coerce a child into abusive sexual activity (incest). Parents may use this commandment to rationalize their physical abuse of a child in retaliation for a child's lack of obedience.

For Christians, the meaning of the third commandment is made very clear in Ephesians:

Children, obey your parents *in the Lord,* for this is right. "Honor your father and mother" (this is the first commandment with a promise) "that it may be well with you and that you may live long on the earth." Fathers, do not provoke your children to anger, but bring them up *in the discipline and instruction of the Lord* (Eph. 6:1–4, RSV, emphasis added).

Children's obedience to their parents is to be "in the Lord"; it is not to be blind and unquestioning. In addition to instructions to children, instructions are also given to parents to guide and instruct their children in Christian values—love, mercy, compassion, and justice. Any discipline of a child must be for the child's best interest. The caution to the father not to provoke the child to anger is most appropriate. If there is anything which will certainly provoke a child to anger, it is physical or sexual abuse by a parent.

Jewish tradition deals with the same concern, making a distinction between children based on maturity.

One is forbidden to beat his grownup son, the word *grownup* in this regard refers not to age but to his maturity. If there is reason to believe that the son will rebel, and express that resentment by word or deed, even though he has not yet reached the age of Bar Mitzvah (13), it is forbidden to beat him. Instead he should reason with him. Anyone who beats his grownup children is to be excommunicated, because he transgresses the Divine Command (Lev. 19:14). "Thou shalt not put a stumbling block before the blind" (for they are apt to bring sin and punishment upon their children).[6]

Even though Jewish law gives great authority to the father in relationship to the children, the requirement for restraint is clearly indicated. Again, the priority is on the welfare of the child.

The other scriptural injunction commonly used to justify abusive discipline of children is the proverb, "Spare the rod and spoil the child." This proverb is commonly interpreted to mean that if a parent does not use corporal punishment on a child, the child will become a spoiled brat. This is a good example of a misinterpretation based on a contemporary understanding. In fact, the image referred to in this proverb is probably that of a shepherd and the rod is the shepherd's staff (see Psalm 23:4: "Thy rod and thy staff shall *comfort* me"). A shepherd uses his staff to guide the sheep where they should go. The staff is not used as a cudgel.

With this image of the shepherd guiding the sheep in mind, it is certainly clear that children need guidance and discipline from parents and other caring adults to grow to maturity. Children do not need to be physically beaten to receive guidance or discipline. Beating children as discipline teaches them very early that it is all right to hit those you love for their own good. This kind of lesson fosters early training for persons who grow up and subsequently physically abuse their spouses and children.

CONFESSION AND FORGIVENESS

The need to admit wrongdoing experienced by an abusive family member is a healthy sign that he or she is no longer denying the problem but is ready and willing to face it. The offender may seek out a minister or rabbi for the purpose of confessing.

Sometimes, however, an abusive father confesses, asks forgiveness, and promises never to sexually approach his daughter again, or a mother swears never to hit her child in anger again. The minister/rabbi is then put in a position of assuring forgiveness and evaluating the strength of the person's promise not to abuse again. While the abuser may be genuinely contrite, he or she is seldom able to end the abuse without assistance and treatment.

The minister/rabbi needs to assure the person of God's forgiveness and must confront the person with the fact that he or she needs additional help in order to stop the abuse. For some people, a strong word from a minister/rabbi at this point is an effective deterrent: "The abuse *must* stop now." Sometimes this strong directive can provide an external framework for beginning to change the abusive behavior.

For the Jew the Hebrew term *teshuvah* is the word for repentance. "Teshuvah" literally means "return," clearly denoting a return to God after sin. In Judaism there is a distinction between sins against God and sins against people. For the former only regret or confession is necessary. For sins against people, "teshuvah" requires three steps: first, admission of wrongdoing; second, asking for forgiveness of the person wronged (here abused); third, reconciliation, which can be accomplished only by a change in behavior.

The issue of forgiveness also arises for victims of abuse. A friend or family member may pressure the victim: "You should forgive him. He said he was sorry." Or it may arise internally: "I wish I could forgive him." In either case, the victim feels guilty for not being able to forgive the abuser. In these cases, often forgiveness is interpreted to mean to forget or pretend the abuse never happened. Neither is possible. The abuse will never be forgotten; it becomes a part of the victim's history. Forgiveness is a matter of the victim's being able to say that she or he will no longer allow the experience to dominate her or his life—and will let go of it and move on. This is usually possible if there is some sense of justice in the situation, officially (through the legal system) or unofficially. Forgiveness by the victim is possible when there is repentance on the part of the abuser, and real repentance means a change in the abuser's behavior.

Another issue is timing. Too often the minister/rabbi or counselor's need for the victim to finish and resolve the abusive experience leads him or her to push a victim to forgive the abuser. Forgiveness in this case is seen as a means to hurry the victim's healing process along. Victims will move to forgive at their own pace and cannot be pushed by others' expectations of them. It may take years before they are ready to forgive; their timing needs to be respected. They will forgive when they are ready. Then the forgiveness becomes the final stage of letting go and enables them to move on with their lives.

CONCLUSION

This commentary addresses some of the common religious concerns raised by people dealing with family violence. It is an attempt to help the reader begin to see ways of converting potential roadblocks into valuable resources for those dealing with violence in their families.

Personal faith for a religious person can provide much-needed strength and courage to face a very painful situation and make changes in it. Churches and synagogues can provide a much-needed network of community support for victims, abusers, and their children.

It is clearly necessary for those involved in Jewish and Christian congregations and institutions to begin to address these concerns directly. In ignorance and oversight, we do much harm. In awareness and action, we can contribute a critical element to the efforts to respond to family violence in our communities.

9. A Theological Perspective on Sexual Assault

MARY D. PELLAUER

Institutional resources to help victims of sexual violence have mushroomed over the last decade. Tragically, however, the new understandings and attitudes generated by rape crisis centers, feminist coalitions, and the like have had little impact upon religious communities. As a result pastors and the church in general have all too often been unhelpful to victims of sexual violence. As one woman put it:

> The aftermath was almost as bad as the act itself. When people read about the rape in the papers I was actually shunned, even in church. The women whispered behind my back. They thought I must have brought the rape upon myself. Some even asked me why I didn't fight back. . . . The church? Months passed before the gossip subsided. Had I not come to the rape crisis center, I would not have had anyone to help and support me. Even my husband listened to those voices. The pastor? He did not know how to handle the situation. He never said anything to me. Never.[1]

The gossipy salaciousness of the church members stems from the confusion of sex and violence, which is a central myth about rape; it illustrates all too well the disastrous effects of such conventional attitudes for the church. If we are serious, then, about providing justice and healing to rape victims among us, we will have to demand changes in seminary curricula, in the priorities of judicatory bodies, in notions of stewardship, and in relationships within local religious bodies. But by themselves these changes will not be enough. We will also have to begin changing our theological understanding of the experience of sexual violence.

Recently the pioneering work of Marie Fortune has brought to light explicitly theological questions that many rape victims ask:

Why did God let this happen to me? Is this a punishment for some sin I have commited? Even when victims do not use traditional religious language, however, the experience may have profound spiritual dimensions. To see these implications, mostly ignored by our conventional or patriarchal understandings of religion, will enable all of us to confront the reality and meaning of rape and child sexual abuse. It will enable clergy in particular to help victims without blaming them.

There are at least four spiritual dimensions inherent in crises of sexual violence: (1) The fundamental experience that they are life-threatening; (2) the sense of shame and humiliation, sometimes expressed as a need for cleansing; (3) issues of trust and betrayal, particularly as they relate to our capacities for relationship to God; (4) the need for others to provide and for victims to accept help in healing the wounds.

RAPE AS A LIFE-THREATENING EXPERIENCE

The change from perceiving rape as an act of sex to perceiving it as an act of violence came directly from *listening* to the accounts of victims.

When the New York Radical Feminists held our first speak-out on rape, a majority of the women who testified said that once the aggression had begun they were convinced they were going to die. "This wasn't an act of sex I was going through—I felt I was being murdered," one woman recalled.[2]

This listening went on all over the country. The first empirical study of victims who came to a Boston emergency room, for instance, created a new concept, "rape trauma syndrome," precisely to express this new understanding:

The primary feeling expressed was that of fear—fear of physical injury, mutilation, and death. It is this main feeling of fear that explains why victims develop the range of symptoms we call the rape trauma syndrome. Their symptoms are an acute stress reaction to the threat of being killed. Many victims feel they had a close encounter with death and are lucky to be alive.[3]

Many assailants are verbally explicit about these threats.

But he kept threatening to kill me if I did certain things, like if I got to the phone. . . . He said, "I don't want to kill you, but if you do these things, I'll have to kill you. . . ."[4]

Others combine threats with weapons that make the menace crystal clear:

And he kept the gun on me all the time. He showed me the bullets in case I should think it unloaded.

But whether assailants are verbally explicit, or whether victims are beaten, strangled, threatened, or manipulated into submission does *not* matter. Women who are raped are frightened and terrorized. They are in shock, in varying ways, during the attack and after it. They are *afraid.*

They have a right to their fears. No one can tell in the course of an assault whether this one—this one right in front of me or right behind me—will kill or not. The woman who survives a rape has done the right thing: She has come out of this nightmare alive. For that reason, second-guessing victims—asking, for example, "Why didn't you resist?"—is *never* helpful. The victim, after all, is the only one who had direct access to all the information about the threats facing her.

The woman who has been raped has not confronted death as a distant abstraction ("We are all mortal"). She has confronted it directly, concretely, specifically, at the end of a knifepoint at her jugular, at the end of a gun pointed at her head, or at the end of those fingertips around her throat. Moreover, she has confronted her own death as being arbitrary, at the whim of another who has taken it upon himself to play God with her for the sake of his own anger or for the sake of his own fantasies of power or for the sake of his dangerously beloved violence.

Death, especially my own death, is always a religious issue. We acknowledge this reality when religious leaders preside over funerals. Often rape victims undergo the same grief processes that have become so familiar to hospital chaplains. Needless to say, such a life-threatening experience is also a confrontation with the stark facts of one's own powerlessness and vulnerability, with the realization that one may be unable to cope reasonably with the events of one's life.

Confronting the specific menace to her life also shatters the victim's *world.* Being a self always involves a careful interweaving between self and world, so much so that some have called human being "Being-in-the-world." All women live with the knowledge and fear of rape as a component of our knowledge of and feelings about the world. Still, there is a qualitative difference between the worlds of those who have experienced rape and those who merely factor it in among the possible risks. The compromises, the risks, the timidity, and the occasional brashness with which women confront a world in which our violation may happen at any time render our worlds fragile. The victim's world, however, is shattered. As Julia Classon, a crisis worker, has put it,

No matter how much we live in fear because we know the dangers, we still disbelieve, we don't believe it can happen to *us* because if we did we wouldn't be able to stir, we'd lock ourselves in. We have to disbelieve in order to get through the day. And all that is shattered when we *are* raped.

The woman victimized by rape, then, faces the interrelated tasks of healing her person and reconstituting her world. She must be healed, physically and emotionally; she may experience nightmares and flashbacks; she may feel as though she is going crazy. At the same time, she must put her shattered world back together again; she must learn situations that make her feel safe and secure once again; she may face encounters with legal or medical procedures alien to her; she may locate resources previously invisible; she must come to terms with the naked face of terror once concealed in nebulous shadows.

Similarly, our efforts cannot center on the personal healing of victims alone. We must also be dedicated to changing the world in which victims have been endangered.

CLEANSING AND PURIFICATION

Within the feminist understanding that rape is an act of violence, it is confusing to notice that victims' stories sometimes resonate with feelings of being unclean, of needing to wash:

When I realized he was gone, I wanted to pour Lysol all over me. I wanted to be cleansed. I took a bath, and then I thought about calling the police.[5]

This theme, far from being opposed to the violence inherent in rape, may be more deeply connected with it than we ordinarily assume:

I didn't resist because I was afraid for my life. I felt I had to give in and humor them, or they would probably kill me or beat me up. . . . After each rape I felt dirty and disgusting. . . . It was a source of shame and humiliation. . . . After it was over, I was aware of pain and dirtiness in my body, and I was hurt in my pride and confused about why they had raped me and why they were laughing at me and making fun of my body and taunting me.[6]

This feeling of being unclean may be the result of the combined beliefs that rape is sex and sex is dirty, or the result of the myths about rape that insist that the victim is "dishonored." Certainly our Western tradition's messages to us, especially to us women, make such an interpretation possible.

But it is equally possible that these women experienced the violence and the domination of themselves as what was "dirty" in these encounters, and that such acts of cleansing spring from the "need to wash away the knowledge that one's body has been invaded and brutalized by another."[7] The sense of being *degraded* by the rape is quite common:

This is the first time I've really discussed either of these things because they left me with a feeling of being used like so much toilet paper.

There's something worse about being raped than just being beaten. It's the final humiliation, the final showing you that you're worthless and that you're there to be used by whoever wants you.[8]

The fact that many assailants explicitly use obscenely insulting language during the assault indicates that the victim's brutalization is precisely part of the purpose of the act. It may be also that women experience rape as uniquely degrading precisely because its hurts and humiliations have been accomplished by sexual means—our capacities for expressing mutuality and love have been turned to an end that is the opposite of their purpose.

The sense of being dirtied is also frequently shared by victims of incestuous abuse. Because of the unique nature of the sexual abuse of children by parents and other relatives, the results are even more deeply internalized as a stigma upon one's very being.

As the victim quoted by Summit in his essay later in this volume put it,

I am a filthy, sick animal trying to act like a human being and doing a pretty poor job. I'll never be anything but sick and inhuman. I am covered with green slime that can be seen by all. I am scum. I am a slut and a whore. . . . I belong in a hole where decent people don't have to associate with me. I am shit. I destroy everything I care for. My soul either kills off or chases away everyone who comes in contact with me, especially those that become dear. I make myself sick.[9]

We have learned from anthropologists of religion that dirt is not simply a matter of hygiene. It is also an entree into a cosmos. As Mary Douglas tells us, "Dirt is essentially disorder. . . . Eliminating it is not a negative movement, but a positive effort to organize the environment." This, I believe, is precisely what victims who feel the need to wash are expressing—a positive effort to organize an environment that has been suddenly ripped out of shape, befouled by violence.

Dirt, Douglas continues, is relative; it is "matter out of place."

Shoes are not dirty in themselves, but it is dirty to place them on the dining table; food is not dirty in itself, but it is dirty to leave cooking utensils in the bedroom. . . . Dirt is the byproduct of a systematic ordering and classification of matter, insofar as ordering involves rejecting inappropriate elements. This idea of dirt takes us straight into the field of symbolism.[9]

Extending this notion of symbolism to the experience of victims, we can make better sense of the need for cleansing. For most of us, peaceful mutual consent is the bottom line of our expectations for intimate relations. For the rape victim, then, the semen, blood, bruises, and ripped clothing all mutely testify to the radical disordering of the world. Byproducts of male ejaculation left on oneself after a violent encounter are truly "out of place" because the victim did not consent to them.

We should notice also that the mythology about rape identifies the woman herself as the dirt, as the matter out of place. Thus, the incest victim quoted above called other people "decent" and herself "scum"; she later added, "I do not deserve life." Such a person may be at risk for a suicide attempt partly in order to keep the world and other persons from being contaminated by her worthlessness. But consider also our ordinary statements about rape. When we ask victims "What were you doing there anyway?"—as though by being on the street at night or in a bar they deserved to be raped—we are expressing the same sense that *they* as women are "out of place."

Our reactions can either relieve or exacerbate the victim's feelings of guilt and shame. One woman put this quite clearly:

At first the doctor appeared kindly as the victim tearfully told her story. Then he asked if she had been a virgin, and when the young woman said no, he began to seem wary. . . . The doctor examined her and then called in a colleague. The two men discussed "how untorn and unbruised I was down there, and how it didn't look as if I had fought at all." They berated the victim for being out alone at night. . . . The young woman felt devastated. "I left feeling worse than I have ever felt in my life—*shamed and unclean.* I felt I was not believed and that the rape had been my fault. . . ."[10]

The connections between violating conventional notions of sexual propriety, being "out alone at night," and being held responsible for the rape are all quite clearly made in this account. Unfortunately, no simple washing with water will relieve this woman, and many like her, of the sense that she was and is somehow unclean.

The notions that *women* are dirty, that we are to blame for rape, that we are bad, are of course fundamental to the patriarchal society in which we live. It is extremely important, therefore, to distinguish the cosmos that is implicit in the notion that women are dirty from the one that is implicit in the experience of victims, that the *violence* is dirty. The insight of rape victims that being dominated and degraded by a violent sexual assault is an expression of a fundamental disorder in the universe is a more accurate and trustworthy sense about the world's fundamental meaning. It is our myths about rape that are a massive reversal of the true order of the universe. To make matters clear, we must engage, in Mary Daly's phrase, in a "reversal of the reversal."

This sense that violence and violation disturb the order of the universe is also inherent in the archaic meanings of these words, which define them as "desecration." These ancient meanings need to be brought more forcefully before our "modern" minds as we consider rape as a spiritual crisis: The experience of victims suggests that the integrity of the body is sacred. Rape demeans precisely that which we ought most fully to cherish.

TRUST AND BETRAYAL

It is not easy to change a perception of the world as radically unsafe when the perception rises out of intense, real, personal experience. It may take great lengths of time for victims to work through their fears. Two months after her rape, one young woman reported:

I keep jumping when I walk anywhere. People really frighten me. So many things scare me. I never used to be frightened; didn't fear things. Now I can't stand it.[11]

Like this woman fearing "people" in general, many victims may be tense, nervous, easily irritated with everyone after the sexual assault.

Such issues are at their most pointed when the other resembles the assailant—particularly in gender. There is virtually a chorus of voices rising to express fear and distrust of men after rape.

I still seem upset and edgy all the time. I just don't feel like being with people. I just couldn't stand to be near guys.

It made me more wary of men. . . . I'm really angry at all men. I'm gradually disassociating myself from men.

Well, I don't trust men. . . . I see a man who's built big, and I immediately become paranoid.[12]

Of course all distrust of men by women does not necessarily stem from rape. But we should not underestimate the effect of the pervasive fear of such violence in creating this atmosphere of discord.

Issues of trust are particularly poignant in cases of the sexual abuse of children. Our family is the fundamental matrix in which we learn the basic values with which we relate to others, the basic structures of our personality, and our underlying stance toward the world. The atmosphere of terror, fear, immense secrecy, and manipulation in which incest victims live, often for the most formative years of their lives, takes a terrible toll upon their capacity to relate to others. In order not to give away the "secret" that rules their lives, children may withdraw from their feelings or from the world around them:

I felt so different from the other kids in school. I was sure that if I wasn't careful they would be able to tell about me. I was sure I was going to give it away by something I might say or do in school. I was very careful to be quiet, never raise my hand and not draw any attention to myself. I never even laughed out loud until just a few years ago. I tried to be invisible.[13]

This child's world and identity have been damaged. Should she turn to someone else in the adult world and fail to receive a caring response, her sense of betrayal will only deepen.

Religious people simply must begin paying serious attention to these destructive effects on human capacities for trust. What we trust, what we deem trustworthy, how we develop trust and mistrust, may have far more to do with our basic capacities for religious faith than any number of convictions about sin or specific commands of a particular deity. Such at least was the conviction of Erik Erikson, one of the few thinkers to have been concerned about this: "Trust born of care is, in fact, the touchstone of the actuality of a given religion."[14]

The metaphors and language that we use for God are directly related to these issues of trust, and they affect whether we see the church as a place to ask for help. Victims often make these connections crystal clear.

I was raised as a Catholic. . . . In those days the church was very judgment-oriented, and as a child you felt—I felt—like a worm in the church because I was so low and God was so high and I was just about as worthless as a piece of sand. So trying to deal with the church and trying to deal with my home life was hard, because I couldn't even go up and say, "Father, I think I'm doing something wrong, but I'm not sure. Is this right or wrong?" You couldn't go to a priest and say that. If there was a doubt in your mind if something was right or wrong, it was automatically wrong—that's the way I was raised. So I began to withhold this kind of information in the confessional, and to a Catholic girl the confessional is sacred. So this ended up building guilt on top of guilt. . . . I clung to the church . . . because it was the only solid thing in my life, and as I clung to it the thorns kept going deeper and deeper into my own flesh.[15]

The notions of God and self ("God was so high; I was so low") this woman received from the church did not make the church a trustworthy place to go in her agony and confusion.

Other victims point to other dimensions of our traditional notions about God as creating particular problems in incestuous situations. Recall Martha Janssen's account of her experience:

I was in intense conflict within myself. That conflict was magnified in church because of a most common image—that of God, the Father. How could God be like a father? As far as I could tell, fathers did bad things.

That such young women experience in our church's continuous, repeated, and virtually exclusive use of "Father" as a metaphor for deity a deep alienation and pain can be readily understood. Simply to replace half of the "father" references for God with "mother," however, will not begin to resolve these issues, for incest victims also feel anger at mothers for having failed to protect them. Rather, a richer and wider experimentation with a full range of metaphors and images may be necessary. These issues cannot be ignored, whatever directions our theological perspectives are to take.

HEALING AND SUSTAINING

It is helpful, almost a relief, to remember that victims of sexual violence need not suffer forever. Indeed, to many in the antirape movement, "victims" need to be considered "survivors," lest we unrelentingly label such women by the crises in their lives and so distort their strengths and capacities to heal themselves. Thanks to countless workers across the country, rape need no longer be considered "a fate worse than death."

Healing, however, is not the same as "returning to normal," for the woman who has confronted her own death can never do that. She may, however, grow, finding new strengths and riches within herself and her life. She may become whole once again, finding a new wholeness appropriate to the crises she has faced.

That is, she may find healing—provided that she can find a supportive network of people who care about her enough to listen to her feelings and pains. Locating such a network is the single most important factor in the length of time assaulted women require to recover. In one of the few long-term studies of the recovery of rape victims, women without social support had still not come to terms with the crisis *four to six years* after the assault.[16]

A sustaining and empowering presence enables victims to garner their own resources of strength. The contribution the rest of us can make will depend crucially on how successfully we internalize certain truths that are or ought to be self-evident. These truths have now been empirically validated in studies of the healing process, and yet they are far from universally understood and accepted, even in the churches.

In the face of the confrontation with a life-threatening experience, persons who have been assaulted need concrete care expressed for their safety and well-being. They need reassurance that their reactions are normal for persons who have faced such extreme crises; they need concrete help in finding medical care and in increasing the safety of their surroundings.

In the face of fears that they are to blame for the attacks upon themselves, victims need exoneration. *No one deserves violence.* They need to have their stories believed, seriously believed, by those to whom they speak. They need to be assured that they are good people, regardless of what has happened to them.

In the face of the realistic mistrust victims may feel toward others, they need a reassuringly consistent presence that can allow them to rebuild their abilities to trust other persons. Confidentiality is always fundamental, and the nonjudgmental acceptance of their feelings as expressed. A context of trust also implies empowerment; doing things for the victim instead of enabling her to do things for herself only extends the powerlessness she experienced in the sexual assault itself.

In the face of a world that allows and encourages the victimization of women, rape victims also need action that can heal the wounds in the social order that perpetuate such crimes, as surely as they need a sustaining personal presence to heal their own wounds.

In giving sustenance and support to those assaulted and abused, rape crisis centers, friends, and families are performing genuinely spiritual acts. They are performing the pastoral acts that ordained clergy all too often are either unwilling or unable to perform. As human beings whose very selves are constituted in and through our relationships with others, those relationships may (or tragically, may not) become the locus of healing and reconstituting the meaning of the universe. As Adrienne Rich has put it,

> My heart is moved by all I cannot save:
> so much has been destroyed
>
> I have to cast my lot with those
> who age after age, perversely
>
> with no extraordinary power,
> reconstitute the world.[17]

10. Theological Perspectives on Sexual Violence

PATRICIA WILSON-KASTNER

During the last few years, American society has become increasingly aware of the extent of sexual violence in the home and in the society at large. Slowly and cautiously, the churches have begun to acknowledge and discuss the complexity and extent of a problem they have long minimized. An important element of our efforts to minister helpfully in the painful human anguish of sexual violence is a firm grasp of our theological understanding of such human situations. In order to assist ministers in clarifying their own theological perspectives, I have attempted first to identify the issues, then explore the traditions and look at the theological roots of hope and transformation for victim, perpetrator, and the wider community.

IDENTIFYING THE ISSUES

Any clergyperson or religious professional encountering an episode or situation of sexual assault or abuse meets a reality that tries the limits of our emotional and theological resources. In order to respond compassionately and helpfully to each individual event and to the massive extent of this societal evil, every minister needs to be conscious of his or her own theological perspective and its contribution to the pastoral needs of such situations.

Another section of this book outlines the statistical extent of this massive social problem. No percentages prepare us for the shock of visiting in the hospital the unconscious body of a four-year-old girl raped by her thirty-five-year-old father, or the seventy-two-year-old woman beaten and assaulted in her apartment by an intruder. Or perhaps we encounter the agitated college sophomore who is visiting home this month and reveals to her disbelieving parents her rape on a date last month. As we listen to person after person, we expand our notion of sexual violence even beyond the pervasive male rape of woman to see the extent of male violence against girls (even infants), boys, and sometimes other men. We acknowledge our growing awareness of women's usually more subtle but nevertheless real sexual violence against girls and boys, and sometimes even adult women and men.

We view these events and trends woven into the fabric of a society in which violence is condoned. Sexual violence represents a violent (not erotic) assault upon the most fundamental human drive aside from the most basic biological urge to survive. Sometimes even life-threatening violence is a part of sexual assault. Sexual assault threatens the core of the human psyche—its capacity to reach out, to trust, to respond to another, to experience pleasure.

The perpetrator of sexual violence is both a victim and assailant, who acts out our society's perverted notion of power as the ability to *do something to somebody* by exercising his own power by hurting another at the place of the other's greatest physical and psychic vulnerability. It is not surprising that women and children are the most frequent victims of assault, when our religious and civic traditions have conspired over the centuries to institutionalize their powerlessness. Nor is it accidental that most frequently those who assault others feel themselves internally or externally helpless and choose to prey on those who are weaker.

A minister who tries to respond theologically to issues of sexual violence thus confronts an extraordinarily complex social and personal question. Its roots lie deep in a religious tradition that at first appears to be of ambiguous value in its understanding of power and the relationship of the sexes.

EXPLORING THE TRADITION

Theologically, the most fundamental question to which one must respond is: What does it all mean? More personally phrased, Why does God let this happen? The only honest answer is, I think, that we don't know. We can identify social and personal factors that explain *ex post facto* or even point to the probability that the evil will occur, but we can give no satisfactory explanation in the deepest sense. Evil is ultimately unintelligible. We know what happened, and sometimes even how it happened, but not why.

But even if evil is mysterious, as a sort of negative image of the mystery of divine love, we can still identify different perspectives and aspects of our religious tradition. These illumine and give meaning and hope in the midst of the destructive chaos of sexual violence. The rest of this essay is an attempt to identify the elements of the Christian tradition that I find most useful in grasping the healing and transforming work of grace; each minister must participate in a comparable effort from his or her religious perspective.

WHAT DOES THE TRADITION SAY?

The Christian tradition itself gives mixed messages about human sexuality and the use of force and violence against others. Much could be said about this ambivalence. At the very least it means that the minister, the one who has been assaulted, and most probably the assailant and the wider community share in a heritage containing elements that both discourage but also encourage or permit sexual violence.

For instance, in the Old Testament, some sexual assaults and violence are clearly condemned (for example, Deut. 22:23–29). The rape of a woman is condemned, yet the assault is not banned for the reasons we might expect. The unmarried woman, for instance, is regarded as the property of her father and compensation is to be paid to him for his loss. Children are not named in the legislation, and later interpretation did not even count the assault of a girl child less than three years old. Thus the roots of the religious and legal tradition about sexual assault of women rests upon a consideration of them as property, not as persons.

On the one hand, Jesus' inclusion of women and children as persons points in the direction of a sexual ethic respecting every person's right to her or his bodily and sexual integrity. On the other hand, much in the development of the Christian tradition supported the notion of women's inferiority and encouraged an environment in which sexual victimization of women was at least covertly permissible, because women were not considered as fully human as males.

The question of women's full humanity was debated quite seriously at times and places in the early church. Scholasticism in the Middle Ages adopted a philosophical anthropology based on women's inferiority to men. At times (for instance in the Middle Ages), women were portrayed as voraciously sexual, seducers of men; at other times, as in the Victorian period, women were pictured as sexless angels, responding to the needs of lustful men. We must clearly recognize the ambivalence of the tradition about women because so many victims of sexual assault are women. Even male victims of sexual violence are those who, in the eyes of the assailant, are like women—helpless and inferior.

Further, the Christian tradition is also ambivalent with respect to the issue of our exercise of power. This ambivalence contributes to an environment in which assault is a possible response to another. The victims of violence, overwhelmingly women and children, have been consistently exhorted in the Christian tradition to be meek, submissive, and obedient. In the classical Catholic theology of marriage, for example, the notion of contract dominated. The woman was understood as owing her husband sexual use of her body as a marital obligation. Although in theory the obligations were mutual, men were seldom exhorted to reciprocate. Even though moral theologians would be horrified at some of the consequences of their theories, unquestionably these notions gave religious sanction to female submissiveness and male force in the exercise of power over a woman's body.

Christian theologians also reinforced ideals of male domination through the assumption that males were superior and would do what was best. Because possible victims—women and children, and even less powerful men—were not given permission to develop their own counterbalancing strengths, assailants never learned other useful ways to exercise power than to use force and ultimately violence. The popular religious image of a father-god who killed his own son to satisfy his own anger, and who was able to reward or punish his whole creation to do his will, served to reinforce the image of power as coercive and even intrusive.

Family and friends and even the wider community have been theologically alerted to their responsibility for one another in the communion of saints, but they also have been warned about the dangers of violating other relationships that God has ordained, such as that between husband and wife, parent and child. This reluctance to intervene, combined with the normal human unwillingness to acknowledge evil in someone known and perhaps loved, produces a profound resistance to viewing clearly a situation of violence. Consequently, most people have accepted as divinely sanctioned their own propensity to attribute high motives to those in authority, not wanting to believe that they would abuse their trust of those who depended on them for nurture and protection. Because of this misplaced faith, members of the community have in effect denied their own responsibility for one another—both perpetrator and victim.

THEOLOGICAL ROOTS OF HOPE

Even though the Christian tradition has offered profoundly ambivalent traditions about sexuality and violence, it still contains elements that offer hope and strength to victims of sexual assault and abuse. These elements counter the human tendency to distort our power over other persons and to assume that this twisted order of things is what God has created and intends for us.

One of the most fundamental insights of the Christian tradition in considering sexual violence is the insistence that there really is evil. We do not understand it, we cannot explain how or why there is evil. (Consequently, the quest for a satisfactory theodicy will never be truly successful). Nonetheless, evil is not an illusion or a product of our imaginations or a misjudgment about others. People do indeed hurt others; basic human urges can be twisted to cause pain and damage to others and the self. This is evil, a radical distortion and perversion of deeds and of the human heart.

Evil is a reality that humans can and sometimes do choose to allow into their lives. Although one may identify many contributing factors, ultimately a person chooses good or evil, even if the choice is within a limited range. An assailant or abuser may be in pain, buffeted by various external and internal forces, but ultimately that person chooses to victimize another. The victim is just that—one who has had evil done to her or him through the violence of another. The victim never deserves evil (assault or abuse) and has a right to expect it to stop.

The second theological notion is that both victim and assailant are invited to a new life. Neither are bound by inexorable laws to live as doers of evil or sufferers of its consequences. Good and evil both may be brought to the life of the new creation, to the hope of existence transformed by the love of God active in the world. Fundamental to the new creation is the notion that God created the world and its inhabitants in love, that evil is a twisting and distortion of creation and God's love for it, and that God can and will heal the wounds of creation if we will allow it.

Human beings are invited to respond with repentance, rejection of evil, forgiving and being forgiven, acceptance of divine and human healing, and the living of new life at one with God and humanity. Although the path to and the living out of this transformation may be quite different for victim and assailant, each is called to a life of healing and transformation.

The third major theological insight is that in our common life we are children of God. Our lives are intertwined with and interdependent on one another. If we are children of God, we are also responsible for one another's well-being; we are our brother's and sister's keepers. That is, if we share a common life, we are also called to live in ways that do not harm others and actively protect and nurture them.

If one accepts such a vision, then as individuals and as a human community, we must take account of ways in which we do and do not nourish the interpersonal, social, economic, and other needs of people around us. Unquestionably, the perpetrator of assault or abuse violates these fundamental responsibilities to each other. The victims of assault have found their trust in these human interconnections radically violated; perhaps that loss is the most serious effect of this violence. But all of our lives are bound in the network of interrelationships. Each of us is part of a society in which such serious abuse can happen. Directly or indirectly we contribute to conditions that foster or permit abuse, and we often do nothing to stop the cycle of violence in which one generation of victims learns and chooses to abuse the next. As human beings and as Christian believers, we are called to a more responsible life together. As children of God, joined together in community, by nature and by grace we are bound together in a mutual interconnection whose failure is clearly manifest in abuse and violence.

HOPE AND TRANSFORMATION

Because of the complexity of all human situations, and especially because of the difficulties in understanding such a blatantly evil event as sexual violence, we cannot simply identify relevant theological themes. We must ask how the theological themes illumine the lives of the participants in the events of sexual assault and violence. Further, we must ask how these realizations move the persons involved toward healing and transformation. If one simply hurls theology at persons in such a painful situation, one might be better doing nothing at all. Instead, I would prefer to explore the positive contribution theological insights can make to healing the raw wounds left by sexual violence.

THE ASSAILANT

The perpetrator of sexual violence must struggle with his or her own humanity before God and with others in a direct and painful way. The assailant must accept and admit that he or she has abused his or her own freedom and the humanity of another. This recognition, on its most basic level, requires an acceptance of human freedom and of one's own misuse of that freedom. Ultimately, the one who commits violence chooses to do so. The victim, girl or boy or woman or man, has been wounded and violated because the assailant chose to do the wounding and violating. Various factors, such such as alcoholism, poverty, sexism, a heritage of pain, mistrust, and the experience of abuse contribute to and motivate a person to hurt others, but they do not *force* the person to commit abusive acts. Other choices were possible, but the assailant chose violence towards another. Without that choice, the violence would never occur.

This basic reality of human freedom, which may be severely limited by internal and external factors, must be genuinely recognized and understood by the assailant. If the person can accept his or her own freedom, then the person can take responsibility for his or her own violence towards another. Many studies have demonstrated that true healing can only happen in the doer of violence if that person admits and takes responsibility for the abuse. Only if he or she assumes responsibility for the violence can any healthy relationship with the world begin to grow.

To make this confession of one's own wrongdoing may be a new experience for an individual who has a limited sense of self and of his or her own relationship to God and to others. The violent and abusive person may never have considered himself or herself as a child of God capable of making decisions. Commonly such a person will mask responsibility with the excuse that strong emotions or drugs or alcohol overcame one's will.

It can be a moment of great spiritual insight and growth for a person to say: I hurt someone seriously, and I wish I had not. To do so is to claim one's own personhood, to recognize another's, and to acknowledge a possibility of respecting one another. Such an acknowledgment, if honestly offered, can grow only from conviction that we are children of God who come from, depend on, and are related to this God, and who find relationships to each other and themselves in context of the fundamental rooting in God. In an atmosphere recognizing responsibility and accepted freedom, the assailant can begin to grapple with the reality of the destructiveness done to another individual and to the whole human community through his or her violence. The perpetrator of abuse must explore with honesty the reasons for acting in such a way as to damage the self and another. Untangling layers of self-deception and accepting painful truths about oneself can take place only by becoming willing and able to live honestly in relationship with a God who strengthens and sustains us.

But to confess the truth about oneself is a beginning step, not the whole. Part of the truth the assailant discovers before God is that he or she is called to be different, to leave the old destructive ways of relating in order to accept and act in new ways. In biblical language, this person is called to repentance, *metanoia.* This means turning violent and hateful behavior into constructive, humane, and loving ways. Such a transformation may be the work of a lifetime, proceeding in fits and starts. Nonetheless, it is essential that the assailant who has abused and violated another clearly feel from the midst of one's own pain and confusion a clear call to a new way of life.

A repentant life will involve this person in a painful acceptance of his or her own weakness and the evil done to others. But it will also impel the individual to an ongoing search for self in a God who is adequate to all we might ask or expect. The repentant assailant can find true power, the power of life and constructive freedom, in God, in a restored inner self, and in a community to which he or she can relate positively. Rather than victimizing others, the perpetrator of evil can become one who works healing for the self and others by being open to God's transforming life offered through the human community.

VICTIM

The victim of sexual assault and violence is also a survivor. But how fully human can the survivor be? Has she or he been so scarred and damaged that a fully human life is impossible? The victim has been hurt profoundly, and no words or subsequent actions can unmake that reality. Evil has really been done; the person has survived moral evil of the most destructive and radical sort. Just as the doer of the evil must acknowledge and repent of his or her destructive behavior before positive change or growth is possible, the victim cannot grow or be free without a clear and straightforward admission of the evil work of another, which assaulted the core of one's personhood. The appropriate human response to such a twisting of God's intention for all of creation and for each of us can only be a cry of anger and of pain at such violation.

The victim of sexual assault and violence embodies an extreme expression of the effects of evil directed to another person; both the psychic and the physical self are violated and to some extent will always retain the scars. The victim is both a damaged individual and also a representative of all of us in the fragility of our creatureliness, subject to the pain and destructiveness that another person or persons can work upon us.

Such anguished experience raises in the victim and survivor the most basic questions that a human being can ask. Can anyone— God, parents, strangers, even my own body—be trusted again? Is everything hostile and potentially or actually destructive? Are the victim's own feelings of trust and love only lures to evil and destruction from the very ones to whom one might be attracted? Is God the maker of a hateful world? Or am I in my created being so offensive and guilty before God that I deserve evil happening to me? Is healing possible to one who has been so violated, or am I doomed to isolation and shame and my own sense of abnormality? Is there any hope for me in my radical pain and anger?

A Christian response begins with a firm affirmation of the image of God in each of us through creation. God creates humans in the divine image; this resemblance and longing for God is each person's most essential gift. If even sin cannot obscure the divine image in the sinner (Wis. of Sol. 2:22–23), then by no means can the evil done *to* someone take it away. The victim may feel evil, destroyed, and deserted by God. She or he needs pastoral and theological help to regain contact with her or his powerful relationship with God through creation. Recovering the sense of God's presence will restore a core of health and wholeness that provides resilience and the power and dynamism for life.

For a Christian, the cross and resurrection lie at the heart of the living out of the victim's recovery from the damage of sexual violence and assault. Much cheap and trivial writing has come from Christian pens as people have tried to find answers for their pain. But even the bad advice given to suffering people should not obscure for us the centrality of the cross and resurrection to the mystery of human agony. The cross of Christ emerges from a world created good, which has been damaged by evil that causes suffering. The cross does not answer the question of why such evil is in the world. The cross is rather a sign that although evil is among us, through God's presence and action with us it will be overcome.

Jesus incarnated God's suffering with the world, even to accepting destructive and degrading treatment at the hands of others. Jesus, the Gospels are careful to point out, did not ask for suffering, tried to avoid it when he could, and begged in the Garden of Olives to be delivered from pain and death. Nonetheless, when evil moved in to arrest and destroy him, he accepted his death in solidarity with all the other innocent sufferers of the world.

In the extremity of his suffering, he could not even see what his suffering meant; he was thrown up against a wall of his own loss of understanding and trust in the God who sent him and whom he expected to protect and guide him. "My God, my God, why have you forsaken me?" both Mark and Matthew report as his last words. Jesus articulated for suffering humanity, and especially for the victim of assault that strikes at the fundamental integrity of body and spirit, the cry of one who could see neither meaning nor hope in the depths of pain.

And yet, through the suffering of the cross, Jesus was raised to new life. Jesus' resurrection bursts forth as a sign of hope to the victim and survivor that new life is possible from even the most violent and destructive situation. Because God is active with and among us, sustaining and strengthening us in our suffering even when we neither feel nor acknowledge it, death and destructiveness can never be the last word. Even in the most desolate situations, transformation is possible for the victim. Radical assaults upon the person's deepest being can be healed. The victim need not be chained or entombed by old pain and wounds, with their limits, twistedness, and numbing of life in the self. The cross is not only a sign of God's suffering with us in Christ; it is the hope of resurrection for all who have been hurt and victimized by the evil that haunts our world. As the very wounds of the crucified one testify to the strength of God's love overcoming evil, so the painful experiences of body and spirit are not to be denied but are transformed in the power of healing love.

FRIENDS, FAMILY, COMMUNITY

All of us are children of God. Cain asked God, "Am I my brother's keeper?" From God's point of view, the answer was so obvious as not even to call for a direct response. From a Christian perspective, we are children of God and brothers and sisters of one another. Most of Christian history is the tale of our endeavors to avoid our ties and responsibilities to one another. We can shake off our isolation and self-centeredness by serious consideration of a central Christian notion, the communion of saints.

To assert that we are members of one another, joined together in the body of Christ, is not simply a metaphor but the expression of a profound reality. We are bound to one another because of our common relationship to God through Christ in the life of the Spirit of God. We form one interdependent whole, the body of Christ, the communion of saints. At the very least, this language underscores the closeness of the interrelationships and the responsibility we have one for another: the hand for the eye, one member of the team for another.

If we take these images even with moderate seriousness, the very occurrence of one act of sexual violence is an affront to the community. It raises serious questions about our responsibility for each other. How could this sort of act happen at all among people who are caring for each other? Why are we so seldom aware of these acts or the painful consequences of them? Why do we raise and allow to come to maturity assailants who are able and willing to so damage another human person? Why are we so inept in identifying and healing the pain of those who have been victims of sexual assault and violence? What can we do in our process of repentance and transformation to become agents of prevention of violence and healing of those who have been victims and those who have attacked another?

Our sense of the vast distance between the way we actually live and the way the communion of saints would live united with all of God's people goads us to reform ourselves. We so often lead lives of covert violence, of failure to attend to the needs and hopes of others. We press on through life, bending others to do our will, depending on emotional manipulation, the power of money, status, or other forces to move others. Although we may not assault others sexually, we may attack and violate them in other ways. Our approach to life and our confidence in the right of power to compel others who are less powerful than ourselves build a society in which sexual violence and assault are merely the extreme expression of a system of violence and exploitation. God calls us to reform ourselves from such a way of life.

If we are truly members of one another, we are also invited to listen to the pain of others in order to heal it. Deploring sexual violence verbally is a modest beginning. We are called to see the pain of the wounded children who cannot even articulate the assault on their developing selves; the fear in women who dare not go outside at night; the confusion in the faces of those who have been raped by friends and acquaintances, and who believe themselves responsible. We are also invited to be open to the confusion and distress of those who have themselves been so damaged that they can only find satisfaction through destroying another person. We are called to hear and heal their pain because we are children of one God and brothers and sisters of each other.

Because we know that we are members of a community, we also are certain that we must rectify the injustices that make possible a society in which assaults can happen. We know that this is an ideal, just as we know that our healing of individuals is always unfinished and imperfect. Nonetheless, we are impelled by the strength of our love for one another to labor to heal the poverty, the sense of hopelessness, the atmosphere of corporate violence, sexism, and oppression of the less powerful that help to make a world of victims and assailants. We rest assured that the community of God's children seeks a transforming of the society in which victim-violator relationships dominate, into one in which we strive to live in fairness, justice, and mutual assistance and love.

3. RESPONDING WITH COMPASSION

Sexual assault and abuse call out to us to respond in new ways. The whole topic invites us to act—to behave in healing ways toward specific victims and to become involved with the social transformations necessary to the hopes of prevention.

The first four of these essays focus on the sexual assault of an adult victim.

- *"Standing by Victims of Sexual Violence: Pastoral Issues" encourages new responses from a classic pastoral stance.*
- *"Support Counseling with Victims of Sexual Assault" provides basic information about the recovery process and counseling victims. These basic guidelines are relevant to all the varieties of sexual violence. We encourage you to make them second nature when you respond to victims.*
- *"Sharing the Crises of Rape: Counseling the Mates and Families of Victims" extends our concern to the needs and possibilities of those people intimately concerned with victims.*
- *"The Male Minister and the Female Victim" reflects upon issues which may arise for a male pastoral counselor.*

Sexual violence, however, is broader than rape. The next four selections explore needed responses to other varieties of sexual violence.

- *"Sexual Harassment: Victim Responses" shares information about typical victim responses and guidance for counseling.*
- *"Beyond Belief: The Reluctant Discovery of Incest" provides an in-depth discussion of the responses of incest victims and implications for treatment and prevention.*
- *"Confidentiality and Mandatory Reporting: A Clergy Dilemma?" addresses some concerns that may arise for clergy who become aware of a child victim of sexual abuse or incest.*
- *"Responding to Clients Who Have Been Sexually Exploited by Counselors, Therapists and Clergy" explores the newly discovered problem of abuse by professional caregivers. This essay addresses these concerns from the point of view of the victim's recovery process. "A Client Bill of Rights" is one example of a new statement of ethics explicitly spelling out a professional commitment against sexual abuse by counselors.*

As important as good counseling is for victims, ministry is more than counseling. "What the Church Can Do" points to possible programs for the local congregation. "Resources for Ritual and Recuperation" offers some examples of the array of symbolic resources that we need in order to deal holistically with sexual assault and abuse.

We invite you to let these guidelines for compassionate and healing responses to victims inform your ministry. We invite you to seek out further training from crisis centers and shelters and to participate in the new discoveries for response still being made today.

11. Standing By Victims of Sexual Violence: Pastoral Issues

JANE A. BOYAJIAN

As religious leaders, our call is to be *celebrants*. We affirm joy and grace in human life—and despair and pain. Remembering what endures, imagining possibility, finding assurance and self-forgiveness, moving toward healing and wholeness—these are the work of liturgy. So we must ask ourselves: How do our liturgies inflict pain and afflict the despairing without our knowing?

We would *bring aid*. Ours is a responsive work. We would stand by and "suffer with," hearing human need even when it cannot be stated and responding effectively and warmly. We must also press the question: How could it be otherwise?

And so we are *social transformers*. Our theologies envision *shalom*, that time when the oppressed will know justice and hope. We would transform, cocreate in this world, so that *shalom* might come. So we must also consider the question: How do we subvert that work by our silences, habits, institutions?

We are *morally alert*. We know well that ethical sensitivity includes the ability to reexamine closely held values, exploring the fit of those values in new contexts. And so we will also examine our own practice as religious leaders to ask: How do our habits and allegiances to principles or colleagues undo our commitments and our calling?

Unintentionally, we clergy sometimes add to the pain, shame, and alienation of sexual assault victims. I look now at my own practice as a clergywoman; I wonder about the ways I too perpetuate the myths about sexual violence, increasing the shame that victims feel. As clergy we are particularly alert to the disempowered and the alienated. Responding sensitively to those in need and effectively addressing the factors that create those needs are central aspects of our clergy work. These twin tasks are also central to our work with the sexually assaulted and sexually abused.

We bring much skill and experience to these tasks. But sexual violence differs from many other of our concerns, since it is an especially sensitive area. Much of what feeds victims' shame is hidden from our eyes. Our language and the biblical passages we read may deepen her sense of guilt.[1] Our closely held values may unintentionally blame victims. So we must examine the particularities of sexual violence and underline issues that call for our special care as religious leaders.

Standing by another who is suffering means not abandoning her even when her reality hurts or threatens us. Admitting that sexual abuse is an actuality even in our congregations means recognizing the limitations of our own ministries. Owning the reality of sexual violence highlights further work for us to do. It can break our hearts. When we acknowledge that there are victims in our pews, we must know that there are also assailants. So, as we ask how we can better respond to victims, we must also ask what responsibilities we have to assailants and their families.

Our religious institutions, liturgical traditions, and sacred writings provide justification for the victimization of children and (primarily) women. Acknowledging this reality means seeing that we clergy add to their pain when we support the *status quo*. How shall we change our institutions, metaphors, symbols, and personal values—even our selves—to be both responsive and socially transforming?

Sometimes we may see a colleague sexually involved in serial affairs with parishioners. We may acquiesce in his being transferred to another congregation, silently closing ranks behind him. Thus we place professional etiquette before caring for those in our charge. Do we really mean to convey, by our actions, that collegial loyalty is always our primary responsibility?

We commit ourselves to work not only for the social transformation of our communities but also of the institution we love and serve: the Church. To do that well, we must look at the language and the myths we perpetuate institutionally. And we must look at our personal values. As religious leaders, our work is in moral ground. Yet like other leaders, we too must examine our choices.

How do we balance one value against another when we cannot serve both equally?

All this is painful work. And it can be personally threatening. Acknowledging the reality and extent of sexual assault is frightening. The world seems less safe, the home less a refuge, than we had previously believed.

Working in the area of sexual violence tests us spiritually. The facts of sexual violence are statements about our ministries and our communities. Our faith is challenged when a parishioner asks us: How could God let this happen to my child?

We must reflect. What is asked of us? Where do we miss the mark? How can we do better?

At the very least, we should do no harm.

Of course. But sometimes we do so without intending to harm another.

An example: Several months into this project, I went to the ballet for an evening's respite. The program notes discussed the first ballet, a new work. The choreography was based on a familiar biblical story. The house lights dimmed; I relaxed into my seat with anticipation. The children of David danced before me; it was a gentle sight. Then two figures performed the love duet of ballet, the *pas-de-deux*. Tamar and Amnon relished one another, savored the body of the other through the dance. It was very beautiful and passionate. And then they lay together.

Suddenly my evening's peace was violently jarred. All at once, I remembered that this beautiful scene before me actually depicted the rape of Tamar. I really felt quite undone. I looked around at my companions and the thousands present. They were clearly enjoying this moment. Their faces did not indicate that they had found anything amiss. I was, I thought, obviously crazy or mistaken. Perhaps I had my biblical stories confused. As I turned back to the stage, the dancers were caught in an embrace that embodied mutuality. Of course, I'm wrong, I thought.

Later that night, returning home, I looked up the passage.

And she answered him, Nay, my brother, do not force me; for no such thing ought to be done in Israel; do not do this folly. . . . Howbeit he would not hearken unto her voice: but, being stronger than she, forced her, and lay with her. (2 Sam. 13:13–14)

What had been danced as a *pas-de-deux* of love was, in fact, a *rape*.

That evening's experience was an occasion for a new understanding. That night, victims and assailants both were given strong messages about violence against women through the medium of the flowing garb and muted colors. I truly saw exposed the very heritage I so value, which disguises this violence so that we do not see it for what it is. When I finally did see it, I assumed I was in error.

At the very least we should do no harm.

As religious leaders we are symbols for our religious institutions wherever we are seen and on whatever issues we speak. "Wherever we go we go," says Ernst Bloch. As clergy, our work is the sacred, the mysterium. Even if we do not claim special power, others ascribe it to us by reason of this office. Our office has a life of its own, and our office is ever with us. So our words and actions do not stand alone. Both our language and our presence can do harm or bring aid.

Will we give aid?

To do so, we must rethink our roles as clergy. Most of us do not concur with one scriptural interpretation that a woman's sole responsibility is to serve her husband.[2] As preachers and celebrants, if we do not sensitively air the issues of sexual assault, we do harm. Left in silence, each victim is further isolated, alone with her self-blame and guilt. When she hears traditional and thoughtless interpretations of familiar biblical passages, she may believe that God blames her too. If familiar liturgy exhorts her to "bear what she has to bear," she can hear that as a call to submission, to remain uncomplaining in an abusive home.[3] Even if her reason tells her otherwise, she may look to herself as cause of her own victimization. She is, after all, a child of our culture, shaped by interpretations of our Judeo-Christian treasured writings.

Avoiding harm and bringing aid mean learning the realities about sexual violence and understanding the subtle messages our language conveys to victims. When we speak even of the sexual abuse of children, for example, we need to remember that "children" are usually *girls,* that abusers are usually men, that *abuse* is a word that softens a *criminal assault,* and that *incest* suggests an activity different from other sexual violence, implying mutuality, participation, and responsibility on the part of the assaulted girl.[4]

Bringing aid means using our authority as example. We will own the realities of sexual violence in our congregations and communities. Through sensitive preaching, we will give permission to break the silence about sexual assault in our congregation. We will convey our respect for others' personal timetables by giving clear sermon titles forwarning of the subject. We will reconstruct new liturgies that reach across the isolation of victims to bring healing and assurance, or to cleanse and reclaim the place where an assault occurred.[5]

In counseling sexual assault victims, doing no harm means using the same care we bring to other counseling but with a special new attentiveness. For most of us, the issues of sexual assault require an awakening, a new sensitivity. (See Chris Servaty, "Support Counseling with Victims of Sexual Assault," pp. 124–139.) Much of the guilt and shame victims feel may emerge from their interpretation (correct or incorrect) of theology. Standing by them means patiently working through the theology a victim brings to the counseling situation. She may need our help in reconstructing her theology as well as her world. She may need to learn, inside, that she did not cause what has happened to her. We cannot expect that an individual's theology is always consistent, especially in stress. We will pay special attention to the values and judgments we bring as counselors about which we may have little initial awareness. She may be carefully listening to us for the censure she expects, hearing cues we do not intend but which reflect traditional values about family life. She has been accustomed to traditional assumptions about "woman" that will not help her now.

We must examine our assumptions that passivity is woman's way and aggression is man's way. We need to be attentive to our stereotypes: "She is too old (or too young) to be raped." "He is too nice a guy to be an abuser." "This can't happen in my congregation." "She's too bright to believe that it was her fault."

We need to get the facts straight. For example, children are not usually assaulted by strangers. In 90 percent of the child abuse cases, the individual is known to the child. Most often, that child is between three and six years old.[6] We will remember that recovery from a random attack is most difficult because there is no rational explanation for what has taken place. If we put ourselves in her shoes, we will think about what it means to have one's self and one's home violated. We may begin to understand why it might be harder for people raped in their own beds to recover. We will be patient.

In counseling the sexually assaulted, we will be especially attentive to issues of power. For example, most of us are newly come to the importance of touch as a way of conveying warmth and reassurance. So we may want to touch her. But we may need to break the new habit in this situation. For many women, a male hand, however gently placed on her shoulder, is experienced as "power over": he is claiming her. When an individual has experienced unwanted touching, the last thing she will want is a pat on the knee or an arm around the shoulder. Such a gesture may become a nightmare reborn.

In counseling victims, we will remember what it means to feel deeply powerless. We will ask ourselves how much probing and how many details we really need to hear in order to be helpful. Religious confessional and psychotherapeutic practice, says Sissela Bok, place a high value on absolving oneself of guilt through purging oneself, transforming through revelation.[7] But asking her to divulge too much can intensify her sense of victimization. Hearing too much can magnify the power we have over her. Self-knowledge, a vital tool in any counseling situation, is critical here. After all, we enhance our own power by hearing another's secrets. Conversely, the revealer, too, has a power to call forth responses from us which are manipulative or exploitive. So we must ask: Is my own voyeurism out of control?

Bringing aid to any counseling context means standing by her, being with her. This means ensuring that she has the support she needs, even when we are not there or able to provide it. Self-perception and a willingness to refer are critical. In sexual violence cases, having good pastoral counseling skills may not be enough; referral to a local sexual assault center may be the best we can do for her. If we do not like her (or respect her) or do not understand her values, and therefore, her value conflicts, we cannot support her.

Standing by her means taking her seriously—legitimating her reality however shocking or surprising it may be to us. Among the most poignant cases are those of elderly women who have been sexually assaulted but whom no one believes. They are thought to be "too old" to be sexually assaulted. These are people twice victimized—first assaulted, then denied. Their listeners forget that sexual assault is a hostile act rather than a sexual one; they have become victims because they are vulnerable.

Like all counselees, sexual assault victims need respect for their values and their timetables. The guilt and turmoil of each can be exacerbated when we superimpose our judgments. It may seem clear to you that this wife is not safe at home. But she is struggling with an agonizing conflict of values asking herself: What is my responsibility to my children, my husband, my marriage vows, myself? You may ask how an incest victim can still love her father while she permits the abuse to continue because she fears tearing apart her family and losing the father whom she loves. Choosing self-sacrifice may seem the only apparent course. If we encourage her to leave the situation and she will not or cannot, then among the most responsible actions we can take is to help her to do contingency planning. If the worst happens at 2 A.M., what can she do? If she wants or needs to remove herself from the situation at some later time, what shall she do?

We will avoid superimposing our own timetable for change on the victim. Changing and growing take time, after all. Remembering our own responses to a disaster or crisis helps us here. Often our first response to crisis is denying this new reality that now threatens our life and well-being. We do that by pretending it is not so, by seeking others who will support that pretense, by "going away inside" to avoid facing disaster, by creating a world of our own in fantasy, or by returning to the past. Facing a crisis takes energy; we must reorganize our life in the face of this new reality.[8] This means acknowledging our own responsibility to take life-saving action to protect ourselves from further harm. Since disaster changes our lives profoundly, none of us makes those crisis-driven changes easily. If we have been hiding the crisis from ourselves for a long time and are now recovering an incident buried deep in our past, we may not recall it or change easily. The gradual recall of abuse as a child, for example, may be a slow and anguishing process. That victim's family may resist and resent a process dedicated to the retrieval of dark family secrets that they prefer to be forgotten. They will not thank you for "meddling," and her process of recovery may be difficult and slow. Respecting a person means validating her reality and her personal process of recovery. Letting her set the pace is one way of restoring her sense of control.

Informed consent is an issue. Respect for persons means informing them, in advance, about the values we bring to this counseling setting. What is the likely outcome of this counseling? What are our goals? We will review with her the options before her and consider what might happen if she chooses to do nothing in her own behalf. What are the likely effects of surfacing her anger, of her possible radicalization? Having been informed of these issues, she will be able to make an educated and informed decision about being a partner in our counseling. To assume that we know what is best for her is simply another way of taking control away from her, of victimizing her further.

Some abuse counseling will ask more of us as counselors than we can give; then we must take special care. Here are some examples. We may not like the counselee or respect her values; then we should stand aside and live with our guilt for doing so. But our responsibility is to see that someone else does stand by her. We may find it impossible to stand by an assailant or the family of the assailant. Similarly, care is needed when counseling a mother in an incest case because she is often the second and silent victim. She is blamed for the incest. ("She must really have known all along," or "If they had had a good sex life, he wouldn't have turned to his daughter.") Abused children are often removed by the court to "safe" homes. These children are victims of violence who, during a life-shaking disaster, are taken from all the support systems (family, friends, school, church) on which they normally depend. They may even believe that they themselves are the cause of the violence and of the family breakup. We clergy can provide a sense of stability and needed news of home. We can provide support by our presence when children are asked to give depositions. All these actions take energy and time to convince public officials responsible for their case that our presence is appropriate and right.

As religious leaders, we know that individuals do not feel hopeful if they believe they are without options. Bringing aid, then, means empowerment, helping the victim find options so she can recover her sense of control and hope. Empowerment means recognizing that it is *she* who must decide what is in her best interests. Empowerment means protecting her privacy—not sharing her information with others without her permission nor pressing her for more information than she wishes to give. It also means respecting her intuitive skills. She, after all, knows her situation. Jean Baker Miller reminds us that the racially and sexually oppressed depend upon a well-developed skill in detecting the moods of those who have power over them.[9] We call this skill intuition; it is a sensing device—a survival tool—that both you and she should respect. Some night you may believe that she is safer at home than her intuition tells her she is; trust her.

Regaining self-respect and empowerment both take time and practice. Carol Gilligan's studies indicate that women make decisions based on an ethic of responsibility. That is, women place highest value on their responsibility to others expressed by an ethic of care, caring for others first. The counselee may need help in adding herself into that caring equation. We can help her to understand that "it is moral to care not only for others but also for [herself]."[10] Thus she can gradually move from self-sacrifice and self-denial to self-care. The challenge for us clergy is to legitimate the ethic of responsibility while also helping her find solutions that include her own self-care.

Clergy are powerful educators and enablers. If we want to give aid, we will encourage support groups for sexual assault victims and their families, of course. We will also provide opportunities for educating adults and children about unwanted touching and about the community resources available to them if they are victims of bad touching. These are obviously pastoral responses. We also have a responsibility to transform our religious education programs, following a careful rereading of the curriculum, attentive to stated and hidden messages. We will be sure that our curriculum in no way teaches victims to believe that they caused their rape or that it is they who are shamed. Language will be gender-inclusive, indicating that women, like men, have hopeful and open futures. These tasks are time-consuming; such transformation often involves major rewriting.

Even more difficult is reconstructing symbols and metaphors of successful, happy, Jewish, Christian, feminine, loving "woman." Girls learn early that they should make themselves sexually pleasing to men. The codes of femininity indicate that it is all right for men to talk about women's bodies and to use women and that women should let them do so. These are social norms to which women adjust without thinking. Like the Chinese women of past generations whose feet were bound so that they would be dependent, women in this culture learn helplessness. They learn to hobble too.[11] Says Susan Griffin, "Chivalry is an age-old protection racket that depends for its existence on rape."[12] As religious leaders, we need to develop curricular materials that move women beyond hobbling.

We need educational programs that validate the uneasiness women feel in many situations, feelings based on reality rather than paranoia. We need to teach young women to protect themselves while being careful not to make them solely responsible for their own well-being. As religious leaders, we value highly the ability to make peace and to mediate differences. But there are times when personal safety may require a response other than nonconfrontation or politeness. Thus we will also teach children that there are times when it is appropriate for them to say no, unequivocally, and to require that others respect the boundaries they set.

Churches have a specific responsibility: We are a primary socializer; we teach people the "ethical" way to live. . . . Because the church exists for the person, the family, and the neighborhood, it is ideally suited both for the transformation of social values and the caring of persons in that change process. . . . Finally, there is the whole matter of teaching people about power. . . . A theology of power must be articulated and experienced, in which the church demands from the society some level of self-determination for all people.[13]

Bernard Loomer asks us to reconsider our own conceptions of power. He reminds us that our traditional concept of power is that of power over another; it is hierarchical. "If I have the power, then you don't." I can have power, in this traditional approach, only if I have taken it away from you. Loomer offers another conception, that of relational power.[14] It is power to which all have access. He does not mean that everyone is equal in the sense of "same." Rather, relational power is power shared. To share power means lifting up, respecting, and validating others—those different from me. All these elements of power sharing are vital aspects of working with those who feel powerless or victimized. Sharing power means making ourselves accessible to another, being with another in the deepest sense of that word. This is the suffering with another, the self-emptying, of which theologians of hope speak. If we suffer with another, we are affected. We are so open to the other that we are changed by what they know and feel.

If we act in the spirit of relational power and are open to being deeply affected, then we will rethink our roles as religious leaders in working with sexual assault victims. We will ask: How do we miss the mark and how can we do better? We will also be profoundly changed by that work. The guilt and the shame rightly belong with us all. The anger of victims should also be ours. And the transforming power of their ability to grow through and to reach for more will be ours as well.

12. Support Counseling with Victims of Sexual Assault

CHRIS SERVATY

This article provides an overview of the crises of sexual assault from the victim's perspective and practical strategies for responding to the victim's immediate needs. Because sexual violence includes a broad range of abusive behaviors, this article will focus on general guidelines for clergy to follow to provide crisis intervention and support counseling to victims. Readers are also encouraged to refer to other chapters in this book and to the bibliography for in-depth study of counseling victims of specific types of sexual assault, for instance, incest, marital rape, child victims.

The role of support counselor with sexual assault victims is an important role for clergy to perform. Victims commonly experience intense spiritual loss and pain and often first seek comfort and guidance from clergy. When their lives seem out of control, hopeless, and overwhelming, victims may view clergy as possible sources for support, intervention, spiritual guidance. Victims choose to talk about their sexual assaults with clergy they can trust to believe them and to give them the support they need.

Frequently, survivors of sexual assault will present clergy with patterns of symptoms or series of personal crises that may disguise the fact that they were sexually victimized. These symptomatic patterns may include chronic depression, suicidal thinking, alcohol or drug abuse, self-destructive behaviors, phobias, and marital problems. Symptoms can be viewed as ways the victim has learned to cope with, deny, or suppress the sexual assault trauma and its effects. Ongoing abusive relationships and multiple victimizations tend to increase the variety and severity of symptomatic behaviors. Changing these behaviors falls outside the counseling limitations of most clergy, but clergy can play an essential role in identifying indicators of sexual abuse and in supportively directing the victim to appropriate treatment.

THE ROLE OF SUPPORT COUNSELOR

Crisis intervention and support counseling begin when the victim directly or indirectly discloses the sexual assault experience. It continues through the victim's process of regaining stability or, when appropriate, of seeking treatment with a therapist. Sexual assault is a traumatic, externally imposed crisis event in an individual's life, when normal coping skills no longer apply or are temporarily disrupted.

The crisis of sexual assault generally results in:

- Emotional responses—fear, anger, guilt, shame
- Emotional needs—for safety, for personal control, for support
- Physical needs—for safety, medical care for injuries, pregnancy, or sexually transmitted disease
- Problems and conflicts—telling friends, family, and coworkers; practical considerations such as transportation, childcare, or changing locks; deciding whether to report to the police

The primary goals of support counseling are to help victims identify their strengths and resources and to empower them to make their own decisions about how to resolve the above needs and problems. This process helps victims to regain a sense of stability, power, and control in their lives.

In order to empower the victim, the support counselor assists the victim in clarifying needs and problems, clarifying choices and options, and facilitating the victim's own decision-making process. The support counselor works with the victim to prioritize problematic areas, thus decreasing the victim's sense of being overwhelmed and out of control.

Many recent victims of sexual assault initially experience shock and confusion (see "recovery process" below). In responding to these victims, clergy in the supportive counseling role should first attend to the victim's needs for physical safety and medical care for injury, gathering evidence, and testing for disease and pregnancy.

Victims should be asked directly whether they feel safe and whether they need medical attention. If the victim has needs in these areas, the supportive clergyperson should seek the victim's permission to contact the police, hospital, or ambulance to secure appropriate emergency services for the victim.

PRIMARY CONSIDERATIONS AND TECHNIQUES FOR COUNSELING VICTIMS OF SEXUAL ASSAULT

1. *Believe and support the victim.* Victims say that the most important messages they can receive from the person they tell are that they are believed and that they are not to blame.

2. *Sexual assault is an act of power and aggression.* It is important to distinguish sexual violence from consensual sex, and to define sexual assault as an act of violence using sex as the weapon. This distinction rightfully places the responsibility for the assault on the offender. It also validates the victim's experience of loss of power and control and helps the victim see sexuality as separate from the sexual assault.

3. *People do not become mentally ill as a direct, single consequence of sexual assault.* Victims need to be assured that they are not "crazy" or mentally ill, and that they can recover from crisis. Prior to their sexual assaults, most victims led normal, functional lives. Often confusion, anxiety, and drastic behavioral changes lead victims to fear for their sanity. Messages that victims are incapable of making their own decisions reinforce this myth about mental illness resulting from sexual assault.

4. *When indicators or symptoms of sexual victimization are present, ask questions.* Because of societal taboos on the subject of sexual abuse, threats from the offender, or the victim's internalized shame, victims are often reluctant to tell anyone about their sexual abuse. They fear that they will not be believed, that they will be further shamed or judged, and that they will be punished in some way. The victim the clergyperson encounters may have already had a negative experience from telling someone. Adults victimized as children commonly say that as children they gave several clues—cries for help—that they were being abused. These adults wish that someone had asked them what was upsetting them and whether someone was abusing them.

The following examples may be helpful to clergy who need to question possible abuse:

- "Many people who come here for help have been sexually abused. I'm wondering whether this has happened (is happening) to you?"
- "Some people keep the secret of being sexually abused because they fear they will be blamed or punished if they tell. If you have been abused, I will believe you and I won't blame you."
- "Have you been sexually abused?"
- "Has someone forced or tricked you into touch that you didn't like or that felt uncomfortable to you?"
- "Sexual abuse can happen with someone you know and trust. Has this happened to you?"

Because there is no single right way to ask whether someone has been sexually abused, draw on what you know about the person before you. Make questions sensitive, specific, nonjudgmental, and relevant to individual characteristics such as age, education, and cultural background. For example, a child may not understand that sexual abuse can involve a family member or caregiver as well as a stranger. It may be appropriate to ask children whether *anyone* has touched them in a manner that felt uncomfortable or confusing. As indicated in another article, suspected child abuse must be reported by helping professionals, and in some states there is mandatory reporting of suspected abuse of vulnerable adults. See the essay by Marie Fortune, pp. 198–205 for further discussion of such issues as they relate specifically to clergy.

5. *Although some victims may initially deny their abuse, it is still helpful to have asked the question.* Some victims will initially deny their abuse because they are not ready to face their victimization and attendant feelings, or they may need more time to trust the clergyperson who has asked them. Regardless of the motivations for denial, by asking whether someone has been sexually abused, clergy give the message that they are willing to believe and help victims of sexual violence. Another reason to ask the question is to give the assurance that the victim is not alone, that others have experienced sexual abuse and have similar reactions.

6. *Victims need to learn new coping skills and to be reminded of existing*

strengths and resources. While it is essential to validate the victim's pain and struggle, it is also important to reinforce positive coping skills. Surviving the sexual assault can be given as a strong example of coping successfully with a life-threatening event. It is also useful to draw on a victim's method of coping with a previous crisis, to remind the victim of what has worked successfully in the past and what resources may be available to assist them through the current crisis. The process of facilitating problem solving and decision making, a core function of support counseling itself, can present victims with opportunities to learn new coping skills.

7. *Many victims accept as truth myths about sexual assault.* It is important for clergy to be aware of and to understand how victims blame themselves through myths regarding sexual violence. Myths are false beliefs generally supported by society that put responsibility for sexual assault on the victims. Myths also imply that there is an identifiable profile for victims and offenders. Common myths regarding sexual assault are discussed on pp. 5–9. Educating victims about the facts of sexual assault can help them redirect responsibility for the assault onto the offender, where it belongs.

8. *Victims are affected by others' acceptance of these myths.* Not only do victims blame themselves with the above mythology, society and people close to the victim verbalize these false beliefs in blaming the victim. An important question for clergy to ask victims is whether they have told anyone else about the abuse and the nature of the response. This will provide significant information regarding the extent and nature of the victim's support system. For example, if a husband believes that victims provoke sexual assault, he may accuse his wife of "asking for it" by the way she was dressed, the way she acted, or where she was.

PATTERNS OF RESPONSE TO SEXUAL ASSAULT: VICTIM RESPONSES, RECOVERY PROCESS, AND COMMON FEELINGS

Crucial to any counseling intervention is an understanding of broad patterns of the responses of victims to sexual assault. Each individual reacts in a unique way. But these general guidelines provide a useful framework for supportive responses.

VICTIM RESPONSES

Each victim's set of responses and recovery process is unique, based on the following interrelated factors.

1. *Age and developmental stage.* Developmental tasks, conflicts, and crises are highlighted by sexual assault. The particular meaning that the assault takes on for the victim is largely influenced by the prominent life themes of the victim at the time of the assault. Adults victimized as children experience gaps in their development related to specific issues corresponding to the age at which the abuse occurred. Their development may be arrested at a particular stage of emotional development. Due to sexuality and separation conflicts, adolescents find it very threatening to tell parents that they have been raped, particularly by an acquaintance or boyfriend. Some young adult victims have sexuality and intimacy issues brought to the forefront at a stage in their lives when they are struggling to form long-term intimate relationships.

2. *Unresolved issues.* Sexual assault triggers unresolved conflicts, feelings, and crises that the victim experienced prior to the assault. These unresolved issues become part of their response to the current crisis. Adult victims of rape may suddenly recall childhood abuse, previously blocked from memory. Issues like trust and intimacy become major themes in a victim's response, especially when these issues were prominent before the sexual assault. Since sexual assault takes away normal coping skills and defenses, unresolved issues are allowed to surface to the victim's consciousness.

3. *Existing coping skills.* The victim's recovery is greatly affected by the existence of functional coping skills and by the ability to learn new ones. Victims who have already experienced a major loss, such as the death of a loved one, may be better equipped to grieve the losses engendered by sexual assault.

4. *Nature of the sexual assault.* The extent of physical injury and the relationship of offender to the victim present several factors that affect the victim's perception of the assault. Victims who experience physical battering are faced with traumatic life-threatening elements as well as physical injuries. Victims who did not experience physical abuse may have difficulty identifying themselves as true victims, based on their acceptance of the myth that rape always involves physical battering. A dilemma for victims who did

not overtly resist their attacker is that they should have fought back or escaped, even when the reality was that the attacker could have caused greater harm had the victim resisted or attempted to flee.

The relationship of the offender to the victim presents another set of issues for the victim. Victims who knew or trusted their attacker will often feel ashamed that they allowed themselves to be vulnerable, that they somehow should have known the offender's intentions. When sexual assault occurs within a long-term relationship, victims feel betrayed, since their trust of the offender was used against them. They feel confused because positive aspects coexisted with abuse in the relationship. It is extremely difficult for marital rape to be identified as such by the victim, partially due to societal messages that do not recognize the right to refuse sex within the marital bond. Acquaintance or date rape often leaves the victim confused about responsibility for the assault; the victim may have been attracted to the offender prior to the assault. The myth that sexual assault only occurs between strangers plays a strong role in a victim's conflicts in this area.

5. *Support systems.* Whether the victim has an intact, responsive support system of family and friends plays a major role in the recovery process. Two reasons for the effectiveness of victim support groups are that groups provide peer support and validation, and that groups provide opportunities for victims to learn new social skills for building healthy support systems.

The victim's support system is an important factor for clergy to assess when providing supportive services to victims. Concerned persons (those close to the victim) experience their own trauma and recovery process as a reaction to the assault on their loved one. Because support systems play a crucial role in the victim's recovery process, clergy should determine who, if anyone, gives support to the victim and the extent and nature of the support. Concerned persons may give mixed messages to the victim, sometimes blaming the victim through their expressions of anger and pain that the victim was harmed. Concerned persons may need support and validation for their own losses such as loss of intimacy, loss of interdependency, or loss of perceived ability to protect their loved ones.

One common experience involving concerned persons and victims is that the concerned person's anger and powerlessness is projected onto the victim through blaming messages such as "Why didn't you get away?" or "What were you doing there in the first place?" This is an expression of the concerned person's frustration (and maybe some mythology) at being powerless to prevent the assault or protect the victim. Clergy can help family and friends identify their own feelings and issues and can assist them in seeking support counseling for themselves. Daniel Silverman's chapter, "Sharing the Crisis of Rape," provides further treatment of these important issues. Sexual assault centers are available to provide support counseling or referrals to concerned persons.

RECOVERY PROCESS

Professionals in the sexual assault field have identified a common set of stages for recovery from sexual assault. Based on the response factors above, each victim's process of recovery will be unique. It is not uncommon for victims to experience stages out of the sequence given here. Symptoms from one stage can overlap into another. The stages of recovery essentially represent a grieving process for victims of sexual assault; it is a process that takes victims from crisis and loss to new coping skills and growth. There is no specific timetable given for stages. Some victims need outside intervention such as counseling or therapy to complete their process of recovery. Others need no intervention beyond having a natural support system that is responsive and positive. Knowledge of this recovery process can provide clergy with a framework for interpreting the victim's behavior as normal outcomes of the underlying process of recovery from loss.

Stage One: Impact

This stage immediately follows the sexual assault, can last for a few hours to several days, and is chiefly characterized by shock, disbelief, anxiety, and fear. The victim experiences disruption in normal coping skills and may appear disorganized and confused. A variety of behaviors can be observed as outward expressions of this crisis state: crying, laughing, withdrawal, hysteria, mood swings, calmness, or lack of any visible affect.

Although victims in this stage are often disorganized and confused, they need to make urgent decisions at this time. Among these decisions are: Whether to report the assault to the police;

whether to obtain an evidentiary exam and medical care; how to get to a safe place; how to repair damage to the home such as locks and doors; and how to obtain childcare if the victim is unable to care for children.

The clergyperson in a support counseling role should first assess the victim's needs for safety and medical care. Although these are priorities in terms of the physical well-being of the victim, attending to the emotional well-being of the victim means providing opportunities for the victim to make decisions and to regain control. For example, asking victims where and by whom they want to receive medical care gives them the power to make this decision for themselves. It is essential to avoid making decisions for the victim and instead to be sensitive toward giving power back to the victim. One must not assume that victims are incapable of making choices; only when victims are assessed as not being capable of taking care of themselves (unconscious or a danger to themselves or others) should the helper temporarily assume control to get them to a secure place or medical care.

Another decision that can be difficult for victims in this stage is whether to report to the police. Victims are frequently ambivalent about reporting. While they may want the offender apprehended, they may also have fears of retribution by the offender, of not being believed by the police or court system, of being embarrassed by having to testify about the assault, or other personal fears. Some victims may not want the offender put in prison or jail, particularly if the offender is known to them. Clergy support counselors should not make this decision for the victim (exceptions are child abuse and vulnerable adult abuse), but clergy should instead help victims explore the pros and cons of each choice and explore how each choice could affect the victim. Should the victim choose to report, the clergyperson can offer to accompany the victim to the appropriate law enforcement agency and provide support through the reporting process. Another resource available for support during the reporting process, as well as crisis intervention in general for victims, is the local sexual assault center.

Stage Two: Denial

This stage may last a few days, weeks, and sometimes years. The victim in this stage may appear to have adjusted to the effects of the sexual assault trauma, but is instead denying, suppressing, and rationalizing these effects. This is a natural and necessary phase in the victim's recovery. It represents the victim's attempt to return to a precrisis level of functioning. When entering this stage, victims feel overwhelmed and disorganized; denial helps them refocus their energies toward performing tasks with which they can exercise some control. During this stage the victim's primary needs are for security, comfort, and control. Victims may firmly state that the sexual assault is in their past and that they want to forget what happened to them. It is important for clergy to allow victims to progress through this stage at their own pace, to validate the victim's attempts to regain control and normal functioning, and to be aware that the victim will need further support once denial has served its purpose.

Concerned persons are frequently alarmed at the sometimes sudden change from shock to denial in the victim's behavior. Clergy can educate family members that denial is normal and that when the victim has regained control of daily functioning, the victim will again need their support and encouragement to continue the process toward recovery.

Stage Three: Process

The process stage usually begins when the victim is no longer able to suppress the sexual assault experience. Since this is the primary stage through which resolution occurs, it may last a few months to several years. This stage is precipitated by emotional distress and/or an event that triggers the victim's need to talk about the sexual assault. Depression, anxiety, nightmares, flashbacks, and constant thinking about the assault are some indicators of emotional distress. Events that trigger the process stage include the anniversary of the assault, seeing the perpetrator, having to testify about the assault in court, and other crises such as marital conflict, losing a job, and loss of a relationship. The victim discovers that the coping skills previously used to suppress feelings about the assault are no longer effective.

The process stage is the key stage for counseling to occur because the victim is now ready to talk about the assault and has a desire to resolve painful feelings. Clergy who do not have training specific to counseling sexual assault victims should provide the victim with support and with assistance in seeking other resources for counseling the victim through this stage. Local rape and sexual assault centers have counseling services and referrals that specifically address the needs of victims and concerned persons. They are also available to provide consultation to clergy who request information and training on sexual assault issues.

Stage Four: Integration

The final stage of integration is a culmination of the previous stages in that the victim has processed through the feelings connected to the assault and has integrated the sexual assault into the whole of the victim's life. The victim no longer feels controlled or dominated by the effects of the sexual assault and views the assault as a painful but significant event in the past. The victim has changed from accepting personal responsibility for the assault to directing anger and responsibility onto the offender.

It is normal for some victims to recycle through any or all of these stages of recovery, such as when a new crisis triggers an unresolved issue. Clergy can assure victims that whatever form or time their struggles take, the end result of their recovery process is new growth. Many victims have shared that their progress through recovery stages become shorter in duration and less painful each time. This experience reinforces the belief that learning new coping skills through losses produces a positive spiritual effect: from crisis there *is* growth.

COMMON FEELINGS

In addition to a general recovery process, victims experience a common set of feelings in response to sexual assault. These feelings can appear in any stage of recovery. Like the recovery process, they are unique to the individual and to circumstances of the assault, but there are common themes that explain the sources of these feelings. Awareness of these themes and resulting feelings can assist the clergyperson in validating feelings and giving appropriate feedback to the victim.

Fear and Anxiety

Because of the life-threatening nature of many sexual assaults, victims fear recurrence of violence in general and by the perpetrator in particular. Even when the victim's life was not overtly threatened, the losses incurred by this violation of self and well-being results in a heightened sense of vulnerability. Some victims will avoid any situation that they sense has a potential for repeated attack. Other victims generalize their anxiety even toward familiar surroundings and people.

Behavioral symptoms of fear and anxiety include sleeplessness, nightmares, edginess, uncontrollable shaking, withdrawal, and isolation. Victims may also express distrust of people who resemble the perpetrator in some way (gender, race, occupation), or they may distrust people in general.

Since the victim's fear and anxiety stems from true loss of control experienced in the sexual assault, it is helpful to explore options to regain control and safety in the victim's life. To begin this process, ask the victim what would make her or him feel safer. Identifying concrete actions to increase the victim's sense of security and allowing the victim to make choices regarding these options give the victim an opportunity to address fears in a realistic manner. It also gives the validating message that the clergyperson understands the source of this fear and that there are actions that can be taken to feel more secure. Changing locks on doors, moving to a security building, taking the bus instead of walking, and alerting a neighbor to watch the home are some examples of options to explore. When making choices to increase safety does not alleviate the victim's fear and anxiety, the clergyperson can provide support through active listening and validation of these feelings.

Guilt and Self-blame

As indicated in the section above on response factors, victims feel guilty in relation to the circumstances of the assault. Victims may seek additional reasons to blame themselves, recounting what they could have done differently to avoid the assault. They may blame themselves for being careless, acting seductive, not finding a method (or choosing not) to fight back or to escape, initially trusting the offender, and other personal reasons. At the level of support counseling, clergy should respond that the victim did what she or he had to do in order to survive and that the perpetrator *chose* to act on the victim's vulnerability in the given situation. Victims can learn new coping skills to decrease their vulnerability, but they are *never* responsible for the violent action chosen by the perpetrator.

When clergy recognize victims who repeatedly place themselves in vulnerable situations, it is essential to refer them to a counselor or therapist who is experienced in treating victims of sexual assault. Treatment can involve learning new skills to decrease vulnerability in a manner that is sensitive to the special needs and issues of victims.

Shame and Embarrassment

These feelings originate from violations of the victim's body and privacy. Often the perpetrator has verbally humiliated the victim as part of the attack, demeaning the victim's body and sexuality. If the victim underwent a medical exam following the assault, the victim may feel further exposed and violated. Questions asked during a police report may also embarrass the victim who is ashamed of what the attacker said and did during the assault. Victims also may not know medical terms for body parts and functions, or they may be too embarrassed to say these terms.

Shame tends to encompass the victim's entire self-concept. The victim may feel dirty, damaged, unworthy, unlovable, and incapable as a result of the violation of her or his body and self. Clergy should reinforce positive qualities in the victim and give affirming messages to counteract the victim's shaming process. Since shame is so deeply rooted and pervasive in a victim's self-concept, therapy is frequently recommended to heal and rebuild the victim's self-esteem. Groups are especially helpful in that they allow victims to express their shame in a supportive setting.

Anger

Victims frequently have difficulty finding a constructive outlet for their anger. Clergypersons should allow victims to recognize and express their angry feelings and should help victims to focus their anger on the perpetrator. When anger is consistently directed inward through depression or self-destructive behaviors (such as self-mutilation or chemical abuse), the victim should be immediately referred to a professional who is qualified to treat these behaviors and is sensitive to sexual assault issues.

Clergy can also assist victims in finding constructive outlets for anger that suit the victim's personality and needs. Some victims find that by reporting and testifying against the offender, they can experience justice and compensation for the crime committed against them. Others choose to confront the perpetrator directly with their anger. (This is *not* recommended if the perpetrator could further harm the victim.) Victims can become involved in organizations that promote nonviolence and advocate for victim rights. Victim support groups provide another healthy outlet where anger is validated and suggestions for expressing anger can be given.

It is important to convey to victims that anger in itself is not an unhealthy emotion; it is when anger is misdirected and expressed destructively that anger is harmful. Victims need to express their anger for what the perpetrator did to them as a necessary step towards integration of the sexual assault experience.

SPIRITUAL AND RELIGIOUS ISSUES

Victims of sexual violence experience crises in their spirituality and conflicts in religious values. Victims struggle to integrate their beliefs and values with the losses imposed by sexual assault. They may challenge the values practiced and held by their religion, and they may question the existence of God. Victims may also express anger and distrust toward the clergyperson who is trying to help them.

Spiritual crises are compounded by experiencing rejection or judgmental responses from clergy or church. These victims become further alienated from their religious community or sink deeper into despair and shame. Clergy must listen nonjudgmentally and openly to the content and feelings expressed by victims. By allowing the victim to evaluate and struggle with spiritual and religious issues, clergy can play an important role in the victim's process toward resolution and healing. Spiritual hope, guidance, and support, offered in a nonintrusive manner, create a nurturing climate for the victim to move from spiritual crisis to spiritual growth.

It is difficult for victims to resolve the contradiction of being a good person, of "following all the rules," with the experience of having a most degrading violation of their spiritual and physical being perpetrated against them. It simply does not mesh with the religious values they have learned, implicitly or explicitly: "If you are good, good things will happen to you," or "if bad things happen to you, you must be a bad person." Some victims thus conclude that they must have done something wrong or that they really are inherently bad or sinful in God's eyes. Whatever the clergy counselor's perspective on original sin, such theological positions need to be disentangled from the specific facts about sexual assault. These victims need patient guidance and consistent feedback that they are not to blame and that they did nothing to deserve the sexual assault. They also need continual validation that they are truly good people.

Another spiritual area that causes great confusion for victims is whether they really ought to "forgive and forget." This is not a realistic nor healthy practice for victims, particularly in the first three stages of recovery. They *can* find inner peace by clearly placing responsibility onto the perpetrator, a process that allows integration to occur and is actually a "letting go" process for the victim. The "forgive and forget" practice too often becomes a form of minimization and denial and does not serve to heal the internal wounds of the victim. Healthy anger, focused on the perpetrator, acts as an energizing and healing force for the victim. The victim always has the right to deny forgiveness to the offender.

A third area of spiritual crisis involves loss of hope. Victims are naturally very sensitive to, and consequently may feel overwhelmed by, the violence in their lives and in the world around them. This reinforces their feelings of insecurity and powerlessness. They may temporarily lose their coping skills for maintaining a spiritual balance and perspective. If this balance is not regained, the victim may become immobilized with depression and despair. Clergy can play a powerful role in instilling hope by reminding the victim of what is of value in that person's life, of what control the victim does have to make choices, and of those who care about the victim, including the clergyperson. When victims question whether they will ever feel hopeful again, encourage them to accept this struggle as part of the grieving process and assure them that they will indeed heal spiritually.

SUMMARY OF GUIDELINES FOR CLERGY

1. *Believe* victims and validate their feelings. Know common myths about sexual assault, and be sensitive to how victims and con-

cerned persons blame victims through these beliefs. Victims need to hear that it is *not their fault* they were assaulted.

2. *Empower* victims by providing options and allowing them to make their own decisions.

3. *Be nonjudgmental* in allowing victims to explore spiritual issues.

4. *Refer and assist* victims in obtaining appropriate services. Identify local sexual assault programs, law enforcement agencies, and medical services. Know how to refer victims to community resources that are experienced in providing services to sexual assault victims.

5. *Know your limits.* Do *not* counsel victims beyond your skill level. There is a difference between providing support and providing therapy. Both functions are important but address different needs.

6. *Get support for yourself.* You will have your own responses to the experience a victim has shared with you. Consult with professionals experienced with sexual assault to obtain assistance and personal support. Local sexual assault centers are available to provide training, consultation, advocacy, and counseling or will know appropriate local resources for these services.

13. Sharing the Crisis of Rape: Counseling the Mates and Families of Victims

DANIEL C. SILVERMAN

Male mates and family members may find it difficult to respond to the female rape victim in an empathic and supportive manner for a variety of cognitive and emotional reasons. This paper will describe common patterns of reaction among the husbands, boyfriends, and family members of rape victims; it will attempt to understand the dynamics of such responses and their effects upon the relationships involved; and it will offer technical suggestions to the counselor, who must deal not only with the intense feelings of mates and family members but also his or her own emotional responses to the affectively laden topic of rape victimization.

Increasing clinical experience in rape crisis counseling has led to the inescapable conclusion that therapeutic and didactic work with males and family members may be critical in attempts to help the victim.[1] Just as rape represents a traumatic event that precipitates a crisis in the life of the victim, it may also assault the psychological equilibrium of the victim's couple and family systems. Abrupt changes in the balance of interpersonal relations and family functions may occur in direct parallel to the intrapsychic disharmony experienced by the rape victim.

There are four important ways in which counseling interventions may be indispensable in assisting mates and family members to provide a truly supportive environment for the victim's reconstitutive efforts in the post-traumatic period: (1) by encouraging the open expression on the part of mates and family members of their affective responses to this shared life crisis; (2) by facilitating cognitive understanding of what the experience of rape actually represents to the victim; (3) by educating the people close to the victim about the nature of the crisis she's experiencing and helping them to anticipate future likely psychological and somatic sequelae of the traumatic episode;[2] and (4) by providing direct counseling services to individual family members whose personal responses to the shared crisis are so profound as to affect their ability to cope adaptively.

VENTILATION OF FEELINGS

RESPONSES OF HUSBAND AND BOYFRIENDS

Persons close to the female rape victim may be subject to the same misunderstandings, prejudices, and mythologies surrounding the crime of rape that are held by the general public.[3] A common tendency in this regard is that of reacting more to the sexual than the inherently violent aspects of the rape. To understand the responses of male mates or family members, it is important to remember that they may be firmly of the opinion that ("nice women don't get raped," "only sexy young women are ever raped," or "any woman who is raped must have asked for it."[4] These kinds of thoughts are inevitably linked with feelings of resentment and anger towards the victim, although the individual may not be consciously aware of it. One boyfriend of a rape victim, when asked if he believed his girlfriend to be in any way responsible for her rape, revealed his unconscious feelings when he remarked emphatically, "Of course not! I have no doubt she *was* responsible."

Not surprisingly, feelings of anger toward the victim are expressed openly with considerable difficulty and often are manifested indirectly. Subtle derivatives of angry feelings may be observed in doubting the veracity of the victim's story, criticizing the woman for "not having been more careful" (even when it's clear that carelessness played no part in precipitating the rape), or wondering whether she "enjoyed" the experience. One husband was distraught to learn that his wife had experienced an orgasm during the rape and felt enraged because he was certain that he "would never be able to give her as exciting a sexual experience again." It is possible that this man's anger served to defend against the emergence of difficult feelings about his own sexual adequacy and an unfavorable comparison with the rapist, who was viewed as possessing special prowess. While the basis of such feelings may be understandable, the critical problem here is, very simply, that such attitudes and the emotions they generate make the "revictimization" of the woman a real possibility. Counselors must be alert to the presence of such misapprehensions and their associated feelings and must work gently to mobilize them into direct expression. This is crucial, as the unearthing of such feelings and their causes allows for far greater control of the potentially damaging covert or mixed communications they may engender between the victim and her male mate. (Individual sessions with husband or boyfriend may allow the emergence and clarification of such material in an environment that lends the safety of privacy and confidentiality to the man and protection to the absent victim.)

Another attitude commonly expressed by boyfriends and husbands is the view of the woman as the "property of her man."[5] Male mates may feel personally wronged and attacked by the rape of "their woman," and may display a proprietary indignation that serves more to protect against their own unconscious sense of vulnerability than to express a deeply held personal philosophy. It is important for the counselor to realize that these feelings are multiply determined. They may reflect common male attitudes about feminine sexuality, the veneration of virginity, and a sense of entitlement to "exclusive rights" to that sexuality. More deeply, however, there may be unconscious concerns about homosexuality stirred by having been "had" by the rapist when "he took my woman," or discomfort associated with the excitement of "sharing a woman with another man." Other misapprehensions that may impede supportive behavior on the part of males include anger over the fact that the victim has "allowed herself" to become "devalued" or "damaged merchandise."[6] One boyfriend wondered whether he would ever be able to escape the thought that his girlfriend was "tainted" by her experience. Another felt that his lover would bear a permanent emotional wound, "like a scarlet 'R' on her forehead." A husband described feeling physically disgusted when approaching his "unclean" wife sexually, immediately following her rape. Obviously such responses may reinforce the victim's sense of humiliation and devaluation.

A potential difficulty for the counselor is the negative personal reactions such "unenlightened" or "chauvinistic" feelings may evoke. Being openly critical of the man for expressing these sentiments is only likely to heighten his sense of feeling attacked, which may already be present as a result of identification with the loved one. It may serve to further increase defensiveness and anger, mitigating against the useful ventilation of the affects. A helpful counseling maneuver could be to focus supportively on the man's injury as a result of the rape of his mate, suggesting that whenever a loved one suffers a trauma or loss of any kind (for example, through illness or injury) he too experiences pain and loss. Furthermore, mates and family members should be helped to realize that, while rape is a terribly traumatic experience with subsequent sequelae not unlike a grief reaction,[7] the victim need not be permanently debilitated by it. It may be useful to explain that, while an individual may never "forget" unfortunate or tragic experiences such as the death of a beloved person, these memories do not make it impossible to go on living a rich and satisfying life after an adequate opportunity to mourn the loss.

Perhaps the most important point to be made here is that the counselor must remember that, to no little extent, the mate's frustrations may grow out of a shared sense of devaluation and shame. One woman's husband, depressed and tearful, expressed this clearly when he remarked, "I feel as if I'd been raped too." Mates must be allowed to discuss difficult feelings fully in an atmosphere of noncritical acceptance and understanding. Only then should the counselor consider beginning didactic work to disabuse the man of his misconceptions.

The importance of involving the male partner of the rape victim in cases of stable or married couples cannot be stressed enough. The crisis precipitated by rape is a mutual one, and the man is potentially his mate's prime support. Clearly, the rape experience will add stress to vulnerable areas in any relationship.[8] For example, the sense that the man failed to protect his woman from being raped could precipitate feelings in the victim or mate about how good a protector or provider the man is in general. Couples whose sexual relations have been problematic prior to the rape are likely to experience considerable new stress in that area; this aspect of the relationship may have to be carefully explored and evaluated by the counselor to determine whether specific therapeutic intervention for sexual dysfunction is needed.

While the rape may serve as a catalyst that crystallizes previously unaddressed conflicts, it may also stimulate a total reevaluation of the quality of the relationship, a newfound closeness and common sense of purpose in response to the external crisis the couple shares. The goal of couples counseling interventions, then, is to make these facts conscious and explicit so the closeness may be solidified and adaptive strategies for coping mobilized. In situations where the rape experience "unearths" significant individual or couples issues of long standing, it may be necessary to allow the crisis intervention to develop into a more traditional ongoing counseling experience or to refer the victim or couple for longer-term therapy. Clearly, such clinical decisions must be made on a case-by-case basis in harmony with the needs, wishes, and motivations of the clients.

RESPONSES OF FAMILY MEMBERS

In the acute posttraumatic period, parents and siblings of rape victims may experience a sense of shock, helplessness, rage, or physical revulsion that parallels the affective responses of the victim.[9] Immediately following her rape, one father drove his daughter to the apartment of a friend who had also been a rape victim: "She seemed so helpless; I felt so helpless. I didn't know what to say and the only thing I could think of to do was to get her to talk to her friend."

In their anxiety to aid the victim and contain their own feelings of helplessness, families may attempt to rally the support of the victim's women and men friends, clergy, coworkers, teachers, supervisors, and so on. At times (particularly in the acute posttraumatic period) the woman may experience these attempts as invasive. The woman may still be in a period of relative denial of what has happened to her or may wish to share the reality with only a chosen few. Her need for privacy, confidentiality, or simply not to discuss her crisis at all must be respected by families and helping professionals alike. The family may find it useful to ventilate their concerns and sense of frustration over being unable to help "undo" the victim's plight by talking to the counselor in the victim's absence. This may be particularly important in those situations where victims refuse any follow-up contact with rape counseling services because of their need to deny difficult feelings of vulnerability and helplessness. Families may use counseling services in these situations to understand the bases of the woman's resistance to counseling, as well as to develop useful strategies for assisting the victim through their supportive efforts.

Fathers and brothers (as well as mates) of victims may experience frequent thoughts of extracting violent retribution from the rapist on behalf of the woman. One brother of a rape victim spoke in lurid detail of how he would "rip the SOB apart with my bare hands" if given the opportunity. These thoughts may function to protect the man against his own sense of utter helplessness and the impotent rage he shares, albeit unconsciously, with the victim. In some cases, the underlying dynamic of powerful fantasies of revenge may be an attempt to "act out" the woman's desire to see her victimizer suffer in the way she has. Ironically, this may result in the woman having to bear the additional burden of calming, placating, and reassuring the men who would be her avenging protectors. Counselors should be alert to this situation, and be ready to point out the potential disservice done the victim by the man's overzealousness.

The above reactions on the part of family members seem to represent both an affective identification with the victim as well as personal responses and attempts to cope with the stress of the life crisis they are sharing. In some cases of rape, interpersonal difficulties in the form of intense parent-child or couples conflicts seem to lead individuals to place themselves at greater risk of personal harm. People who care less about themselves because of disordered relationships tend to take less care of themselves. One woman, angry at her husband because of his late working hours and unavailability, left their apartment following a heated argument, insisting upon taking the dog out alone at 2:00 A.M. During this unprecedented late night walk, she was raped in the unlit public park in which she sat. A seventeen-year-old woman, following an especially vitriolic exchange with her parents over issues of independence and life style, stormed from her home in the late evening and, for the first time, hitchhiked alone to a dance her parents had demanded she forego. She was raped by the young occupants of the car that had picked her up. In both cases, the family members of the rape victim experienced considerable guilt and sense of responsibility for precipitating the rape. Anger with the victim for "retaliating by getting herself hurt" was clearly present as well. In difficult situations such as these, the counselor must help sort out responsibility and clarify the way in which the conflicts and events leading up to the rape may have reflected self-destructive attempts to deal with ongoing interpersonal problems.

Families often mobilize themselves to cope with the crisis precipitated by rape in predictable ways. Patronization and overprotection in the aftermath of the rape are common responses. Immediately following her rape, one woman's parents quickly rented and moved her belongings to an apartment in "a good neighborhood where they couldn't afford to send me before." Another family, whose daughter had been assaulted in her own apartment, insisted upon chauffeuring the daughter by car to and from work, to the store, and to visit friends, despite the fact that she had previously lived alone and used public transportation. Other families urge victims to move to a new city or return home "where we can watch you and keep you safe."

These maneuvers may represent an attempt on the part of the family members to assuage feelings of guilt and responsibility for having failed to protect the "defenseless" woman from being raped in the first place. While such gestures of concern are undoubtedly well intentioned, there is a ready danger in such actions because they may communicate the idea to the victim that important people in her life see her as a vulnerable child in need of caretaking. This can reinforce the victim's own sense of "I am indeed helpless and defenseless" and prevent her from using her most adaptive strategies for coping with the crisis—strategies that might not be as regressive or costly in terms of self-esteem and sense of autonomy. Counseling interventions that support the family's earnest desire to be caretaking and helpful but that also indicate the counterproductiveness of "infantilizing" the victim are important contributions.

Another coping tactic used by families is that of "distraction." The idea here is to keep the victim occupied with group activities, vacation trips, shopping sprees, and the like in an attempt to deny and undo the effects of the rape. In some situations, in direct contrast to overinvolvement and intrusiveness, the victim may be encouraged by her mate or one member of the family to keep the rape a "secret between us" to "protect" other family members from being traumatized. Examples of this include "protecting mother from upset," "not letting dad know because he will be enraged" with the victim, and "sheltering" younger siblings (or children, if the victim is a mother). As is generally the case, family "secrets" tend to become great burdens and destructive of potentially adaptive behaviors. The reasons for a conspiracy of silence vary, but they may include parental discomfort with one's own or a child's sexuality, fear of blame for negligence, or simply hidden alliances and long-standing family problems. Obviously, chronically disturbed family relationships may impede supportive efforts as much as the foregoing specific maladaptive family responses to the rape crisis. Attempts either to hide the truth or distract one from it are based upon the family's conviction that open, ongoing discussion of the trauma keeps painful, disorganizing memories alive in a destructive way. The impact of such a stance is to deprive the woman of the opportunity to mourn the personal loss inherent in her rape experience, deny her much-needed support, and communicate by inference that "What's happened is simply too terrible to discuss," confirming the victim's worst fears and doubts.

EDUCATION OF FAMILY MEMBERS

As indicated earlier, a significant component of the counseling intervention with families and mates of rape victims must be educational in nature. Following opportunity to discuss fully the difficult kinds of feelings described above in an atmosphere of noncritical acceptance, the counselor should make efforts to teach the family and mates about the nature of the crisis precipitated by rape. The focus should be on:

1. Explaining the inherently violent nature of rape as a crime, helping family members to understand that the victim's experience has been more of a life-threatening one than a sexual episode. It must be made clear that the predominant feelings experienced by victims posttraumatically are those of powerlessness in the face of a life and death situation, vulnerability, devaluation, and fear of loss of ability to control the events in their lives.[10] Family members may need considerable assistance in helping the victim to remobilize her most effective coping behaviors. Understanding the kinds

of feelings she is experiencing is a crucial first step in laying the groundwork for family responses that will not undermine the woman's attempts to help herself. In addition, families may require guidance in identifying and demythologizing long-held attitudes about women who are raped. Using one's position as an authoritative but nonpunitive teacher, with a fund of knowledge concerning the crime of rape,[11] the counselor can do much to disabuse families and mates of their misunderstandings and biases.

2. Preparing the family for the predictable psychologic and physiologic sequelae of the rape, described as the Rape Trauma Syndrome. The counselor should explain carefully in advance that, following a period of apparent outward readjustment, there may be an emergence of nightmares, insomnia, somatic symptoms, anxiety attacks, phobias, depression, crying, and, more significantly, feelings of fear, humiliation, anger, and self-blame. Foreknowledge of these possible reaction patterns may help to lessen family members' concerns when they occur, and it may allow the family to respond to the victim in a more calm and reassuring manner.

3. Helping the family understand that they are most productive when they assist the woman in mobilizing *her* own best coping abilities[12] as an autonomous adult rather than a sheltered child. This would include encouraging the family to allow, but not force, the open expression of the victim's feelings, conveying strongly the idea that rape, like other life crises, need not destroy the woman's potential for normal functioning in the future, and helping the family learn how to control their desires to intervene forcefully to "undo" the rape trauma.

4. Teaching the family and mates the concept of "containment" of the victim's feelings may be the counselor's most important contribution. This means explaining how to provide an accepting and safe "holding environment"[13] into which the woman can release her troubling thoughts and feelings without fear of condemnation or critical response born of a shared sense of helplessness. The counselor, by way of example, must model containing behaviors of empathy, willingness to address difficult material with poise, gentle reassurance, and an avoidance of the tendency to be overly directive. More importantly, it implies helping the family to

grasp the very difficult reality that there is no single "magical" or "right thing" that can be said or done to make "everything better." This necessitates not only sharing the family's disappointment over this unfortunate fact, but also helping them to realize that, in being emotionally available to, caring of, and genuinely concerned about the woman, they are offering her much that is immediately invaluable and eventually restorative.

CONCLUSIONS

Growing clinical experience makes clear the absolute necessity of involving important members of the victim's social network in the postrape counseling intervention. The possibility for the mobilization of decisive support and help with guided family participation is great, just as the potential for increased burdening and revictimization of the woman is considerable if such efforts are lacking.

Interventions follow two distinct paths, one of facilitating expression of emotional response to the shared life crisis, and the other of disabusing misconception and preparing constructive strategies of coping through education in the nature of the crisis. Typical crisis responses of mates and family members are observable, and foreknowledge of these patterns may be extremely helpful to the counselor in determining and adapting clinical approaches and maneuvers. The typical responses can be summarized, following Lazarus's[14] behavioral classifications of coping reaction patterns, which include: (1) actions aimed at strengthening the individual's resources against harm; (2) avoidance; (3) attack; (4) inaction. Examples of the first category would include seeking out and obtaining postrape counseling and gynecologic services, joining rape victim support groups, family attempts to protect the woman, physical relocation, or the highly adaptive behavior of cooperation with the criminal justice system to work toward removing rapists from the general population. Avoidance is seen in the technique of "distraction" or maintenance of a "conspiracy of silence." Attacking behavior may be represented in the stimulation of fantasies of retribution or the displacement of anger onto would-be helpers. Inaction, in the form of failure to avail oneself of professional counseling and medical assistance, is at once potentially dangerous and tragic in its consequences.

The most significant idea that the counselor can share with his or her clients is that of containment of the incredibly difficult human emotions provoked by rape victimization. To a great extent, this is done more by deed than word, and it demands that the counselor attain a considerable knowledge of and ease in dealing with the affectively charged crisis of rape.

14. The Male Minister and the Female Victim

COOPER WIGGEN

I write this article with an attitude of humility and hope. I have few credentials to support my convictions, but the few are important. I am male, an ordained United Methodist minister, and I have experience working with victims of sexual violence. Like most male pastors, I received limited exposure to sexual assault issues in seminary, although I studied within a small but strong feminist community. Fortunately for me, I have received some training from the Sexual Violence Center of Hennepin County, Minnesota, which is located in a building that belongs to my present parish.

In most congregations, the majority of members are women. We rarely discuss whether a male minister can really understand and cope with the dynamics of women's lives. That many sexual assault victims may not want to deal with a male figure in any part of their processes regarding rape may be a jolt to a male pastor. Obviously, a clergyman must just accept this. Often he may never know the limits to his effectiveness if female victims never let him know they have been assaulted. But if a male minister communicates openness and awareness about sexual assault dynamics, and shows by his behavior that he respects the experience of victims, he may be invited to hear the stories of victims and to participate in their healing. This is a privilege and a challenge.

I shall first summarize the roles and directions of our work by employing the traditional models of ministry: pastor, priest, and prophet. Next I want to reflect on how male anxiety influences pastoral work, particularly in regard to victims. This anxiety can diminish my effectiveness, but it may also provide energy for my own spiritual growth as well as for creative ministry. Last, I want to offer a prayer for male pastors who willingly give time for authentic ministry with female victims of sexual assault.

THE ROLES OF A MINISTER

The belief governing ministry in general, but especially ministry with victims, lies in trusting God's loving force as being sufficient for the healing of every victim, regardless of how great the violence. What follows from that trust in God is our belief in ourselves —however flawed we are—in being instruments of God's love. We require the wisdom of compassion in our work.

The first and central factor that colors all I do in regard to victims is my commitment to compassion and justice. What I have to give—and as an ordained minister must give—is an attitude of personal caring as well as moral outrage. Regardless of what the victim has come to believe about herself (for instance, that she deserved to be assaulted or that her rape was not all that significant), I need to preserve an attitude that holds to the judgment that rape is terribly wrong. Perhaps more importantly, even when I may feel little affection or respect for the victim on a personal level, I am bound to give her the respect and care a child of God deserves—especially one who has been victimized. This is not to say that my convictions must be directly expressed, certainly not preached to her in private. But my spiritual orientation and hence the intuitive or feeling tone of my work needs grounding in commitment to compassion and justice. Prayer is the most significant preparation in this grounding of myself.

A victim needs and deserves healing. Her assault, however personally traumatic, creates wrongful pain in her and beyond her being. She does not live in a vacuum. Others are affected. Damage can occur in relationships. Fear grows. The God of life is outraged and calls us to heal and transform these wounds. Likewise, her healing and growth help herself and others too. So I am committed to help the healing process, however small my role may be.

Encountering a victim happens in many ways. Sometimes I am the first person taken into the victim's confidence. Often I hear about the sexual assault long after the healing process has begun. Sometimes I am briefed by innuendo or an offhand remark.

My responsibility is to relate as a pastor. First, I offer a safe and accepting environment for conversation. If the victim wants to talk, then I am available. I run through a priority list of concerns. Her bodily safety comes first. Especially if I am hearing from a person recently assaulted, I ask myself and her: Is she living in safe circumstances? Does she need health care? Has she a counseling and/or support community? Does she need support in going through institutional processes such as medical examinations, police and court procedures? Often a professional sexual assault center can provide the needed services. I make myself available to walk through the necessary procedures of getting help. I may be the victim's advocate in suggesting and encouraging the best possible measures of self-care.

Then there are possibilities for priestly ministry. My role is to represent Christ's redeeming love. I choose to think of confessional conversation and prayer as a helpful construct for this work. There is an irony here. By hearing the victim's "confession," I am receiving the confession of a sin committed *against* the victim, not *by* the victim. The confession requires complete confidentiality. Through conversation I seek to help the victim express her deepest and darkest feelings. Rape so deeply violates people that they suffer severe psychological wounds. Often there will be great bitterness and fear. Trust has broken down with other relationships. Guilt or self-blame is easily evoked. A victim often feels unclean. Often victims question how they can ever again live with a positiveness or freedom in normal circumstances.

As the victim adjusts and heals, a psychological or spiritual "scar tissue" may develop. Soft places in her being are toughened. Innocence has been taken away. As one friend put it, "I hate to live by suspicion and caution, but I must. I cannot help myself." The priest faces an awesome challenge. In hearing the intimate story of a victim, with her grave doubts and fears, I am allowed to meet her in her most vulnerable place. I become a witness to what the victim perceives to be unclean. In effect, I am invited to relate to the scar tissue, perhaps even the soft place beyond.

When I am the priest hearing a confession, healing is the point. Forgiveness is not of immediate importance. Forgiveness has meaning only in the context of relationship. My role is to hear and care and gently guide the victim in her need to care for herself. She is the most critical factor in her own healing. She will help the healing process by sorting out what she is feeling, by naming the ugly things that stir within as well as without, and by surrendering to God what seems to her as unmanageable. Often feelings become attitudes that control her. Bitterness, guilt, or both can become her boss, so to speak, or part of her scar tissue.

At some point in our confession experience, I offer her the opportunity to ask God into her scar tissue. She can make a decision to expose her trauma to God in the hope that God will actually effect her health. As priest, I listen, I pray for her, and I encourage her to pray for herself. "O Lord, I believe you can help heal me, help thou my unbelief in me and you." Absolution can happen through this simple prayer: "Lord, I give to you that over which I am powerless." Having identified the factors that have power over us, we can risk their loss of power over us by offering them to God.

Absolution by itself is helpful but inadequate. It requires a follow-up, a discipline of behavior faithful to the healing. The victim may benefit from receiving the sacrament, from rituals of healing, and from the common Sunday worship. In her own privacy she can offer her vulnerability to God during a public service of worship. But finally, she needs to practice herself-in-the-process-of-healing through relationships with people. Often victims can gain this practice and positive reinforcement through a rape support group. Some will need or prefer a church-based group; others will not. As priest, I recognize that my job is not finished until I can offer or affirm groups of people where the victim works out her healing.

A further reflection upon our priestly role is necessary. I believe the pastor and church can be adequate in the ministry of healing. Professionals in the sexual violence field have special wisdom and resources to give. They are the experts. But a problem can arise. It can be confusing to the victim to face very different vocabularies and theories of healing. Professional therapists may discount or ignore the place of God in healing. Sometimes I have felt myself on the verge of competition with the victim's other counseling guidance. I need to remember that I am first pastor and then priest. Mine is not to prove the worthiness of my priestly function but to offer my listening and my advocacy. Her choice is the important choice. I may be most helpful to the victim by helping her to reintegrate herself into church life rather than by providing a church-based healing process. In any case, there may well be significant issues for the victim to face in practicing her Christian faith.

We also have a role as prophet. In ministering to the individual victim, one cannot help but observe wider social issues of injustice and violence. Despite the fact that most members are women, we function through a male-dominated church. We worship using a male-dominated tradition, often perceived as sexist, and we confess a male savior in sharing our faith. A rape victim may feel uncomfortable with or offended by the male expressions of salvation such as God the Father. The culture in which we live continues to impose male dependency on women. The primary helping institutions available to the victim such as the police, the courts, and the hospitals, also reflect male dominance. When drawing upon the charge to compassion and justice, we face a challenge of biblical magnitude. Who among us will speak words of God on behalf of the "lesser ones" over against the forces of domination?

I will not take time here to argue the case that prevailing powers of dominations, often through various forms of violence, govern our culture. I trust your sensitivity in discerning the cries for justice from so many minority groups. How does the male pastor respond prophetically? The answer lies, I believe, in two parts.

First, we recognize the prophet as God's messenger to God's people. The prophet addresses the governing bodies, the people who have power, to call for change or for the godly distribution of power. Our national covenant of citizenship is very different from our religious covenant. In striving to change society, the prophet presses to change the core values of that society. This task is so large as to be truly awesome. It resembles Jesus' call to God's coming rule on earth. We can, however, make a witness within this great struggle. This witness must be public, and it must clearly communicate an identification with victims. The male pastor begins to be prophetic when he joins with feminist groups and others in public advocacy. Participation in public rallies, legislative lobbying, and public speaking are some illustrations of the prophetic witness.

The second part of the prophetic response lies in contesting within our own churches. In order to assume God's call to challenge society, I must challenge myself and my church. Here we have a shared covenant and value structure. Here we can hold one another accountable in Christ. This challenge for me is the more troublesome because I see myself, my church, and our power persistently cooperating with the majority values. Whatever our theology, however we view the role of prophet, we share through ordination a responsibility to articulate the gospel of Jesus Christ and to lead the church in its faithful witness. There are many ways to frame this and to implement it. Liturgies can be changed, sermons preached, classes taught, programs to change sexual violence carried out. All this and more we can do. But we need to bring our pastoral concern and our prophetic call to that place within the church where the power lies. We go to the governing body of our local church to call for solidarity with victims. We challenge our churches to make their central mission emphasis a reflection of God's compassion and justice, especially for the oppressed. The challenge remains to raise prophetic witness to the top of our priorities.

MALE ANXIETY

A paradoxical factor that deeply affects our ministry is male anxiety. Many of us experience anxiety when faced with our own sexuality or that of others, and particularly when sexuality is a dimension of violence. When hearing a woman's account of sexual assault, I inevitably feel queasiness in my gut. While I realize that rape is not really a sexual act, but rather a physical expression of violent domination, I also realize that the victim's sexuality is involved. The assault itself will often make me shudder. The sexuality part makes me nervous. Inevitably, my sexuality is involved.

Male pastors have been shaped by a culture that inhibits our ability to care effectively. Who among us has not learned to associate manliness with sexual success with women? That success has so often been portrayed through the male ability to pursue, persuade, win, or gain sexual pleasure from a woman. We learn to court, impress, and sometimes to intimidate a woman into submission. Paradoxically, our sexuality is perceived as both in control and as totally dependent upon the woman. One way or another, we must gain her giving. Of course, many of us have been trained to be kind and gentle and respectful. But we live and move in a culture that advertises female sexuality as a commodity, a product to be purchased and used. Our adolescent rites of passage remain strongly suggestive of male control. The double standard still applies to virginity. Perhaps younger male pastors possess a different perspective, but I remain deeply affected by double standards and confusing messages concerning sexuality.

One of the ways sexuality can create anxiety stems from years of learning that good boys don't discuss sex. Open learning about sex—especially male issues—is rarely encouraged or even tolerated by the church. What little we do offer may be unrealistic, moralizing, and boring. Locker room discussions among peers are easily more entertaining and often more popular. Thus, one may learn a kind of voyeuristic pleasure around sexual conversations. Some have learned that open conversations about sex with another person can easily be construed as a come-on. Most of us have little practice in sharing intimate issues except with our closest of friends or most trusted persons. It is the case for me, and I believe for many others, that we lack the confidence to converse with nonintimates about deeply sexual or intimate matters.

These factors may all influence what occurs when we talk with a victim of rape. Inner whispers of "voyeur" may be heard. Embarrassment may set in. We are struck by the maleness of sexual assault: I am male. One of us has committed this horrible act. Or memories of pornographic media may appear. Through all of this, one may feel guilt, male guilt, guilt for being a member of the group that did this, guilt for feeling responsible for the others like me. This guilt can emerge regardless of how determinedly good one has been in the matter of sexual conduct. It's as though all the hidden desires and fantasies of male domination flit onto the mental stage.

What I am trying to describe here is anxiety, particularly colored by our male acculturation, as a female shares extremely vulnerable and sexuality-related issues with a male. We can become so anxious with our own feelings and issues that we diminish personal touch with the victim in order to protect her from what we are thinking or in order to keep these inappropriate thoughts out of the way. This is not to say that pastoral reserve is wrong. On the contrary, a careful and gentle conversation is crucial. But this male anxiety may strongly influence our interior life with an inevitable effect on our work. Our inner static can so busy us that we fail in allowing space for the victim. To paraphrase Henri Nouwen, we can practice hospitality or respect for the other only when we can touch our own feelings and so create a listening space for the other.

Male anxiety is also related to power. A female victim has been overpowered. In a real way, she has been robbed of her fundamental person power, an experience that injures her spiritually as well as physically. In sharing her wounds with us, she is working to empower herself. However, she is also risking herself to the power of the pastor, in this case a male pastor. The sheer fact that one is taken into confidence by a victim means that one gains a power of knowledge over her. Herein lies another crux of our anxiety. How shall we act as stewards of this knowledge? Aware that her power has been ripped from her by a male person, we may become especially fearful that we not do a similar thing to her in a very different way.

It is important to remember that anxiety is energy. The queasy stomach or sweaty palm is not the only result of anxiety. Creative listening, a mental discipline of compassion, can also result. I try to use male anxiety positively in this way. I can translate the diffuse fear of anxiety into efforts to be especially careful with and about *her*—especially careful to listen, think, and feel about what she is going through and what she needs, careful to match resources I know about with her situation. When I am anxious, it is because I care. My anxious energy can be used to fuel gentleness. That gentleness, in turn, becomes a gift of power shared with the victim. She deserves what spiritual energy I can give whether she recognizes or appreciates it.

For me, the key exercise in using our anxiety for healing is prayer. I am by no means an accomplished prayer artist. Nor do I need to be. Prayer happens to me when I become aware of my inner tension or frustration. They become signals for me to listen carefully to myself with God's help. Then it occurs to me to pray.

One format that works for me, therefore, is to practice self-listening as I listen to the other. Between us is God. When I need a mental image, I create Jesus in mind and ask for his guiding attitude. I see his firm confidence in God's love for the victim. I sense his powerful gentleness, his knowing faith in healing. I pray for him to use me as an expression of love.

Another important element in prayer lies in breathing. To center myself into my relationship with God, I breathe deeply and regularly to release body tension and inner static. Calming my breathing helps me to center into my feelings. I pray for help in drawing those feelings into my whole being. This happens before, during, and after conversation with the victim. It helps.

Another prayer I may practice focuses on the victim. First I pray for the clarity and receptiveness of my eyes. Then I concentrate my energy on her, her story, and her needs. I try to make nonintrusive eye contact and pay attention to her body language as well as her words. By listening with my eyes as well as my ears, I aim to make intuitive connections with her and with myself. While I listen, I ask for God's presence in her as well as in me. Sometimes, while prayerfully listening in this way, the conversant will suddenly change her pattern of behavior, as if something has happened to her that touches deeply. For instance, once a friend who had been stuck for a long time in bitterness and self-pity suddenly began discussing ways she herself could make a difference in herself. I renewed my intent eye contact to discern what was going on with her; she responded by asking, "What's going on here?" I responded by affirming her willingness to help herself; she laughed and continued. An energy happened between us, a positive loving healing energy. I do not take responsibility for all that happened in that moment. She was ready to make that step in her healing process. But by my discipline of prayer and self-examination, I was ready to support her in it.

Other pastors may have other practices that help them to use male anxiety creatively and gently for healing.

My hope for us is that we can be inspired through God's creative love to a more humble, more courageous, and more Spirited ministry. Self-examination and cultural criticism are basic to our growth, as is sensitive listening to the victims in our midst. We are called to a more effective ministry. We are needed by those who suffer. Their voices and their wounds are a word of God for us all.

So I end these reflections on the male clergy's ministry with female rape victims by sharing a prayer:

Dear God, I pray for your loving presence. As a minister of your church, I face many obligations and opportunities. Often I become overly busy with doing important work so that I forget to listen. Help me, Lord, to listen. I ask especially to hear your call through the cries and whispers of rape victims. Give me strength to face their pain. Free me to see my selfish desires and to feel my anxieties. Remind me again and again of how you work in and through us for healing. Despite all the abused sexuality, the domineering and dominations, and the violence vying to control your world, I remain steadfast in my devotion to your power and your will. In Jesus' name, I pray, Amen.

15. Sexual Harassment: Victim Responses

BARBARA CHESTER

Sexual harassment is a complex, multidimensional issue. Although often treated as a trivial or rare phenomenon, sexual harassment is widespread, pervasive, and systemic in nature. Studies have reported that 42 percent of women working for the federal government and 20 to 30 percent of all female students have been harassed. Twenty percent of women have reported leaving at least one job because of harassment, and a further 10 percent have been fired for refusal to submit to sexual advances at work.[1] This complicated form of abuse has often been unrealistically simplified, to the detriment of all concerned.

The legal dimensions of this abuse have predominated in the minds of administrators. A plethora of workshops, guidelines, and policies focus upon the goal of protecting individuals and institutions from the horrors of litigation. It naturally follows that most of the information available about this subject concerns pending court actions and some after-the-fact management responses. For the most part, the problem is seen as a collection of individual acts; the solutions involve a denial of the systemic nature of the issue. Often the outcome is a discreet removal of the victim from the workplace or school. If dealt with at all, sexual harassment is treated on a case-by-case basis.

There is an alternative, however, which is beneficial to both the victim and the institution. The majority of victims do not wish to litigate and do not want revenge against the harasser or the institution. For the most part, victims of sexual harassment simply want to work or to obtain an education in an atmosphere that is safe and conducive to optimal performance. Sexual harassment undermines morale, competence, and emotional health. It is always costly to the individuals and systems involved.

Sexual harassment has been defined legally as including "unwelcome sexual advances, requests for sexual favors, sexually motivated physical conduct or other verbal or physical conduct or communication of a sexual nature." As with other kinds of sexual violence, we need to view sexual harassment firmly as a power issue. Sexual harassment is an act of aggression against the victim. It "asserts a woman's sex role over her function as worker," whether she is student or professional.[2]

Based upon more than a year of counseling experience with victims, both on an individual and a group basis, and upon the crisis intervention provided by a metropolitan rape crisis center, this essay shares information about the process of victimization that gives rise to sexual harassment and some typical responses of victims. The data comes from a small number of victims and is therefore more suggestive than definitive. However, despite a range of ages, settings, and situations, there is remarkable consistency in the reactions, feelings, and needs presented by these women. Several case studies will illustrate my points. I hope that counselors and advocates can respond more effectively to victims when we see certain responses as normal, adaptive reactions to the structured victimization that occurs.

VICTIMIZATION AS A PROCESS

Rather than viewing sexual harassment as a series of discrete acts, we must understand it as a process. No behavior or set of behaviors occurs in a vacuum, and victimizing behavior is no exception to this rule. Victimization is a process that begins prior to any overt act. It proceeds through a process whereby both victim and society continue to label, blame, and often condemn the victim.

Social antecedents to any particular episodes of the sexual harassment of an individual woman include pernicious sex-role stereotypes, economic and work-role stereotypes, age-role stereotypes, beliefs and attitudes that hold women responsible for sexuality, and the normalization of sexual violence in our culture. Sexual harassment is therefore intertwined with sex discrimination. It is reinforced and perpetuated by maintaining secrecy about it, by disapproval and disbelief from others, and by the victim's internalizing the shame, blame, and guilt for the abuse.

For example, a systemic belief system that makes assumptions about the types of jobs that women and men should perform leads to an atmosphere that is at best unconducive and at worst hostile to people who choose to pursue "nontraditional" careers. Women in jobs traditionally performed by men often find themselves within a hostile or threatening atmosphere. Even chance remarks or jokes can be and are messages of consequence. We often find overtly sexually harassing behaviors toward women occuring in conjunction with placing women within less desirable working conditions.

For instance, M's employment involves working with electrical cable systems. She is the only woman in her work setting. She is constantly subjected to jokes about wife-beating, rape, and child abuse by her coworkers. Cartoons of a nature insulting to women are regularly hung on the bulletin board in her workplace. Once she found a cartoon on her work station depicting a naked woman; a knife had been thrust through the woman's breast and the caption read, "Death to women." M's job involves a certain amount of physical danger and therefore a need to rely on her coworkers for safety. Thus the cartoons and other acts carry a very real threat. In addition, despite her seniority to many of the men, M is consistently assigned the least popular shifts and is denied vacation time requests. She has been told that her work performance is poor because of an attitude problem—that is, she does not laugh and joke about sexual violence, and she is angry at being denied desirable shifts and vacation time. Furthermore, as the only woman in a hostile environment, M is denied the feedback needed to label these actions toward her as harassment. Inevitably she assumes the shame and guilt. She believes that the problem is indeed her attitude. She has chosen this work and is desperately afraid that her inability to fit in will mean the end of her dreams and aspirations.

Similar dynamics occur in the experience of C, a student intern with a suburban police department. At work C was constantly regaled with boasts by a fellow officer that he had beaten his wife and that women deserve this kind of treatment. She was constantly given the message that women do not belong in law enforcement. Her supervisor told her that instead of patrolling she should be giving him a "blow job." When she complained to her internship supervisor, she was told to go along with the "teasing" and that this situation was all in good fun. As in the previous situation, the onus was placed upon C to understand, accept, and laugh it off. After all, this is what police work would be like for her once she graduated. No responsibility was placed upon the system to behave in an appropriate professional manner—or indeed, even to comply with federal and state statutes prohibiting this kind of behavior.

We need to see therefore that a combination of subjective and structural factors work together to keep sexual harassment in place. Ordinary chains of command and supervision within workplaces rarely use their power to stop such degrading and disempowering behaviors. These real structural events must be understood as a serious and central part of the victim's processes of response to sexual harassment.

VICTIM RESPONSES

Sexual harassment has been compared with tiny drops of water. Each drop may be of minor importance and small effect, but months and years of regular droplets erode even the hardest of substances. Similarly, Dr. Mary Rowe likens harassment to Saturn's rings. Harassment is often composed of "microinequities," subtle acts that are petty enough not to be legally actionable or perhaps even protested. But, like the dust and ice in Saturn's rings, taken together they constitute formidable barriers to people seeking an education or a career and growth as a human being.

Sexual harassment is a long-term erosion of a victim's mind, body, and spirit. The women I encountered endured harassment lasting from six months to six and a half years (average duration was two and a half years). Harassing behaviors involved verbally suggestive remarks ("with your body, you would be too distracting to work around"), sexist comments, and episodes of rape and attempted rape. Harassment occurred in all types of settings including vocational-technical institutes and universities, hospitals, factories, and major corporations. In 56 percent of these cases, the perpetrator was the supervisor or boss. In 31 percent of the cases, the victims were single heads of households and financially dependent on their jobs.

Women in these situations often feel trapped, isolated, and

stuck. As the harassment continues, their self-esteem plummets
and their energy wanes. Maintaining secrecy is an unspoken but
all-pervasive and strongly sanctioned institutional norm. Certain
responses appear to be consistent among victims. The stages that
follow are not discrete or exclusive and should be seen as a continuum rather than as a hierarchy. It is important to stress that
victim responses are survival mechanisms by which individuals
seek to adapt to an increasingly hostile and unhealthy environment.

ADAPTATION

During this ongoing stage, people often try to minimize, deny, or
rationalize what is going on in hopes that the reaction to them will
die down and disappear. They may try to become "one of the
boys." They may laugh at the demeaning jokes or change their
style of dress. They may also accept unreasonable job demands
and even submit to coerced sexual demands, hoping that this will
end the harassment and its attendant fear and anxiety.

D is a twenty-eight-year-old single parent who wished to change
careers. She was admitted to a vocational-technical institute to
learn one of the trades. As the only woman in the class, she was
constantly subjected to many microinequities: condescension, sexist comments, hostility, exclusion, and isolation. Her teachers
made remarks about her not being wanted; they were extremely
discouraging about her aspirations, telling her she would never get
a job in the field. Upon graduation she received a position in a
training and placement program for women and minorities. Her
supervisor assigned her to isolated workplaces where he could and
did continually make sexual advances. These advances escalated
and were accompanied by threats to her continued employment.
D experienced nightmares, headaches, and severe anxiety. She
finally submitted to the coercion, hoping to appease her aggressor.
But rather than ending, the harassment continued. D was forced
to leave the program. She has now filed suit against the vocational-
technical institute, the job training program, and the city.

Because harassment is often confusing and subtle, and its implications so frightening, clients rarely define it as such, even to
themselves. Counselors need to provide a safe place to talk. They
need to listen respectfully and in a nonjudgmental manner. For

instance, when D concluded that submitting to her supervisor was her only option, not blaming her for this response was vital to her healing.

As with other kinds of sexual violence, nonthreatening questions about possible harassment (among other issues) should be considered when a student or employee shows a marked decrease in performance, concentration, or an increase in absenteeism and physical or stress-related ailments. If harassment is occurring, the counselor should validate that fact and use that term. The counselor should also validate that sexual harassment is not permissible behavior, and that the client is not abnormal or alone in this experience. As in other kinds of sexual violence counseling, it is important to affirm that she is not to blame and does not deserve such treatment.

FEAR AND ANGER

As adaptation fails to produce the expected results, feelings of powerlessness, humiliation, and insecurity increase, creating a fear that can only be dealt with through "fight or flight" reactions. Victims may be extremely anxious and fearful. And although it can be expressed in a variety of ways, sexual harassment victims experience intense anger, often overwhelming and seemingly uncontrollable (which may in turn increase fear and anxiety). Because it is unsafe to address these feelings in the workplace, the anger is often stuffed or turned inward. Thus we may observe a myriad of physical problems, including ulcers, back pain, asthma, skin problems, dysmenorrhea, sleeplessness, migraine headaches, weight changes, and even cancer.

It is at the point of developing such physical symptoms that many women first seek help and support. They may turn to coworkers or other students, to counselors or friends. Validation and information are crucial during this time. Family and friends often accept stereotypes and blame the harassment on the victim, further isolating her and increasing her feelings of rage and hopelessness. The anger may also be displaced onto partners, friends, or children; these are safer targets since they cannot terminate the victim's employment or education. Displacing anger may create further feelings of shame and self-hate on the part of the victim.

Strong and responsive internal grievance procedures are crucial at this time. Unfortunately, coworkers, supervisors, and administrators often feel a need to protect the system rather than the person. Thus they may add to the confusion of the victim by denying the problem or blaming the victim. It is unhappily rare that internal grievance procedures respond in helpful and effective ways to complaints of sexual harassment.

Such painful and unhelpful responses by those to whom a victim may turn are exemplified in the following case. S works as a bookkeeper with a firm that handles automotive repair. She was hired in another state and transferred to the present workplace almost immediately. After she had worked for a short time, her boss informed her that she was transferred so that he could date her. She tried making light of it at first, but his demands became more persistent. Finally she told him that she was a lesbian, hoping that this would finish the matter. Instead, he began humiliating her in front of other workers, isolating her from the only other female employee, to whom he began giving preferential treatment. The boss increased S's hours, did not allow her to leave for meals, and told her that if she took so much as a day off she would need a physician's note.

S went to the owner of the firm. He told her that she should consider her supervisor's attention flattering. The other female employee agreed that this treatment was unfair but begged S "not to make waves." S's roommate told her that she was tired of hearing about the problem and believed that S must have encouraged her supervisor's advances in some way. Receiving no support or validation for her anger, S became increasingly anxious, lost weight, and became accident-prone. Her supervisor started demanding that she work odd hours, often when he was the only other person there. He began making "mistakes" on her paychecks. She again went to the owner, who told her that if he had to choose between keeping S or the supervisor, she would have to go. He appealed to her understanding and asked her to remember that working women should expect this kind of thing. By that time, her health problems had become a further trap. The job, which had been instrumental in creating these problems, was the only way she could keep health insurance and obtain medical treatment. Isolated and alone, she became irritable, numb, and withdrawn, shutting herself off from friends and family.

Early advocacy and support for victims is extremely important. Should a victim share her situation with you, be supportive. You can be helpful in strategizing a course of action for her. Help her to evaluate coworkers who might be experiencing similar abuse or who might be supportive; she may need to assess whom she trusts and whom she does not trust. Encourage her to keep a record documenting all incidents, including dates, times, descriptions of events, names of any witnesses. Ask about how she has previously reacted. She may have been trying to avoid confrontation, believing that polite and "ladylike" behavior is best. If she has not yet tried assertive but polite rebuffs, check out the possibility of confronting the harasser. Explore how comfortable the victim feels with sterner approaches, such as reminding him that sexual harassment is against the law or warning him that she will make a complaint. Others suggest that a nonthreatening letter to the accused, including the facts of the harassment, her feelings about it, and a brief statement about what should happen next, may be helpful for those who do not wish to confront a harasser verbally or who wish a written record of their protest. In addition, as much as is feasible, avoid forcing the victim to keep repeating and retelling her story. However, in all these options, it must be emphasized that ending harassment is *not* the responsibility of the victim, but of the harasser and those responsible for the working conditions.

Established and effective grievance procedures within the workplace are central. The creation of a detached ombudsperson specifically for sexual harassment cases may be needed. Local rape centers can also provide information and advocacy services.

WITHDRAWAL AND DEPRESSION

As the preceding case also illustrates, continual stress and unattended anger can create a hopeless exhaustion. With energy and self-esteem at low ebb, the victim may have little ability to find creative solutions. Many victims feel that they have tried everything without result. People in such situations become withdrawn and silent. School and job performance may deteriorate or absenteeism increase. Women report feeling depressed, disgusted, worthless, and incompetent. They may resort to drinking or overeating and have suicidal thoughts. The stress of long-term harassment has infiltrated every aspect of being and created problems in all areas of the woman's life. Her relationships may have become strained and broken; her health may be poor; her feelings about self, aspirations, sexuality, and trust for others may be at an all-time low.

It is at this point that support counseling or therapy become a necessity. Intervention must be carefully balanced. On the one hand, the fact of harassment must be validated. On the other hand, the identity of the woman must not become wrapped up in the harassment. A person is always more than their victimization experience. In addition, her grief and loss must be recognized. She may grieve the loss of aspirations, goals, relationships, and an entire world view. Naming this grief, validating it, and helping the client to mourn is often extremely beneficial.

H is a strong and independent woman who was employed in a factory. Her job was a good one, providing many benefits; after eight years, she had built up a good deal of seniority. For most of those years, however, she was subjected to a great deal of sexual harassment. All aspects of her femaleness were the subject of lewd jokes, including her pregnancy, menstrual cycle, and physical appearance. Her supervisor separated H from the only other female employee, creating isolation and lack of support. At first H tried to change the situation by changing herself. She became passive and quiet, dressed in blue jeans and bulky sweaters. She then tried laughing along, sometimes at the expense of the other female employee. Anger entered when her children became targets of the humiliation. Her anger was met with physical threats and molestation. Eventually, H filed a complaint with the Department of Human Rights and retained an attorney. The overt threats stopped, replaced by hostile silence and complete ostracism. H developed insomnia and underwent great fluctuations in body weight. Her fear and shame made going to work unbearable. Uncontrollable crying spells further increased her embarrassment. The need to concentrate on and to document every act of harassment for her lawsuit led to an obsession with the situation to the virtual exclusion of everything else in her life. Upon finally leaving her job and losing all seniority and benefits, H believed that her identity as sexual harassment victim was an obvious and visible label, a veritable scarlet letter. Therapy for H included helping her to mourn the loss of her job, her marriage, many of her friendships, and her previous self—a self that had experienced the world as a joyful, safe, and caring place with limitless possibilities.

APATHY AND DESPAIR

When the totality of a person's physical, emotional, and spiritual resources are depleted, apathy and despair become an adaptive last resort. This stage involves retreating behind protective walls, not responding to any kind of stimulation, whether negative or overtly positive. Almost any kind of action seems overwhelming. Many women report this, in retrospect, as the most frightening stage of the process. One woman spoke of feeling robbed of her selfhood, of any ability to laugh, smile, or feel joy. In effect, she felt that her spirit had been murdered, leaving only the shell of a person to deal with life. Coping becomes a matter of living day to day or minute to minute. Asking a person in such a position to make big changes and long-term commitments, to handle confrontation, or to become objective and assertive is totally unrealistic. Yet it is often at this stage that a woman pursuing legal recourse is required to do all these things.

Counseling and support at this time can be very beneficial, provided that the individual's exhaustion, lack of trust, and immobility are respected and understood. In a safe and supportive atmosphere, the counselor must slowly built trust. Because many aspects of the woman's personhood have been exposed, intruded upon, and violated, the support person must facilitate rebuilding of personal and professional boundaries. The woman's right to make her own decisions must be respected. For example, though women who have left a job because of harassment are eligible for unemployment compensation, some choose not to go through the process. Although this course should certainly be an option, the person should not be shamed or coerced into choosing to do so.

Counselors may also need to be creative in finding new means of rebuilding self-esteem, hope, and trust. Creative visualization and self-affirmations have proved to be helpful. Teaching clients to turn to images of comfort, nurture, and support, and encouraging them in such practices, may help to rebuild the client's resources from within. Women can also be encouraged to develop and concentrate upon their own affirmations, positive statements for self-reinforcement, which can be repeated aloud or silently to themselves. They may include statements such as "I am a powerful, loving, and creative person," or "I am kind and loving, and I have a good deal to share with others," or "Every day in every way I am getting better and better" may all be helpful. The point is to locate and encourage access to the woman's own internal resources and to support her in following her own internal processes towards renewed health and well-being.[3]

For many victims, and at many points in the healing process, working in a support group with others who have experienced sexual harassment can be an important means towards renewed growth and health. Even a supportive counselor cannot always convey the reality that sexual harassment is a systemic problem, shared by many women in the workforce, in the same concrete way that a group experience can do so. Referring clients to a support group for those who have undergone sexual harassment can be an important part of healing. Helpful topics for group sessions may include: an introductory session (explaining the group focus, its goals, confidentiality, basic myths and facts about sexual harassment); therapeutic retelling of the story, with feelings and experiences and trust issues; survival skills—coping mechanisms, protection planning, recognizing patterns and cycles and escalation; anger and fear, fight versus flight reactions, assertiveness; shame and guilt; boundary questions (accepting the right to say no and set limits); grief and loss; support systems—mobilizing family and friends, advocates, crisis agencies; legal issues and procedures; sexuality concerns; affirmations, mindset of power and healing, letting go.

Undergoing the prolonged stress of harassment produces many physical, emotional, spiritual, and economic consequences for the individual. The responses victims experience can be viewed as adaptive reactions to situations that are perceived as hostile and threatening.

Viewing sexual harassment as a process and noticing the patterns of possible reactions women may display provide resources for adopting the most beneficial strategies and interventions. Unraveling the secrecy, providing safety, respect and support, and helping the individual to know she is not alone and does not have to cope in isolation are all elements that provide for beneficial interventions. They can lead to healing and growth.

16. Beyond Belief: The Reluctant Discovery of Incest

ROLAND SUMMIT

As recently as 1962, there was no climate of belief for the fact that children are at substantial risk of injury at the hands of their parents. While the reality of child battering has emerged as inescapable, a corollary discovery is still largely ignored: children, especially girls, are at substantial risk of sexual exploitation at the hands of their parents and trusted caretakers. As Suzanne Sgroi wrote after years of frustration as a physician trying to encourage protection intervention:

Sexual Abuse of Children is a crime that our society abhors in the abstract, but tolerates in reality. . . . Those who try to assist sexually abused children must be prepared to battle against incredulity, hostility, innuendo, and outright harassment. Worst of all, the advocate for the sexually abused child runs the risk of being smothered by indifference and a conspiracy of silence. The pressure from one's peer group, as well as the community, to ignore, minimize, or cover up the situation may be extreme.[1]

If adult society can learn to believe in the reality of child sexual abuse, there is opportunity for unprecedented advances in the prevention and treatment of emotional pain and dysfunction. If adults cannot face the reality of incestuous abuse, then women and children will continue to be stigmatized by the terrors of their own helpless silence.

Louise Armstrong documents the incredible reluctance of court systems to give voice to abused children.[2] She makes clear also the vested interest of male-dominated society in maintaining secrecy and disbelief. What is not so clear is that the victim of child sexual abuse faces disbelief, retaliation, and revictimization at each level of disclosure within the world of adults. It is not only the court and a community of men that are so incredulous of sexually exploited children. The basic reason for disbelief is *adocentrism,* the unswerving and unquestioned allegiance to adult values. All adults, male and female, tend to align themselves in an impenetrable bastion against any threat that adult priorities and self-comfort must yield to the needs of children.

The child is trapped in a private, impossibly confusing world that gives no validation to the incest experience. The incestuous intruder into the child's private world is something like a monster that inhabits her[3] closet. He threatens her only when she is alone, and she must find her own ways of coping with his overpowering presence. She knows without question and learns through painful experience that nobody will give serious credibility to her fears. Her mother may be the most incredulous and punishing, not because she is indifferent to the child but because she must first protect her trust in the basic decency of her husband and the fundamental security of adult society. Since an adult assumes that other decent adults don't commit incest, and since it is generally believed that children wishfully imagine incestuous experiences or fabricate groundless accusations of sexual assault, it is predictable that most women will reject any hint of incest given by their children. Only an unusually free and perceptive mother can reward a child for sharing with her the bad news of an incestuous relationship.

Across the country and through the years, victims report the same litany of terror: *nobody* could believe. *Nobody* could care. Teachers, doctors, mental health specialists, police investigators, prosecutors, judges, juries, *everyone* in the adult world finds some logical reason to defend the adult against the distress of the child. The monster in the closet doesn't really exist.

"You made him up. You lied. It's *your* monster. All this trouble is your fault. Don't bother us with your childish make-believe world. We have more important things to do in the real world." There is no room for monsters in the grown-up world.

This nightmarish isolation and sequential rejection reinforce what becomes for the victim the most painful reality of incest: "It's my fault. I brought it on myself. I'm so bad I invite trouble and make trouble for others. I'm not worth caring for. There's no place for me in the world of reasonable, decent people. I'll never be reasonable or decent. I'm crazy. I'm nothing but a whore."

Such a victim is likely to live out a life of self-fulfilling prophecies, deprived of a confident core identity and stripped of any capacity for trust and intimacy. If she presumes to be worthy of professional help, she will probably not trust her counselor to share the shame of her childhood. The secret goes unchallenged. If she does claim to be a survivor of incest, she may be told by her therapist that her memories are only distorted traces of old wishful fantasies. Some therapists may recognize the reality of the incest experience yet fail to appreciate the significance of related symptoms. The splitting of self-perception and the need to restructure contradictory relationships, mechanisms that are necessary survival skills of the child entrapped in incest, may be treated as indicators of intractable mental illness. These problems beg for specialized, emphatic attention. Women who have considered themselves hopelessly ill through years of conventional therapy often discover redeeming self-worth and self-confidence after only a few months of contact with other survivors within a specialized incest treatment program. It can be estimated that some five million[4] women in the United States were sexually victimized as children by a male relative. How many such women might benefit from a chance to discover that they were not alone and not at fault?

There is a compelling urgency for all of society to discover incest. Unilateral sensitivity in any segment of the population without concomitant support at other levels only increases the crippling pain and frustration for those who must struggle for belief. Enlightened mothers offer their children the most profound alliance for protection and recovery. But a woman fights an uphill battle unless she is afforded credibility and power within the child-protective, justice, and treatment response systems. And no amount of enlightened agency response can undo the disbelief and disapproval of the extended family and the general public.

The purpose of this chapter is to help establish a climate of belief for the realities of incest. Any woman who can believe that incest happens and who can be confident that children are normally trapped into silence through no fault of their own is empowered to make changes toward prevention and immunity from the most crippling stigmas of incest. Such a woman can be a loving resource to her daughter, to her sister, to her friend, to her neighbor, and, so often most needed, to herself.

Every reader has the capacity to make a difference in the equilibrium of silence. Most people who insist they have never known anyone involved in incest discover the experience among friends and family, and sometimes in themselves, when they are willing to suspend their disbelief. The discovery of incest seems overwhelming only within the habitual stigmas of secrecy, helplessness, and shame. While anyone is understandably reluctant to rediscover the painful helplessness of childhood, the process carries with it also the excitement of a new understanding and empathy. Now that the monster is coming out of the closet as something tangible and physically intimidating, we can use adult systems of investigation, description, and active resolution to reduce the monster to human dimensions.

The following sections provide a map of typical incest experiences, first as statistical data, then as a synthesis of normal patterns of accommodation. Finally, we will examine the implications of these patterns for more effective recognition, prevention, and recovery.

FREQUENCY

For years, incest has been dismissed as statistically trivial, something that is too exceptional for serious concern. Official figures have been drawn from court records in the naive belief that incest is subject to report and prosecution. Not surprisingly, the official incidence of father-daughter incest remained constant for fifty years at one to two per million. In Santa Clara County, California, where the Child Sexual Abuse Treatment Project has invited better identification and coordination of services for incestuous families, annual incidence is approaching one thousand per million!

Several retrospective surveys of college-age females have identified a 20 to 30 percent rate of child sexual victimization.[5] These are not all incestuous or ongoing experiences. The data included one-time-only assaults by strangers. One striking finding, consistent in each of these studies, is that strangers were involved in only 25 percent of the experiences. A girl had a three-to-one chance of being molested by an adult male whom she had been taught to trust. About half (44 percent) of the molesters were relatives, one-quarter (22 percent) resided within the child's home, and about 6 percent were fathers or stepfathers.[6] Projecting these figures to the general population, at least 1.5 percent of all women could be expected to have experienced sex with their father or stepfather, with 9 percent of the female population having a background of victimization by relatives.

These are average figures drawn from a sample of relatively well-adjusted, high-achieving college students. High-risk subgroups show even higher rates. College girls in Finkelhor's sample who were stepdaughters experienced even odds of victimization: 50 percent. Surveys of foster children, runaways, drug addicts, and prostitutes show an incestuous background in the sixty to seventy percent range. Perhaps most significant is the apparent correlation between child sexual abuse and a later tendency toward abusive parenting. Mothers in treatment centers for child abuse report an 80 to 90 percent prevalence of incestuous abuse in their own childhood. Some abusive mothers report that their mothers and their grandmothers were also sexually abused. Yet these most damaged women are often the first to yield power to abusive males and to condemn their daughters as intrinsically evil and deserving of abuse.

What is the power of the incestuous experience to stigmatize generations of women so severely? What are the threats that achieve such perfect secrecy and victim self-condemnation? Why do so few victims seek help, and why are those few so relentlessly ignored? Is there, as Dr. Michael Rothenberg suggested, a conspiracy against children in the United States?[7]

No single system and no simple conspiracy explains the reluctant discovery of incest, but understanding can be gained from a closer evaluation of the dilemmas faced by the child as she tries to survive on the uncharted solo voyage through the tempest of incest. Each wave of involvement in the secret realities of the experience carries her further from the mythical, commonsense "truths" or adult truisms about incest. The more normal the child is in her reactions, the more she will discredit herself. And the better she adapts to the experience, the more she will be condemned.

THE CHILD SEXUAL ABUSE
ACCOMMODATION SYNDROME

Five factors define the progression of adjustment for the most typical victims of incest. These same conditions contradict much of the mythology and misunderstanding that adults apply to their perception of incest. Children's normal reaction patterns defy popular, commonsense, and professional dogma about how children *should* behave in response to incestuous assault. And the unwillingness of key adults to accept the child's behavior leaves the children all the more trapped in a sense of total isolation and self-condemnation. The cycle of disbelief and rejection serves to maintain adult comfort and to reinforce child helplessness until the child learns to behave "normally" and to present the adult world with a credible account of her experience. The first four factors of the sexual abuse accommodation syndrome are secrecy, helplessness, accommodation, and delayed, unconvincing disclosure. The fifth is retracting the complaint and reassuring the world in its insistent belief that the child only imagined the experience, or that she deliberately lied.

1. *Secrecy.* Children rarely tell anyone, especially when they are first molested.[8] The child typically feels ashamed and guilty. She fears disapproval or punishment from the mother (most of the girls in Finkelhor's sample who told their mother found their worst fears justified); retaliation or loss of love from the offender; and, most profoundly, loss of acceptance and security in the home. These fears are often suggested and reinforced by direct threats from the offender.

The emphasis on secrecy and the fearful isolation from the mother define the sexual activity as something dangerous and bad, even when the child is too young to understand the societal taboos involved. Even if the child is carefully and affectionately seduced without fear or pain, the conspiracy of silence stigmatizes the relationship.

2. *Helplessness.* The child feels obligated and overpowered by the inherent authority of the trusted adult, even in the absence of physical force or threats. Helplessness is reinforced by the sense of isolation, secrecy, and guilt, as well as the child's inability to

make sense out of her father's behavior or to find any acceptable way to describe the bizarre relationship to others.

Helplessness is often expressed by immobility. If a young girl is molested during sleep, she typically "plays possum." She does not resist or cry out, even though her mother may be in the next room. A sibling in the same bed may also feign sleep, afraid to become involved.

The natural inability to cry out or to protect herself provides the core of misunderstanding between the victim and the community of adults, as well as providing the nidus for the child's later self-reprisals. Almost no adult seems willing to believe that a legitimate victim would not react with kicks and screams. Attorneys for the offender easily humiliate and confuse the child victim-witness and prejudice the jury with demands for a "normal" protest. Expert testimony on these points is crucial, both to validate the credibility of the child and to help prevent self-condemnation.

With repeated intrusions, the victimized child may lie awake in fright long into the night. Yet, if approached, she remains motionless in a pathetic attempt to protect herself, much as she has learned to hide beneath the covers from imaginary monsters.

Violation of a person's most secure retreat overwhelms ordinary defenses and leads to disillusionment, severe insecurity, and a process of victimization. Well-adjusted adults report lingering terrors and loss of basic well-being after rape or even a robbery within their bedrooms. Children, who have few defenses at best, are even more vulnerable than adults to invasion of their beds.

Finally, it must be remembered that the normal child has no real power or voice apart from the enfranchisement given by her parents. These are not older children or adolescents with strong institutional or peer-group support. The average age of incestuous initiation is eight, with a range from birth to age sixteen. The mean clusters sharply in the middle, with as few teenage initiates as infants. How can a third-grader feel anything but helplessness in confronting a sexually insistent father or stepfather? And how can she blame herself for inviting his attentions or for her failure to forcibly abort his intentions? For a child of eight (or three, five, or eleven, as the case may be), self-blame is intrinsic in the accommodation process unless her mother or some alternate caretaker can give her the power to stop the sexual entrapment.

3. *Entrapment and Accommodation.* The process of helpless victimization leads the child to exaggerate her own responsibility and eventually to despise herself for her weakness. The child is confronted with two apparent realities: either she is bad, deserving of punishment, and not worth caring for, or her parent is bad, unfairly punishing, and not capable of caring. The young child has neither preparation nor permission to believe in the second reality, and there would be no hope for acceptance or survival if it were true. Her inevitable choice is to embrace the more active role of being the one responsible, and to hope to find a way to become good and worthy of caring. This self-scapegoating is almost universal in victims of any form of parental abuse. It sets the foundation for self-hate and what Leonard Shengold described as a vertical split in reality testing:

If the very parent who abuses and is experienced as *bad* must be turned to for relief of the distress that the parent has caused, then the child must, out of desperate need, register the parent—*delusionally*—as good. Only the mental image of a good parent can help the child deal with the terrifying intensity of fear and rage which is the effect of the tormenting experience. The alternative—the maintenance of the overwhelming stimulation and the bad parental image—means annihilation of identity, of the feeling of the self. So the bad has to be registered as good. This is a mind-splitting or a mind-fragmenting operation.[9]

The sexually abusive parent provides explicit example and instruction in how to be good: the child must be available without complaint to his sexual demands. There is an explicit or implicit promise of reward: if she is good and if she keeps the secret, she can protect her siblings from sexual involvement (or have Daddy all to herself, as the case may be), protect her mother from disintegration ("If your mother ever found out, it would kill her"), protect her father from temptation ("If I couldn't count on you, I'd have to hang out in bars and look for other women"), and, most vitally, preserve the security of the home ("If you ever tell, they could send me to jail and put all you kids in an orphanage").

In the classic role reversal of child abuse, the child is given the power to destroy the family and the responsibility to keep it together. The child, *not the parent,* must mobilize the altruism and self-control to ensure the survival of the others. The child, in short, must secretly assume many of the role functions previously assigned to the mother.

There is an inevitable splitting of conventional moral values: maintaining a lie to keep the secret is the ultimate virtue, while telling the truth would be the greatest sin. A child thus victimized will appear to accept or to seek sexual contact without complaint. As Ferenczi discovered almost fifty years ago, "The misused child changes into a mechanical obedient automaton."[10]

Effective accommodation, of course, invalidates any future claims to credibility as a victim. It is obvious to adults that if the child *were* sexually involved, as she claims, then she must have been a consenting and probably a seductive partner. If she is not lying in her eventual complaints, she certainly lied and conspired with her "lover" in her earlier cover-up. In either event, she has no credibility in a criminal court. Again, only expert testimony can translate the child's behavior into concepts that other adults can accept.

Since the child must structure her reality to protect the parent, she also finds the means to build pockets of survival where some hope of goodness can find sanctuary. She may turn to imaginary companions for reassurance. She may develop multiple personalities, assigning helplessness and suffering to one, badness and rage to another, sexual power to another, love and compassion to another, and so forth. She may discover altered states of consciousness to shut off pain or to disassociate from her body, as if looking on from a distance at the child suffering the abuse.

If the child cannot create a psychic economy to reconcile the continuing outrage, the intolerance of helplessness and the increasing feelings of rage will seek active expression. For the girl, this expression is most often self-destructive and reinforcing of self-hate: self-mutilation, suicidal behavior, promiscuous sexual activity, and repeated running away are typical. She may learn to exploit the father for privileges, favors, and material rewards, reinforcing her self-punishing image as whore in the process. She may fight with both parents, but her greatest rage is likely to focus on her mother, whom she blames for driving the father into her bed. She assumes that her mother must know of the sexual abuse and is either too uncaring or too ineffectual to intervene. The failure of the mother-daughter bond reinforces the young woman's distrust of herself as a female and makes her all the more dependent on the pathetic hope of gaining acceptance and protection from a male.

Substance abuse is an inviting avenue of escape. As Barbara Myers recalled:

> On drugs, I could be anything I wanted to be. I could make up my own reality: I could be pretty, have a good family, a nice father, a strong mother, and be happy; . . . drinking had the opposite affect of drugs. . . . Drinking got me back into my pain; it allowed me to express my hurt and my anger.[11]

All these accommodation mechanisms—domestic martyrdom, splitting of reality, altered consciousness, hysterical phenomena, delinquency, sociopathy, projection of rage, even self-mutilation—are part of the survival skills of the child. They can be abandoned only if the child can be led to trust in a secure environment that is full of consistent, *noncontingent* acceptance and caring. In the meantime, anyone working therapeutically with the child (or the grown-up, still shattered victim) will be tested and provoked to prove that trust is impossible and that the only secure reality is negative expectation and self-hate.

The following was written in the midst of transient despair by Stephanie, a thirty-six-year-old woman trying to cope with the apparent caring of her therapist and peer group despite her expectation of rejection. After some twenty years of escape within the role of a psychotic child, she had for the prior year achieved a kind of adolescent adjustment free of delusions and hallucinations. Just a month before writing this statement, she had first recalled graphic images of forcible oral and anal rape by her father. While these acts were entirely consistent with the brutal and humiliating punishments she had learned to expect from this man, remembering the repressed sexual experiences made her all the more fearful of hurt and punishment as a natural consequence of the inherent badness of her participation. For this polyabused child-woman, the omnipotent father's assertion that the child asked for and deserved the sexual punishment was tantamount to reality. In every instance, the labels she applied to herself were the names habitually used by her father some thirty years before:

I am a filthy, sick animal trying to act like a human being and doing a pretty poor job. I'll never be anything but sick and inhuman. I am covered with green slime that can be seen by all. I am scum. I am a slut and a whore. People get nauseated when they look at me because of my ugliness. I belong in a hole where decent people don't have to associate with me. I am shit. I destroy everything I care for. My soul either kills off or chases away everyone who comes in contact with me, especially those that become dear. I make myself sick.

I deserved to be screwed in the mouth and I deserved to be fucked in the ass. I asked for it and I got what I deserve. It was my fault and I take responsibility for it. I deserved to be beaten; I was bad; I still am. I deserved to be molested; I am a whore. I deserved the verbal abuse I received; I am a stupid ass. I deserved to be shocked and locked up alone for weeks; I was crazy and still am and always will be.

I am not deserving of love or respect or comfort. I do not deserve caring. I do not deserve softness or tenderness. I do not deserve to feel warm and good. I do not deserve life.

I am disgusting. I am repulsive. I am useless. I am worthless. I am responsible for the unhappiness of all. I am the scum of the earth. I hate the very thought of me.

It is all too easy for the would-be therapist to join the parents and all adult society in rejecting such a child, looking at the results of abuse to assume that such an impossible wretch must have asked for and deserved whatever punishment has occurred, if indeed the whole problem is not a hysterical or vengeful fantasy.

4. *Delayed, Conflicted, and Unconvincing Disclosure.* Most ongoing sexual abuse is *never* disclosed, at least not outside the immediate family.[12] Reported, investigated cases are the exception, not the norm. Reporting is an outgrowth either of overwhelming family conflict, incidental discovery by a third party, or sensitive outreach and community education by child-protective agencies.

If family conflict triggers disclosure, it is usually only after some years of continuing sexual abuse and an eventual breakdown of accommodation mechanisms. The victim of incest remains silent until she enters adolescence, when she becomes capable of demanding a more separate life for herself and of challenging the authority of her parents. Adolescence also makes the father more jealous and controlling, trying to sequester his daughter against the "dangers" of outside peer involvement. He may become harshly judgmental and punitive in a belated attempt to recapture authority and control. The mother, who has come to resent the favored position of the "spoiled" daughter, is likely to applaud the shift in discipline and reinforce the need for harsh punishment and restrictions. The corrosive effects of accommodation seem to justify any extreme of punishment. What parent would not impose severe sanctions to control running away, drug abuse, promiscuity, rebellion, and delinquency?

After an especially punishing family fight and a belittling showdown of authority by the father, the girl is finally driven to let go of the secret. She seeks understanding and intervention at the very time she is least likely to find them. Authorities are put off by the pattern of delinquency and rebellious anger expressed by the girl. Most adults confronted with such a history tend to identify with the problems of the parents in trying to cope with a rebellious teenager. They observe that the girl seems more angry about the immediate punishment than about the sexual atrocities she is alleging. They assume there is no proof to such a fantastic complaint, especially since she did not complain years ago when she claims she was forcibly molested. They assume she has invented the story in retaliation against the father's attempt to achieve reasonable control and discipline. The more unreasonable and abusive the triggering punishment, the more they assume the child would do anything to get away, even to the point of falsely incriminating her father.

Unless specifically trained and sensitized, average adults, including mothers, relatives, teachers, counselors, doctors, psychotherapists, clergy, investigators, prosecutors, defense attorneys, judges, and jurors cannot believe that a normal, truthful child would tolerate incest without immediately reporting it, or that an apparently normal father could be capable of repeated, unchallenged sexual molestation of his own daughter. The child of any age faces an unbelieving audience when she complains of ongoing incest. The troubled, angry adolescent risks not only disbelief, but scapegoating, humiliation, and punishment as well.

Contrary to popular myth, most mothers are not aware of ongoing sexual abuse. Marriage demands considerable blind trust and denial for survival. A woman does not commit her life and security to a man she believes capable of molesting his own children. That basic denial becomes pathological the more the woman herself has been victimized and the more she might feel helpless and worthless in the absence of a protective, accepting male. The "obvious" clues to incest are usually obvious only in retrospect. Our assumption that the mother "must have known" merely parallels the demand of the child that the mother must be in touch intuitively with invisible and even deliberately concealed family discomfort.

So the mother typically reacts to allegations of sexual abuse with disbelief and protective denial. How could she not have known? How could the child wait so long to tell her? What kind of mother could allow such a thing to happen? What would the neighbors think? As someone substantially dependent on the approval and generosity of the father, she is in a mind-splitting dilemma analogous to that of the abused child: either the child is bad and deserving of punishment or the father is bad and unfairly punitive. One of them is lying and unworthy of trust. The mother's whole security and life adjustment and much of her sense of adult self-worth demands a trust in the reliability of her partner. To accept the alternative means annihilation of the family and a large piece of her own identity. Her fear and ambivalence are reassured by the father's logical challenge:

Are you going to believe that lying little slut? Can you believe I would do such a thing? How could something like that go on right under your nose for years? You know we can't trust her out of our sight any more. Just when we try to clamp down and I get a little tough with her, she comes back with a cock-and-bull story like this. That's what I get for trying to keep her out of trouble!

Among the small proportion of incest secrets that are shared, most are never revealed outside the family. Now that professionals are required to report any suspicion of child abuse, increasing numbers of complaints are investigated by protective agencies. Police investigators and protective service workers are now more likely to give credence to the complaint, in which case all the children may be removed immediately into protective custody pending the hearing of a dependency petition. In the continuing paradox of a divided judicial system, the juvenile court judge is likely to sustain out-of-home placement on the "preponderance of the evidence" that the child is in danger, while the adult criminal court takes no action on the father's crime. Attorneys know that the uncorroborated testimony of a child will not convict a respectable adult. The test in criminal court requires specific proof "beyond reasonable doubt," and every reasonable adult juror will have reason to doubt the child's fantastic claims. Prosecutors are reluctant to subject the child to humiliating cross-examination, just as they are loath to prosecute cases they cannot win, so they typically reject the complaint on the basis of insufficient evidence. Defense counsel can assure the father that he will not be charged as long as he denies any impropriety and *as long as he stays out of treatment.*

The absence of criminal charges is tantamount to a conviction of perjury against the victim. "A man is innocent until proven guilty," say adult-protective relatives. "The kid claimed to be molested, but there was nothing to it. The police investigated and they didn't even file charges."

As outrageous as it might seem, there is an open season on children for the sexual predator. Unless children can be encouraged to seek immediate intervention and unless there is expert advocacy for the child in the criminal court, the child is abandoned as the helpless custodian of a self-incriminating secret that no responsible adult can believe.

Health-care professionals have a critical role in both early detection and expert courtroom advocacy. Professionals can help mobilize skeptical caretakers into a position of belief and protective intervention. And only strong clinical expertise asserting the reality of the accommodation syndrome can compete with the "reasonable doubt" of other adults in the court process. Obviously, the professional must first be capable of a strong position of belief. The professional who can believe in the reality of incest and who has learned to acknowledge the secrecy, the helplessness, the accommodation patterns, and the delayed disclosure may still be alienated by the fifth level of the accommodation syndrome.

5. *Retraction of Complaint. Whatever a child says about incest, she is likely to reverse it.* As a small child, she may deny incest when questioned, yet in later years, she may make criminal complaints when moved by anger. Beneath the anger remains the ambivalence of guilt and the martyred obligation to preserve the family. In the chaotic aftermath of disclosure, the child discovers that the bedrock fears and threats underlying the secrecy are true. Her father

abandons her and calls her a liar. Her mother doesn't believe her, or she decompensates into hysteria and rage. The family breaks up, and all the kids are placed in custody. The father is threatened with disgrace and imprisonment. The child is blamed for causing the whole mess, and everyone seems to treat her like a freak. She is interrogated about all the tawdry details and encouraged to incriminate her father, yet the father remains unchallenged, remaining at home in the security of the family. She is held in custody, with no hope of returning if the dependency petition is sustained.

The message from the mother is very clear, often explicit:

Why do you insist on telling those awful stories about your father? If you send him to prison there will be no one to provide for us and we won't be a family anymore. We'll end up on welfare with no place to stay. Is that what you want to do to us? Forget all this foolishness and come back home so we can be a family again.

Once again, the child bears the responsibility of either preserving or destroying the family. The role reversal continues, with the "bad" choice to tell the truth, or the "good" choice to capitulate and restore a lie for the sake of the family.

Unless there is special support for the child and immediate intervention to force responsibility onto the father, the girl will follow the "normal" course and retract her complaint. The girl "admits" she made up the story:

I was awful mad at my dad for punishing me. He hit me and said I could never see my boyfriend again. I've been really bad for years and nothing seems to keep me from getting into trouble. He had plenty of reason to be mad at me. But I got real mad and just had to find some way of getting out of that place. So I made up the story about him fooling around with me and everything. I didn't mean to get everyone in so much trouble.

This simple lie carries more credibility than the most explicit claims of incestuous entrapment. It confirms adult expectations that children can't be trusted. It restores the precarious equilibrium of the family. The children learn not to complain. The adults learn not to listen. And the authorities learn not to believe rebellious children who try to use their sexual power to destroy well-meaning parents. Case closed.

IMPLICATIONS FOR RECOGNITION AND TREATMENT

The first priority for active response to incestuous abuse is recognition. Dr. Suzanne Sgroi defined recognition of incest as the last frontier of child abuse:

Recognition of sexual molestation of a child is entirely dependent on the individual's inherent willingness to entertain the possibility that the condition may exist. Unfortunately, willingness to consider the diagnosis of suspected child molestation frequently seems to vary in inverse proportion to the individual's level of training. That is, the more advanced the training of some, the less willing they are to suspect molestation.[13]

The adult who responds to the needs of an incest victim can no longer hide in the reassurance that incestuous behavior is beyond belief. The supportive adult, whether parent, investigator, physician, clergy, or psychotherapist, must first be capable of belief and then be willing to move beyond belief to responsible advocacy and intervention.

The discovery of incest as a cause of emotional problems is not unique to the 1980s or even to the twentieth century. That discovery was documented by no less an authority than Sigmund Freud in 1896! In that year, Freud reported in "The Aetiology of Hysteria" that the hysterical problems presented by a series of female patients were caused by early childhood sexual seduction by adult caretakers.[14] He also wrote to his friend and confidant, W. Fliess, "I have come to the opinion that anxiety is to be connected not with a mental, but with a physical consequence of sexual abuse."[15] Such a theory was greeted with professional outrage in Victorian Vienna, and Freud spent years trying to rationalize his own discomfort about believing that so many respectable fathers could victimize their children. As he wrote to Fliess in 1897, he was perplexed by the tendency of patients to block or to abandon analysis at the level of incest discovery:

Then there was the astonishing thing that in every case . . . blame was laid on perverse acts by the father, . . . though it was hardly credible that perverted acts against children were so general. . . . Thirdly, there is no "indication of reality" in the unconscious, so it is impossible to distinguish between truth and emotionally charged fiction. (This leaves open the possible explanation that sexual fantasy regularly makes use of the theme of parents. . . .)[16]

That "possible explanation" became the basis for one of the major tenets of psychoanalytic theory. In 1924, Freud renounced his earlier belief in the seduction theory and suggested the Oedipus complex instead. The Oedipus complex assumes a universal attraction of children toward the parent of the opposite sex, with inevitable conflicts, jealousy, and fear directed toward the parent of the same sex. Freud postulated that successful emotional maturation depended on the resolution of those conflicts and that neurotic problems could be traced to the child's unsuccessful resolution of that fantasied family romance:

Almost all my women patients told me that they had been seduced by their father. I was driven to recognize in the end that those reports were untrue and so came to understand that the hysterical symptoms were derived from fantasy and not from real occurrences.[17]

Freud apparently came to this recognition through analysis of his own dreams and childhood experiences, as well as a continuing refinement of psychoanalytic techniques with patients. Whatever the basis for the shift to the Oedipus complex, it offered a fortuitous, adult-reassuring alternative to the seduction theory. Children, not their fathers, were responsible for the allegations of sexual abuse. It was the perverse needs of the child that scapegoated adults with undeserved accusations. Finally, whatever children (or adults) chose to say about sexual experiences with their parents must be assumed to be wishful fantasy unless proven otherwise.

Freud's early discovery was therefore an idea ahead of its time. Neither Freud nor the adult-protective world of that era was ready to explore or to validate the implications of the seduction theory. Not only was the theory discredited; worse than that, the adult-protective reaction served to discourage and delay any subsequent reappraisal of that discovery. Freud's precocious, outrageous early speculation led him and many of his followers to arm themselves with a dogma of disbelief. The messenger of incest not only risks provoking ordinary, common-sense denial but also invites charges of heresy among the most highly trained and sophisticated professionals.

As psychoanalyst Joseph Peters has written:

After 1924 the notion that hysterical symptoms were based upon actual events, real sexual assaults upon children, fell increasingly out of favor. Psychoanalysts abandoned the search for a distinction between actual childhood sexual trauma and children's fantasies. In the Freudian theory of psychoneurosis, the fantasies became as important as real events. Since Freud's thinking developed in this way, his earlier followers were relieved from facing the fact that patients sometimes had been real victims of sexual assault. . . . It is my thesis that both cultural and personal factors combined to cause everyone, including Freud himself at times, to welcome the idea that reports of childhood sexual victimization could be regarded as fantasies. This position relieved the guilt of adults. In my opinion, both Freud and his followers oversubscribed to the theory of childhood fantasy and overlooked incidents of actual sexual victimization in childhood.

In their aversion to what are often repulsive details, psychotherapists allowed and continue to allow their patients to repress emotionally significant, pathogenic facts. . . . In addition, it is important to note that because the reported offender was frequently the patient's own father, in order to avoid the fact of incest, my colleagues seized upon the easier assumption that the occurrences were oedipal fantasies.

Relegating these traumas to the imagination may divert treatment into a prolonged unraveling of natural developmental processes in which fantasy is a component. Furthermore, unsuccessful psychotherapeutic evaluation opens the way for prescribing . . . antipsychotic drugs and electroshock. The treatment may compound the patient's original psychologic problems. Ascribing these events to psychological fantasy may be easier and more interesting for the therapist, but it may also be counterproductive for the most efficient resolution of symptoms.

An immediate supportive response by parents, criminal justice personnel, doctors, and nurses is crucial to preserve the emotional integrity of the child. Particularly when the offender is a member of the family, care must be taken by service personnel to insure that the child's needs are put first.[18]

Dr. Peters drew on the experience of a private psychoanalytic practice as well as extraordinary social awareness as director of the Philadelphia Sex Offender and Rape Victim Center. The Philadelphia center is one of a dozen or so specialty centers that have defined new clinical priorities for sexual abuse victims and their families. Child abuse centers, rape crisis networks, women's consciousness-raising groups, incest survivors' self-help groups, and increasingly specialized clinical research and treatment models have led the way to a growing professional and public awareness of the hazards of child sexual abuse.

Many concerned advocates for women and children fear that the issues of sexual abuse will again be submerged by ideological standoffs and adult-protective, male-dominant smoke screens. Children, after all, still have no power, and women may be sidetracked into such adult-oriented issues as equal rights in the workforce. This is hardly the time to encourage women to stay home to protect their children or to devote more energy to saturating their mates with preventive flattery and loving attention.

It *is* a time to discover that men have many needs that they are too proud and too insecure to acknowledge, and that apparently normal men slip rather easily into exploiting whatever potential sexual object is most available and most easily subordinated. It is a time for better clinical and theoretical research to understand the wide diversity of offender rationalizations for incestuous abuse of children, ranging from chronic obsessive desire to apparently thoughtless opportunism. Listening to victims gives a fairly clear and consistent synthesis of common risk factors.[19] Listening to infinite numbers of offenders gives infinite variations of contradictory motivations and choices, with few common denominators except that these men were born of women and determined to express much of their individuality, power, and dependency needs through the exercise of that one appendage no woman can claim.[20]

I believe the time is right for a real and permanent shift in public and professional protective responsibility for children. We are not living in Victorian Vienna. We are no longer unmindful of the realities of parental misuse of children or the helplessness of children to recognize any condition of well-being outside parental sanctions. We understand that successful therapy depends on a creative balance between theoretical expectations and individual behaviors. And the word *incest* is no longer either unthinkable or unspeakable. Perhaps most importantly, women as a group will no longer defer to the unilateral powers and privileges of men. Women are today less impressed by the rhetoric of sexual intimidation. *Virgin, whore, mother, old maid, prick teaser,* and *bitch* are words that are losing their power to stigmatize and confine women within restrictive definitions of sexual behavior.

With a coalition of support from protective agencies, the justice system, treatment agencies, and self-help alliances, adult survivors are no longer condemned to a lifetime of shame and fearful silence. Mothers of present and potential victims are better empowered to make self-protective and child-protective decisions in their choice of adult sexual partners and/or adult living companions. Children, who are assaulted with all sorts of blatant and confusing media images of adult sexuality, might as well be enlightened in this age of sexual candor with honest messages about their own sexuality and their right and power to protect themselves from adult intrusions into their most personal worlds.

PREVENTION

We can start by telling children of both sexes that their bodies are uniquely their own and by acknowledging that they have the right to discover and to express their own limits of intimacy. Kids recognize rather consistently what doesn't feel right in the attentions of adults: tickling or wrestling that doesn't stop on time, "sloppy" kisses, hands poking, rubbing, and probing under clothing. Too often their expressed objections are silenced by parents urging them to be more accepting of adults' affection: "You have to be nice to grandfather, dear, that's just his way of showing how he loves you."

Several good films have been produced for classroom use to empower young children to break intimidating secrets and to say no to unwanted intrusions (*Who Do You Tell?* and *Child Molestation: When to Say No*). Others define the problems of incestuous abuse for parents and secondary-level students (*Incest: The Victim Nobody Believes* and *Shatter the Silence*). Schools need strong parental support to take rape prevention programs beyond the violent-stranger concept to address the three-to-one chance that children will be approached instead by a trusted adult. The helplessness of those encounters thrives on naiveté and silence.

Specific preventive efforts can be directed to high-risk families. Alcoholism, interspousal violence, child abuse, religious insularity, sexual rigidity in one or both parents, or a marked disparity in power and mobility between husband and wife have all been linked to increased risks of sexual victimization for children. A single mother searching for a new mate and a good father for her children is easy prey to a variety of opportunists who are less interested in her than in her children. Of the 50 percent of molested stepdaughters in Finkelhor's sample, most were victimized not by their stepfathers but by some friend of their parents.

In view of all the unknowns in trying to identify potentially abusive males, there must be more support of the vital role occupied by the mother both in protecting a child at risk and in providing support if incest has occurred. Women who have been sexually abused deserve the opportunity to resolve old conflicts, to avoid the risk of stigmatizing their children with projections of fault, and to reduce the likelihood that they or their daughters will select an overpowering and intrusive male as a mate. That is not to say that all sexually abused women endanger their children or that all survivors should be forced to have treatment.

What is needed is greater availability of survivors' groups and other specialized programs for women that invite resolution of any residual conflicts without unnecessary stigmatization. Victim adjustment patterns should not be labeled as mental illness or character pathology.

Many women assume without question that they are bad or sick or crazy because of the assumed guilt and helplessness of their childhood experiences. They view their internalized rage as evil and dangerous, and they tend to live in fear of losing control of their feelings or of losing touch with reality. Those who are not aware of disturbed feelings or thoughts may still have problems with trust and intimacy or inhibition of sexual fulfillment. Finally, survivors who are sure they are free of any stigma of incest may find themselves uncomfortable in their role as parents. Now that these patterns are so well recognized and potentially so effectively resolved, it seems a tragic waste not to provide more effective community education and more assertive outreach through specialized treatment groups.

TREATMENT

Treatment groups for adult survivors are sometimes contained within the more comprehensive specialty programs for all members of currently incestuous families. Mixing these two genera-

tions of experience in discussion groups can have mutually beneficial results. The adult survivor finds a focus for her rage and a new
assurance of her initial blamelessness in confronting firsthand the
power differentials and coercive dynamics in newly discovered
incestuous families. And the protests of the incest survivor within
the parents' group give adult power to the needs of the child.
Fathers and mothers preoccupied with the adult survival issues
surrounding incest disclosure need continuing, insistent remind-
ers of the needs of their children and the reality of child discomfort.

These interactions presume a model of treatment where the
participants are afforded substantial peer-group contact. I believe
that peer-group confrontation and support are vital to the treatment of incest and other forms of child abuse.[21] These groups can
be organized within a self-help model such as Parents United and
Daughters United[22] or within a professional model or peer-group
therapy. The child, especially, needs the inspiration of a peer
group to offset her concept of being uniquely despised and damaged. She also needs to share the support of those who have
experienced the entire progression of the accommodation syndrome to fortify herself against the temptation to retract her complaint.

I believe that proven treatment networks are vital also for the
effective involvement of protective agencies in holding the adult
responsible for his action. Only the combined encouragement and
intimidation of experienced therapists and peers can lead an
offender to accept responsibility for his actions and to hope for
compassionate sentencing. Without immediate and coercive treatment intervention, the offender will usually deny his role and bluff
his way through the court process by shifting responsibility to the
victim. Finally, the availability of a responsible, cooperative treatment resource allows the courts to impose treatment as a condition of sentencing, often with work furlough and other considerations that encourage continuing responsibility to the family.

I believe there is a therapeutic benefit to criminal conviction for
crimes against children, whether the crime is committed within the
privacy of the family or on the street, and whether the child is four
years old or fifteen. With conviction, the primary responsibility of
the offender is clearly defined, bringing what Giaretto called "the

hard edge of society" against the man rather than the child.[23] Conviction also challenges the power of the offender to act as if he is above the law and immune from the discomfort of the child. He can be forced to vacate the home in deference to the child, and he can be forced to remain in treatment and under probationary supervision to guard against future victimization of children. For incest offenders who have not been habitually attracted to children and who have not shown any capacity to victimize children outside the family, the Santa Clara County model of coordinated treatment has proved very effective.[24] For habitual child molesters, there is little optimism for treatment but all the more need for effective sentencing and societal controls. In either case, the man will not be convicted on the strength of the child's testimony without strong and immediate professional and peer-group support of the victim and her mother.[25] The younger the child and the more closely dependent she and her mother are on the offender, the less likely it is that the offender will be charged with a crime unless there is close cooperation between courts and treatment resources.

As Dr. Sgroi has written:

Perhaps the greatest lapse of societal concern for sexually abused children lies in the failure to link punishment of the convicted offender to treatment. . . . the track record in persuading perpetrators and families to undergo voluntary therapy for incest is abysmal. Although referrals to a psychiatric or counselling agency may be eagerly accepted at the outset, perpetrators of incest rarely remain in an effective treatment program when the pressure to participate slackens.

Why do we ignore compelling evidence that an authoritative incentive to change his or her behavior is absolutely essential for the adult perpetrator of child sexual abuse? Why are we so slow to establish a network of family sexual abuse treatment programs patterned after the highly successful Child Sexual Abuse Treatment Program in San Jose, California? It has been demonstrated that there *is* a humane alternative to separation, family breakup, and incarceration for incest. It requires concern, caring, skill, and an authoritative "or else" to insure family participation. . . . Leadership will have to come from the very therapeutic community that has worked so poorly with the criminal justice system in the past and tends to be so uncomfortable with authoritative incentives for treatment. However, we will tolerate sexual abuse of children as long as most of us live in states and communities where no family treatment programs for sexual abuse exist.[26]

Every child of incest deserves a mother who can understand her daughter's position without feeling betrayed or resentful. Every child deserves a mother who can make a clear choice for protection of her child without prejudice, even if that means severing an otherwise rewarding adult relationship. Every woman who discovers that her husband has taken her daughter as a sexual partner deserves help in sorting out her own reactions to such an assaultive discovery. And every mother who has been a partner to incestuous assault, no matter how passive or unwitting her role may have been, should be evaluated by professionals who are sensitive to the dynamics of child abuse before it is assumed that she is ready to assume protective responsibility for her children, with or without the assistance of the designated offender.

These considerations for the mother are not only minimal requirements for the safety and growth of the children but minimal services for the needs of the mother as well.

There are philosophical differences among treatment programs, of course. Some feel that conviction and punishment of offenders is countertherapeutic. Others wish for conviction but will not involve themselves in witness preparation, testimony, or reports to the courts. Some feel that conviction and removal of the male offender offer the only hope for enfranchisement of the child and her mother. Some demand institutionalization of the father but avoid treatment of child or mother for fear of stigmatizing them with labels of mental illness or culpability. Some insist that all members of the incestuous family are linked in a shared vulnerability and must be treated as a unit, carefully avoiding any assignment of independent or individual problems. In the extreme, such an emphasis on family dynamics can obscure the basic understanding that the offender alone had the knowledge and power either to initiate or to avoid the incestuous relationship.

Typical models with contrasting philosophies have been selected and funded as training centers by the National Center of Child Abuse and Neglect, U.S. Department of Health and Human Services. Further evaluation of program effectiveness should lead to increasing availability of reliable treatment programs throughout the United States.

I feel that the trends are already clear and irreversible. We are committed as a society to intervening on behalf of the children we discover to be abused. We are moving toward the discovery of increasing numbers of sexually abused children, as well as increasing numbers of adult women who can acknowledge a history of childhood sexual abuse. Knowledge gained from these disclosures gives us a better definition of the risks as well as more clearly defined patterns of entrapment and accommodation. Emerging treatment networks provide mechanisms for more effective intervention, using the power of the courts to challenge abusive parental style as well as to motivate parents to take the risks of exploring and resolving their conflicts in parenting.

I hope that the treatment programs given this power to act on behalf of the courts will draw on the most client-empathic models currently available to foster maximum self-esteem, self-confidence, and self-control in every member of the family. I hope they will be child-protective as well as adult-supportive. And I hope they will be as endorsing of loving and caring and touching as they are alert to role reversing, possessing, and intruding. I hope that the designated helpers will be selected and trained to be genuine and open with clients and to welcome client participation in treatment planning. If these second-generation treatment resources have learned from the best of the current programs, they will offer resocialization of parents and reparenting of victims. This current rediscovery of incest carries with it a new potential for belief and new guidelines for moving beyond belief to achieve a better climate of nurturance and trust between adults and children.

Some of the job and hope of that nurturing relationship can be seen in this letter from Stephanie to her therapist, Carmen, who with a peer group of incest survivors showed Stephanie the beginnings of noncontingent caring:

Your hugs are warm: When you hold me I feel warm and good; most importantly warm.

Your hugs are caring: They prove a person is cared for. Who can willingly hold someone they dislike or hate? When you hold me I feel cared for.

Your hugs are respectful: They start and stop on time, allowing respect for someone's choice. When you hold me I feel I have the right to say what happens to my own body. Not duty bound or forced. I can say *No*.

Your hugs are deeply satisfying: When you hold me the pain in my chest stops and the longing is fed. They last long enough to fill the whole with your goodness.

Your hugs are free: There are no payments expected or obligations attached to them.

Your hugs are precious: I feel I've been given something precious with each hug; and indeed I have. One of the most precious things in my life.

Your hugs are full: Arms surrounding completely and just tight enough to hold the goodness in and keep it from escaping. Close enough to really feel cared for.

Your hugs are encouraging: They make me feel that the dirt doesn't show. Who could put their arms around a mass of green slime? If it doesn't show and can't be felt, perhaps there is a slight doubt that it exists.

Your hugs are strong: They come from someone strong. I seem to be able to gain strength from them. Things don't look so bad when there's someone more than just yourself to back you up; there's someone there telling you that whatever you decide is okay.

Your hugs are sincere: There's no doubt that every hug you give away is given with true warmth and caring to back it up.

Your hugs are supportive: They make me feel worthwhile and make me want more than ever to get well, not only for myself but for you because you're taking the time and effort to try. Thank you.

Your hugs are clean: They sparkle and they look, feel, and smell as clean and fresh as you do. No amount of scrubbing could make them any brighter.

Your hugs are comforting: In the dark when I'm scared I pretend a hug from you and the dark is not so very frightening anymore.

Your hugs are mine: The hugs you choose to give to me are mine. No one can take them from me or steal their memory. They're mine forever and don't have to be shared with anyone.

Your hugs are special: Just because they come from you they're especially special.

Your hugs are everything a hug should be.

Thank you for your *hugs*.

17. Confidentiality and Mandatory Reporting: A Clergy Dilemma?

MARIE M. FORTUNE

There is increasing controversy surrounding the issue of mandatory reporting by clergy of physical or sexual abuse of children and the privilege of confidentiality within the pastoral role. Some clergy perceive the expectation of mandatory reporting of child abuse by helping professionals to be in direct conflict with their pastoral role. When state law requires clergy (along with all other helping professionals) to report suspected child abuse, some clergy feel that they face a dilemma. Thus we now see efforts by clergy in some states to be exempted from the list of professionals who must report suspected child abuse in any form. Many states (including Washington, California, and Kentucky) already do not require clergy to report child abuse.

Two legitimate concerns expressed by some clergy are an unwillingness to have the state determine their role and function as a religious professional and an effort to protect their relationship with a congregant from incursion by the state. Both of these issues are raised in the context of the separation of church and state provided for in the U.S. Constitution and certainly deserve careful attention.

In states where clergy are relieved of the requirement of the law to report, some seem to feel that the conflict is resolved. They are unlikely to report even though they have the right to do so, as does every citizen.

But the hesitancy by many clergy to utilize the reporting mechanism provided in their state to protect children from further abuse and their desire to be exempt from that which is required of other professionals suggests that the conflict is not just with the mandatory nature of the reporting requirements. The problem may best be stated in terms of a perceived conflict of the ethics of confidentiality and the ethics of reporting certain harmful behavior in order to protect children.

This perceived conflict of ethical demands is the focus of this article. Part of the conflict arises from the interpretation of confidentiality and its purpose, particularly as it rests within the responsibility of the religious professional. The context for an analysis of these ethical demands is the understanding of confidentiality that comes to the religious professional from multiple sources: pastoral, legal, and ethical.

CONFIDENTIALITY

The purpose of confidentiality has been to provide a safe place for a congregant or client to share concerns, questions, or burdens without fear of disclosure. It provides a context of respect and trust within which help can hopefully be provided for an individual. It has meant that some people have come forward seeking help who might not otherwise have done so out of fear of punishment or embarrassment. Confidentiality has traditionally been the ethical responsibility of the professional within a professional relationship and is generally assumed to be operative even if a specific request has not been made by the congregant or client. Sissela Bok suggests four reasons for confidentiality:[1]

1. an individual's autonomy over personal information
2. respect for relationships between persons and for the intimacy that comes with information shared only in a particular relationship
3. an obligation of allegiance and support
4. the safety of a place to disclose information that, if undisclosed, would be detrimental to society as a whole

These four factors represent the *raison d'etre* for confidentiality. Clearly, not only ethical but practical values sustain a commitment to confidentiality.

For the pastor, priest, or rabbi, unlike the secular helping professional, confidentiality rests in the context of spiritual issues and expectations as well. In Christian denominations, the expectations of confidentiality lie most specifically within the experience of confession. The responsibility of the pastor or priest ranges from a strict understanding to a more flexible one, that is, from the letter to the spirit of the law. For example, for Anglican and Roman Catholic priests the confessional occasion with a penitent is sacramental. Whatever information is revealed is held in confidence by the seal of confession with no exceptions. The United Methodist Book of Discipline does not view confession as sacramental but states: "Ministers . . . are charged to maintain all confidences inviolate, including confessional confidences." The Lutheran Church in America protects the confidence of the parishioner and allows for the discretion of the pastor: ". . . no minister . . . shall divulge any confidential disclosure given to him [*sic*] in the course of his [*sic*] care of souls or otherwise in his [*sic*] professional capacity, except with the express permission of the person who has confided in him [*sic*] or in order to prevent a crime." Even within Christian denominations, there is a range of interpretations of the expectations of confidentiality, and it is not necessarily limited to the "confessional" occasion.

The law has traditionally respected "privileged communication" between clergy and penitent if four fundamental conditions are met: (1) a specific context of confidentiality and function as a professional; (2) necessity of maintaining confidentiality in order to maintain relationship; (3) a relationship that ought to be protected in the opinion of the community; (4) injury to the relationship resulting from disclosure would exceed benefit to the community to be gained by disclosure. The primary concern of the law here is that it cannot force a clergyperson to testify against a congregant in a legal proceeding.[2]

Yet all of these parameters shaping the ethical demand for confidentiality for the clergyperson must be considered in a larger context. Are there "reasons sufficient to override the force of all these premises, as when secrecy would allow violence to be done to innocent persons . . ."?[3] The law is unclear as to the clergyperson's duty to disclose intent to commit future crimes and to cause harm to another: is the clergyperson who does not report the probability that a crime will be committed and a person harmed legally liable for damage done to that person? What of the ethical obligation to protect the innocent?

SECRECY

It may be useful in this discussion to make a distinction between confidentiality and secrecy. Secrecy is the absolute promise never under any circumstance to share any information that comes to a clergyperson; this is the essence of sacramental confession. But a commitment to secrecy may also support maintaining the secret of the abuse of a child, which likely means that the abuse continues. Confidentiality means to hold information in trust and to share it with others only in the interest of the person involved, that is, with their permission, in order to seek consultation with another professional, or in order to protect others from harm by them. Confidentiality is intended as a means to assist individuals in getting help for a problem so as not to cause further harm to themselves or others. Confidentiality is not intended to protect abusers from being held accountable for their actions or to keep them from getting the help that they need. Shielding them from the consequences of their behavior likely will further endanger their victims and will deny them the repentance they need.

Neither is confidentiality intended to protect professionals rather than those whom we serve. It should not be used as a shield to protect incompetent or negligent colleagues or to protect us from our professional obligations. Sissela Bok points clearly to this distortion of confidentiality:

> The word *confidentiality* has by now become a means of covering up a multitude of questionable and often dangerous practices. When lawyers use it to justify keeping secret their client's plans to construct housing so shoddy as to be life-threatening, or when government officials invoke it in concealing the risks of nuclear weapons, confidentiality no longer serves the purpose for which it was intended; it has become, rather, a means for deflecting legitimate public attention.[4]

Thus confidentiality may be invoked for all the wrong reasons and not truly in the interests of a particular congregant or of society.

RESPONSIBILITY TO VICTIMS

But another set of ethical principles enters into this discussion from a faith perspective. It has to do with one's professional responsibility to victims of abuse. Within both Jewish and Christian traditions, the community has a responsibility to protect those in its midst who are vulnerable to harm. Thus Hebrew scripture refers to the hospitality code in regard to the sojourner, the orphan, and the widow. These were the persons specifically vulnerable to exploitation and who did not have built-in supporters in family or community. Thus it was the entire community's responsibility to protect them in their powerlessness. In today's society, it is surely the abused child who is most powerless to protect herself or himself and who is in need of support from the wider community.

The other ethical principle that applies here is that of justice-making in response to harm done by one person to another. Christian scripture here is very specific: "Take heed to yourselves; if your brother sins, rebuke him, and if he repents, forgive him" (Luke 17:3 RSV). The one who sins and who harms another must be confronted so that he might seek repentance. Both Hebrew and Christian scriptures are clear that repentance has to do with change: "Get yourselves a new heart and a new spirit! . . . So turn and live." (Ezek. 18:31–32 RSV); the Greek word used for repentance is *metanoia,* "to have another mind." In this context of repentance, accountability, and justice, forgiveness and reconciliation may be possible. This should be the primary concern of the pastor, priest, or rabbi.

It is critical also to keep in mind the context of sexual and physical child abuse as the reference point for this discussion. Aspects of these criminal behaviors must be considered.

- Batterers or incest offenders will reoffend unless they get specialized treatment.
- Offenders against children minimize, lie, and deny their abusive behavior.
- Offenders cannot follow through on their good intentions or genuine remorse without help from the outside.
- Treatment of offenders is most effective when it is ordered and monitored by the courts.
- The secret of the child's abuse must be broken in order to get help to the victim and offender.
- Clergypersons do not have all the skills and resources necessary to treat offenders or to assist victims.

- Quick forgiveness is likely to be cheap grace and is unlikely to lead to repentance.

The question facing the pastor, priest, or rabbi in his or her pastoral relationship to a congregant is: If one receives information in the course of conversation with a congregant revealing the probable abuse of a child and indicating that the child is still in danger of being further abused, what is one's obligation? This question arises regardless of legal requirements of mandatory reporting or exemption.

It is in this context that confidentiality must be understood: when faced with a conflict of ethical norms (confidentiality vs. protection of a child from abuse), how shall we judge which norm should supersede the other? Or can both be fulfilled in bringing forth repentance for an abuser?

In practice, the ethical and pastoral issues are posed somewhat differently. Seldom does an offender against children come forward voluntarily and "confess." It is much more likely that a child or teenager who is being abused or a nonoffending parent or other family member will come to a clergyperson seeking assistance. Hence, what is presented is not confessional on the part of an offender but a cry for help from a victim. Confidentiality is still a concern but not in the sense of the "confessional seal." Instead, it is a matter of respecting the victim's control of the information which she or he shares.

A CASE IN POINT

A fourteen-year-old girl stopped by her pastor's office after school one day. The pastor had been aware that the girl had become more and more withdrawn, but she was still attending meetings of the youth group. The pastor had told her that if there was anything which she wanted to talk about, he was always available. She was now ready to talk. In very hesitant and stumbling sentences, she told her pastor that her father made her uncomfortable and frightened sometimes, that he made her do things she didn't really like. Her pastor asked her if he made her do sexual things. She said he did. This information was very troubling for the pastor on several levels: he had a close relationship with the teenager's father who was previous chairperson of the parish council. He knew him to be

a respected and competent professional who was likable and easy
to work with. But he also knew that the father was not at ease in
relationships on a deeper level. And the pastor knew enough about
incestous abuse to know that it was very possible that the teenager
was being abused and that it was very hard for her to come to him
with this information.

Weighing all these factors, the pastor then explained to her that
he was very glad that she had come to him and that he would help
her. He told her that her father should not be frightening her like
this and that he needed help. The pastor also said that in order to
protect her and to get help for her father that she would also need
to talk with someone else, a worker from the children's protection
service. The teenager became agitated and hesitant. She asked the
pastor not to tell anyone else, that she could get into big trouble,
that she thought she could trust him not to tell, that if her dad
found out he would kill her. She said that she just wanted the
pastor to make it stop.

The pastor acknowledged her fear of others knowing and continued to explain to her why it was so important that other people
who could help be told. They talked for a long time, and finally the
teenager began to understand that getting her father to stop abusing her meant that other people had to help too. She called the
children's protection service from the pastor's office. He remained
with her while she was interviewed by the worker. She went to stay
with a family from the church for two weeks while the CPS investigated the situation and prepared to prosecute the father. The
father called the pastor and in a rage threatened to see that the
pastor was fired. He threatened legal action against the pastor for
interfering in his family affairs. The father was convicted and was
ordered into treatment. Having completed a two-year program,
the family is considering reuniting. The father has returned to the
church and now expresses appreciation to the pastor for confronting his behavior, which he now sees was destroying his family.

The pastor maintained his pastoral relationship, though sometimes strained, with the teenager, the father, and the other family
members throughout this period of disclosure and treatment.
About three months into the treatment process, with the permission of the teenager, the mother, and the father, the pastor shared
this situation with the elders of the church so that they could be

supportive to this family. During the next year the teenager talked with her youth group about her experience so that they could understand what she had been going through. They were very supportive and helpful to her. Subsequently, two more teenagers in similar situations came forward to seek the help of the pastor. The secret of the incestuous abuse had been broken, but the trust of the pastor in his role was maintained. Healing began for the teenage girl. Repentance became a real possibility for the father.

This composite story illustrates the conflict of obligations that many clergypersons feel when faced with information about abuse within a family and also the possibilities of utilizing the available systems to have the most positive and lasting impact on a destructive situation. These situations are never easy or straightforward. They are always complex and time-consuming. But the pastor can play a vital role in supporting the efforts of those who have been harmed to break through the secrecy and get help. Clearly there are many opportunities for judgment calls, and there is seldom a single clear and unambiguous option. But what is important is clarity of purpose: to protect the one who is victimized by the actions of another and to hold the offender accountable. Confidentiality then becomes a means to accomplishing this end rather than a means to sustain the secret of the abuse.

"The premises supporting confidentiality are strong, but they cannot support practices of secrecy—whether by individual clients, institutions, or professionals—that undermine and contradict the very respect for persons and for human bonds that confidentiality was meant to protect."[4] The utilization of reporting of child abuse should be viewed in this context rather than as a challenge to the principle of pastoral confidentiality. It can be a means to assisting a clergyperson to fulfill his or her responsibility to the persons whom he or she serves. Hence the expectations of mandatory reporting and the expectations of pastoral confidentiality may not be as contradictory as they at first appear.

REPORTING THE MISTREATMENT OF MINORS AND VULNERABLE ADULTS

MARY D. PELLAUER, BARBARA CHESTER, JANE A. BOYAJIAN

Abuse and neglect of children and vulnerable adults are against the law. In most if not all states, the law makes it mandatory for most people who work with children or vulnerable adults to report suspected abuse (physical or sexual) and neglect to the authorities. A vulnerable adult includes those residing in facilities required to be licensed and those "unable or unlikely to report abuse without assistance because of impairment of mental or physical function or emotional status."

Physical Abuse includes injuries or patterns of injuries that are nonaccidental. They may include injuries resulting from severe shaking or beating, burns, human bites, broken bones, strangulation, or serious internal injuries.

Physical Neglect is the withholding of or failure to provide the minor or vulnerable adult with the basic necessities of life, such as food, clothing, shelter, medical care, or attention to hygiene.

Sexual Abuse includes the exploitation of a child or vulnerable adult for the gratification of the adult or significantly older child (such as a babysitter). It may range from exhibitionism and fondling to intercourse and the use of children in the production of pornographic materials.

Mandatory Reporting is often a key factor in securing intervention in the abuse or neglect of children or vulnerable adults. If you have contact with or responsibility for children in your work, you are probably mandated to report any suspected abuse. Laws vary from state to state, but statutes are particularly directed at persons in the following areas:

- the healing arts—doctors and nurses
- social services—social workers, probation agents
- hospital administration—emergency room admitting personnel, directors of hospitals
- psychiatric or psychological treatment—counselors, psychiatrists, psychiatric social workers, psychologists
- childcare—employees in day-care centers and nurseries

- education—teachers, school counselors, coaches
- law enforcement—police officers

In many states, clergy are included among those professionals who must make a mandatory report; in other states, clergy are exempt from mandatory reporting. Check the situation in your state. However, even in jurisdictions with a general clergy exemption, it is not generally considered to apply outside of the confessional relationship between penitent and confessor. Thus, ordained persons who are social workers, teachers, or day-care directors, for instance, are considered mandatory reporters even though they are ministers.

However, anyone may voluntarily report any case of suspected abuse. The editors of this volume strongly encourage reporting suspected abuse of children or vulnerable adults to the proper authorities. Experience has shown that reporting is often virtually the only way to achieve protection of the child.

Who takes the report? Each state has a designated agency or agencies. Some states maintain a hotline with a toll-free telephone number. In other states, the local child protection agency or police department is the appropriate agency. Check the situation in your home state.

In some states, anonymous reporting is possible. In other states, if you are a mandated reporter, you must reveal your identity when you report suspected abuse. Especially in states where there are legal penalties for mandated reporters who fail to report, revealing your identity is crucial so that there is a record that you have fulfilled your legal responsibility. Your name remains private information while the case is being investigated; unless it is necessary to employ some judicial proceeding that requires your testimony, your name is not released.

If you are a mandatory reporter, you must report your suspicions personally. Reporting suspected abuse to your supervisor does not relieve you of your individual duty to report the case to the appropriate authority in your area.

When reporting, provide as much clear and specific factual information as you have at your disposal. Reports should contain the identity of the child or vulnerable adult, the identity of the person responsible for the child or vulnerable adult, the nature and extent of injuries, specific instances in which you have observed or have had reason to believe abuse or neglect is occurring. If you observe a child over a period of time, it may be useful to write down such factual information, including dates and times of your observations.

Do not attempt to investigate the case on your own. Let the proper authorities do the investigating. Do not wait to see if you can find out more information or if it will happen again. Most importantly, do not contact the child's parents.

You are immune from civil liability if you provide a good faith report—that is, a report based on the information available to you, a report that is not knowingly false or recklessly or maliciously made.

Authorities are required by law to initiate investigations within twenty-four hours of the receipt of a report.

If you are in doubt about provisions of the laws regarding child abuse and neglect, call the appropriate agency in your areas to discuss it with them.

18. Responding to Clients Who Have Been Sexually Exploited by Counselors, Therapists, and Clergy

JEANETTE HOFSTEE MILGROM AND GARY R. SCHOENER

What brought me to the Walk-In Counseling Center . . . was an incident with a minister that really botched up my faith, my church, my family, a lot. I worked with him in committees, running education at our church, and he would counsel me off and on . . . This happened seven years ago . . . We had one sexual involvement. And my husband and I sought counseling after that. He (the minister) told me not to tell anybody about it. And I held it for a long time.

Excerpt from victim testimony

This article will address the problem of sexual exploitation of clients by counselors, therapists, and clergy. The widespread extent of this problem, and the serious effect it can have on clients, are only recently being recognized. Fortunately, awareness is growing among helping professionals as well as the public at large.

The religious community is demonstrating insight into the problem, as evidenced by written publications. *The Problem Clergymen Don't Talk About* (by Charles L. Rassieur) and *Sexual Contact by Pastors and Pastoral Counselors in Professional Relationships* (by the Washington Association of Churches) are examples. In addition, the 1985 *Legislative Report* by the Minnesota Task Force on Sexual Exploitation by Counselors and Therapists states:

Members of the clergy are sought out for both psychological and spiritual counseling, affording them the opportunity for great power and influence with their counselees. The cases of sexual exploitation by clergy handled by Walk-In Counseling Center and described by victims at the public hearing of the task force (Nov. 12, 1984) indicate the importance of an organized approach to the problem within the clergy. Also, as trusted advisors to whom many people turn in time of crisis, and who are often the continuing resource throughout the life of a counselee, the clergy are in a position to provide support to members of their congregation who have been sexually exploited by other counselors.

A number of clergymen from several denominations testified at the public hearing about the problem of sexual exploitation among their profession. . . .

Sexual exploitation refers to a wide range of behaviors, including erotic talk, seductive behavior, kissing, fondling, as well as sexual intercourse. Counselors and therapists include social workers, psychiatrists, marriage and family counselors, drug and alcohol abuse counselors, psychologists, and clergy involved in pastoral counseling. In order to avoid repetition, the term *counselor* will be used to refer to all the above professions. The terms *client* and *counselee* will be used interchangeably. The emphasis will be on how clergy can respond to clients who tell them about an incident or series of incidents of sexual or erotic involvement with a previous counselor.

THE PROBLEM

The problem of sexual exploitation of clients by counselors is best understood as being similar to incest. What takes place is not so much an expression of human sexuality. It is rather a misuse of power and a breach of trust by the counselor. The counselee often is in a vulnerable state at the time of seeking counseling. For the counselor to initiate sexual activities, to create an erotic atmosphere, or even to allow the client to behave in a seductive manner without pointing out to the client that this is not the purpose of counseling, is unprofessional and unethical in all cases.

Surveys of mental health professionals show that 10 percent of those who respond admit to erotic behavior with clients; in addition, 5 percent report having been involved in sexual intercourse with clients. Here again, there is a similarity to incest in terms of a widespread problem rather than a few isolated incidents as assumed a decade or two ago.

The effects of sexual exploitation on clients can be devastating and long lasting, which is, again, similar to the effects of incest.

EFFECTS ON CLIENTS OR COUNSELEES

Clients who have been sexually involved with a counselor share common feelings. Guilt and shame about the sexual involvement, or guilt felt in connection with a relationship with a spouse or significant other, may be expressed. Many, perhaps all, clients blame themselves. Guilt may center on feelings of having been seductive, or having ruined the counselor's life or career. Some clients are almost obsessed with feelings of responsibility to the point of totally ignoring the fact that the professional counselor is supposed to be in charge and acting only in the client's best interest.

Grief reactions may occur in clients because of the loss and termination of the counseling or personal relationship. The client may have felt dependent on the counselor, so that loss may be a major reaction. Some clients need assistance handling this grief, and some may refuse to separate from the therapist, especially if the relationship has been lengthy and intense.

The client may feel angry about a variety of things: the violation of trust; having been deprived of much-needed counseling during a vulnerable period in her or his life; having left counseling in worse shape than before because of the new burden of confusion; having wasted a critical period in one's life by being focused on a relationship that couldn't last; and having the counselor set up all the rules.

Loss of self-esteem due to the sexual involvement is common. Depression can be severe, to the point of contemplating suicide. The client may feel worthless, since the counselor who knew a great deal about the client later rejected her or him.

Ambivalence and confusion are to be expected on the part of the client. Many clients feel they received some benefit from the counselor. They have a hard time matching their appreciation for the help received with their other feelings. Clients are confused about whether the counselor really cared or meant evil. And clients are confused about themselves and what the sexual involvement said about them.

Fear is another common reaction among sexually exploited clients. They may fear their own impulses to contact the previous counselor in order to express anger, concern, or regret. They may fear rejection by their spouse, family, friends, or the community for having been involved in an illicit sexual relationship. They fear not being believed and being considered vindictive if they report the exploitation. And they fear possible reprisal by the counselor, who in many cases told them never to talk about the sexual relationship with anyone else.

Distrust toward subsequent helping professionals is to be expected from the sexually exploited client, and rightfully so. Since the client's trust was severely abused by the exploitative counselor, the client does well to be cautious when contacting a subsequent counselor. This distrust should be accepted and the client commended for taking care of herself or himself.

WHO ARE THE CLIENTS OR COUNSELEES?

There is no "typical client" likely to be sexually exploited by a counselor. Clients who are victimized cover the range of ages, from children and adolescents to older adults. They include married and single people. Some are not well educated, while others are highly educated. They range from emotionally vulnerable to generally well-adjusted individuals. Women predominate, but there are also male victims. The only thing sexually exploited clients have in common is that they sought counseling and happened upon a sexually exploitative counselor.

WHO ARE THE COUNSELORS?

There are certain categories of sexually exploitative counselors. Counselors, like other human beings, can be subject to poor judgment on occasion. Those counselors who basically function in a professional and ethical manner generally recognize their mistake of overinvolvement with a counselee before too much harm is done and find a resolution for the client and themselves. Other counselors are so self-centered that they don't recognize they are abusing their clients and continue to do so. Yet other counselors are themselves out of touch with reality and carried away with their own power.

RESPONDING TO THE CLIENT WHO HAS BEEN SEXUALLY ABUSED

Following are some guidelines for pastoral counselors to consider in the process of aiding clients abused by previous counselors.

Awareness. Being aware of the problem of sexual abuse of clients by helping professionals is the first step toward helping these clients. Many people do not understand the extent of the power imbalance in the counseling relationship or the degree to which the counselee is vulnerable. More than in cases of rape or incest, the victim may not be viewed as a victim.

Looking for signals and asking questions. The sexually exploited client may tell the pastoral counselor about prior abuse or may communicate this indirectly by showing depression, keeping at a distance, or being distrustful. The pastoral counselor may want to ask if there was any abuse by previous counselors, just as the pastoral counselor may want to inquire about other sexual abuse or family violence.

Listening to the client. It is important to listen carefully to the counselee who relates a story of having been sexually exploited by a counselor. The pastoral counselor needs to determine how the counselee interpreted the incident or relationship. The counselee may, in retrospect, see the sexual involvement as an "affair," or supposedly as part of therapy, or even as "a relationship that was made in heaven" (quote from a client). In order for the pastoral counselor to understand the counselee, listening is the first step.

Believing the client. The pastoral counselor may assume that in the majority of cases the counselee is probably giving a reasonably accurate account of events.

Not assuming particular client reactions. The pastoral counselor's personal reaction to the situation described by the sexually exploited counselee may differ from the counselee's reaction. For example, sexual intercourse may seem like a more serious abuse of a client than erotic talk or suggestive behavior. However, the client may be more thoroughly confused by the latter.

Not overreacting to the client. The pastoral counselor may feel indignant and angry toward the previous, abusive counselor. However, in many cases the client is ambivalent and still has positive feelings toward the previous counselor. The pastoral counselor needs to accept the client's mixed feelings while pointing out that the behavior on the part of the previous counselor was unethical.

Assessing the client's life situation. The client who comes to the pastoral counselor and tells about sexual exploitation may be in crisis, especially if the exploitation was severe and recent. In addition, the client may have marital problems, job or economic stresses, or health problems. If the client is severely distressed, depressed, and possibly suicidal, referral to a psychiatrist or a mental health crisis intervention service may be in order.

Exploring the client's wants and needs. After any life-threatening situations on the part of the client have been taken care of, the pastoral counselor may explore with the counselee the direction in which she or he wants to proceed. It is important to communicate to counselees that they have choices, and that a number of options exist for dealing with their previous exploitation and arriving at a renewed equilibrium in their lives.

In our practice with clients, we like to use the image of a "Wheel of Options"—a circle with the client at the center. Around the wheel are the choices before the client. Each is equally valuable; there is no linear hierarchy among these options for the client. These options include:

- Writing or calling the ex-counselor to express feelings.
- Confrontation or processing session, face to face with the excounselor. (We recommend having a third party present as moderator.)
- Reporting to county or state authorities.
- Individual or group therapy.
- Complaint to the ethics committee of the excounselor's professional association.
- Civil suit for damages.
- Licensure complaint for those professionals who are licensed.
- Criminal complaint.[1]
- Do nothing.
- Notifying agency director (or church hierarchy).

Taking some kind of action often helps the client to put the situation behind her or him. All of these options are possible actions which may be satisfying and therapeutic for the client. The pastoral counselor may or may not assist the client in any of these options. However, getting the client in touch with resources to aid in taking such actions is important.

Resources for the client. Resources for the exploited client vary depending on the community. The client's personal support network may include friends, a parent, sometimes the spouse or co-workers. Self-help groups with which the client has a previous relationship (such as Alcoholics Anonymous and Alanon) may be appropriate.

A lawyer referral service may assist a client in selecting an attorney specializing in this type of case. A community mental health center may be available for subsequent therapy. The local chapter of the Mental Health Association may know of additional referral resources for the client. Rape and sexual assault counseling services may also be available to the client. A support or therapy group for those who have been sexually exploited by their counselors can be of great help; if such a group is not available, it can be formed.

THE SPECIAL CASE OF THE CLIENT
EXPLOITED BY CLERGY

When the client has been sexually abused by her or his pastoral counselor, this has additional ramifications. The client may distrust this and other religious counselors. In addition, the client's faith may be severely shaken. The client is likely to stay away from church. She or he may withdraw from the social contacts and activities related to the church and become quite isolated.

The pastoral counselor contacted by a client exploited by another minister may have difficulty dealing with the implications. If the transgressor is affiliated with one's own religious community, this tends to be a more painful matter than if it were a different helping professional, such as a social worker or psychologist.

SUPPORT AND RESOURCES FOR THE
PASTORAL COUNSELOR

Responding to the sexually exploited client can be stressful. The confidential nature of the matter limits the type of people with whom the pastoral counselor can discuss the situation. However, it is important not to do this work in isolation. The pastoral counselor needs at least one other person to ventilate to and share his or her indignation, frustration, successes, and failures in dealing with the situation. This person likely should be a pastor in the same denomination.

Building a professional network for dealing with sexual exploitation of clients is helpful. The pastoral counselor may want to consult with a therapist, a lawyer, or an agency administrator. Information may be obtained from professional organizations such as the National Association of Social Workers (NASW), State Psychological Association, or State Psychiatric Society. In short, by seeking support and consulting with resource persons the pastoral counselor can lighten the burden for himself or herself and be of most benefit to the exploited client.

PREVENTION OF SEXUAL EXPLOITATION

Sexual exploitation can have a traumatic and devastating effect on the client and her or his family, as well as on the offending pastoral counselor and the congregation as a whole. Preventive strategies within religious communities could include: addressing in seminary classes the issues of sexual attraction and the pastor's power over the counselee; offering seminars on all kinds of sexual abuse, including abuse by counselors; emphasizing self-care for the pastoral counselor so he or she is less likely to feel needy and look to clients to meet his or her needs; and early assistance for the pastoral counselor who is about to engage in unethical behavior. Sexual exploitation of clients is preventable. Like other helping professionals, clergy need to take active efforts to minimize its occurrence.

Awareness of the damaging effects of sexual exploitation by counselors is growing. Healing for clients may be facilitated by other professionals. Awareness of the patterns and of effective responses is crucial.

CLIENT BILL OF RIGHTS[2]

Clients have rights in the following areas:

COMPETENCY

Counselors or therapists must have specified formal training in order to be licensed or certified in the field of sexual assault.

CONFIDENTIALITY

Counselors and therapists are required to keep all information about you confidential unless you give written permission to tell someone else, with the exception of laws that mandate the reporting of child abuse and/or abuse of a vulnerable adult.

PROFESSIONAL FEES

Counselors and therapists should be willing to discuss their fees with you and to come to a clear understanding of costs for other associated services.

SEXUAL BEHAVIOR

Counselors and therapists should not, under any circumstances, be involved with you in any sexual manner. This could include sexual intercourse, kissing, touching breasts or genitals by either you or the counselor/therapist. Counselors and therapists should not "date" you or be in any way romantically involved with you. They should not suggest being sexual with you or verbally demean you in a sexual way.

CONFLICT OF INTEREST

Counselors and therapists should not work with you if you are a friend, relative, employer, or otherwise closely associated.

DATA PRIVACY

Counselors and therapists should provide access to your own records. They or their staff should be available to assist you in explaining written material and answering your questions.

COMPLAINT PROCEDURE

If you feel that any of the aforementioned rights have been violated in any way, you may take the following steps:

1. You may confront or tell the individual with whom you have a complaint how you feel about the way you have been treated.

2. If you are not satisfied with the response or feel that you cannot speak directly with that person, you can request a meeting with that individual's immediate supervisor. The supervisor may ask or assist you in putting your complaint into writing. You or the supervisor may request a meeting with all participants involved.

3. If you feel that the outcome of this meeting is unsatisfactory, you may ask to speak with the executive director of the clinic with which the counselor is associated.

4. You may send a written copy of your complaint to the Board of Directors of the clinic.

5. If the nature of your grievance or complaint is an illegal behavior, you may wish to file a police report or take civil action.

19. What Can the Church Do?[1]

PEGGY HALSEY

A major social problem is making itself known to us. A first step is the intentional breaking of the silence. We must speak about these issues, taking the initiative as both clergy and laity in saying the words—rape, incest, child sexual abuse, battering. We must make it clear that we see the church as a refuge for people who are hurting and an entirely appropriate place for these issues to be addressed. We must find ways to demonstrate that the church is a place where people can feel confident in turning first, not last, for comfort and healing.

A church committed to breaking the silence and offering effective ministry to church and community members experiencing sexual and domestic violence has a number of concrete options for action. All should be entered into thoughtfully, after careful discussion in appropriate committees and groups. In a local congregation, there are several groups which might initiate such efforts, working as appropriate with the others: committees on mission, women's organizations, committees on social responsibility or on family ministries.

1. *Set up a study group* or groups in the church to work on self-education on issues of sexual and domestic violence and to take leadership for promoting awareness of these issues throughout the congregation. Contact programs in the community or region that address these issues for resource suggestions; they may be eager to send a speaker to meet with your group.

2. *Reexamine the theological messages* that are being communicated in your church through sermons, Bible study, and church school curriculum. Is sexual hierarchy implied? (Do teachings assume that men have God-given authority over women and that wives should be subordinate to their husbands?) Is it assumed that children are the property of their parents and that physical abuse of children is justified by such scriptures as "Spare the rod and spoil

the child"? (In fact, the rod referred to in that Proverb is the shepherd's rod, used to guide sheep, never to hit them.)

Consider sponsoring a Bible study series that examines such themes as marriage as a covenant relationship and the religious community's mandate to be a refuge for those in trouble. Ask your pastor or other trained resource persons to assist in exploring the implication for victims of other religious issues as the meaning of suffering, confession and forgiveness, reconciliation and restitution.

3. *Sponsor an educational event or series of events for the church or community.* Most communities have experts on sexual assault or sexual abuse who are eager to contribute to public awareness. A panel made up of such persons as a social worker, a mental health professional, a crisis line or shelter worker, a chaplain or pastoral counselor, a police officer or hospital worker familiar with violence in the community, could be extremely helpful. Adequate time should be allowed for questions. Excellent films on these issues are also available and can be used effectively in educational events.

4. *Assess the resources currently available in your community.* You may be surprised to find rape crisis lines, child abuse prevention programs, shelters for battered women. Even if such direct services are not available, you may find counselors, police, medical, legal, and pastoral professionals who have developed programs and services for victims and offenders. Make certain that your pastor and other pastors in the community are aware of these services and that their availability is widely publicized.

5. *Set up peer support groups.* One of the most devastating consequences of sexual abuse is the isolation victims experience; most believe that they are alone, that no one else has the same problem. The church can provide a valuable service to these persons by forming groups where women who are abused or have been raped can come together to share their experiences and support each other in making decisions about living a healthy life. Similar groups can be formed for adults who were incest victims as children, or for battered women. Such peer support groups may be open to both church members and to persons from the wider community. A trained resource person should be consulted for assistance in setting up such groups. Check with area women's

centers, universities, mental health centers, and pastoral care centers for such resource persons.

6. *Volunteer your services* to existing programs such as crisis centers and shelters. Most are in constant need of committed dependable volunteers and would probably welcome a group of volunteers that could take responsibility for its own recruitment, scheduling, and substitutions. Be sure to ask for, even to insist on, training before beginning work as volunteers.

7. *Initiate new programs* to fill gaps in services identified in community assessment. Move cautiously in this area, undertaking new programs as a single congregation only if an ecumenical or community coalition is impossible. The more broadly based the effort, the better the chances for viability and effectiveness. In addition to the peer support groups mentioned above, the following services may be ones that your church can initiate:

- A telephone crisis line for reporting rape, battering, incest, or child abuse, and for making referrals to community resources.
- "Safe homes" for battered women and their children, where families volunteer to temporarily house women and children leaving abusive situations. Safe homes are usually an alternative to establishing a shelter, particularly appropriate for rural communities where security and transportation may be drawbacks to a shelter.
- A residential shelter for abused women and their children. This is a massive undertaking (as, to some degree, are all of these) and requires careful planning. Outside assistance should be sought, especially from groups who have experience in developing shelter programs.
- Programs for offenders. Increasing numbers of local communities have programs for batterers, sex offenders, and child abusers. Insofar as these issues are crimes, it is important to work together with professional resources in your community.
- Crisis nurseries and childcare centers where parents in imminent danger of abusing their children may leave them safely while they seek assistance with their problem.

8. *Become advocates for prevention* of sexual and domestic violence in your church and community. Press for training of local police and hospital personnel. Monitor public school sex education pro-

grams for quality and inclusion of abuse prevention in curriculum.

Provide training for church school teachers in identifying abuse and in teaching abuse prevention. Strengthen family life education programs in the church, focusing on equality and nonviolent conflict resolution. Urge your pastor to include explorations of anger, conflict, power, and violence in his or her premarriage counseling sessions and in sermons. Provide your pastor with continuing education opportunities in these areas.

Press for including such issues in the seminary training of church workers, both ordained clergy and lay professionals. Sponsor resolutions regarding the church's role in sexual and domestic violence at your regional or national denominational meetings.

20. Resources for Ritual and Recuperation

MARY D. PELLAUER, BARBARA CHESTER, JANE A. BOYAJIAN

In pain or in health, a human person is a rich and many-layered tapestry. A person is always a complicated and multidimensional being, with aspects of the self interlaced and interwoven. As we have tried to exemplify in the many essays above, the wounds made by violence and abuse are not only on the surface but extend into the depths of the self. While the trust relationships of support-ive counseling may extend into these depths, still other resources may be needed to touch and move us in ways as rich and many-layered as is the whole person. Poetry, music, song, images, sym-bols, rituals, prayer—all operate in these complex intertwined ways. While we cannot always explain or articulate why they work as they do, we know that these forms touch us in special ways. They are not like information, concepts, or ordinary "talk." They in-volve the whole self. They nourish and refresh us with a surplus of meaning.

Frequently the symbols and rituals of established or traditional religious communities offend and harm women. As the essay "Don't Tell Mother," pp. 62–66, poignantly notes, for many vic-tims male language for the divine, like God the Father, may echo victimization and oppression. For other women, such traditional rituals may simply be irrelevant, not communicating with the depths of our lives. Traditional religious practices by and large have not even included the experiences explored in this book, let alone spoken from and to them with perceptiveness and power. Our religious communities do not feature a vast array of song, poetry, prayer, and litany from the experiences of rape and sexual assault, child sexual abuse and incest, sexual harassment, batter-ing, and other violence.

We desperately need such resources. We need them to express

and transform the anguish and the hope, the pains and the longings. We need them to connect these experiences with the breadths and depths of all that is or could be. We need them to move us to weep, to rejoice, to act. We need them to embody the terrible beauty of the experiences of survivors. We need them to bless us as we struggle.

We provide here only a sample of the kinds of resources emerging. There are litanies, psalms adapted to the experiences of victims, devotional readings on selected scripture texts. Some of these are explicitly Christian, including references to Jesus Christ or to trinitarian formulas. Some are more neutral, adaptable to varying settings such as a women's ritual community or a Christian worship setting. We include a ceremony of purification from a Native American tradition, with an explanation by its compiler. Some of these resources express anger; others express desolation, consolation, determination, oneness, and communion with the whole or with the spirits. This whole range of feelings and of spiritual options feels important to us. We are not concerned about whether this material is "orthodox." We must reach for a wide range of spiritual insights, methods, and resources for nurturing and invoking our powers of life and celebration.

The flexibility of several of these forms is built into them. Litanies may be used for private meditation; psalms may be cast for community use. We encourage readers to take advantage of this adaptability, revising such forms to suit the concrete needs of your situation. We hope that these materials will be put to use in your lives and communities. Creativity is found both in generating novel resources and in connecting resources created elsewhere to specific circumstances.

And we must create more. We hope that you will sample from this small selection, adapt and use these materials in your own life and work, and be sparked to create and share your own resources.

Litanies, Psalms, and Songs

LITANY OF CONFESSION

PHILADELPHIA TASK FORCE ON WOMEN AND RELIGION

LEADER: We confess that we have failed to love ourselves.

PEOPLE: We remember that we have looked on our own bodies with dislike and distrust. We have denied our own feelings. We have confused assault with flattery.

L: We confess our failure to touch each other with love.

P: We remember the trap of secrecy that kept us from sharing our fear and pain. We remember that we believed violence could only happen to other women. We remember that we believed we were responsible for preventing rape and that we suspected those who were raped.

L: We confess that we have put our trust in men.

P: We remember that we have denied ourselves freedoms in order to buy male protection. We believed ourselves to be helpless. We have not trusted in our own strength and potential.

L: You are now invited to share your own confessions . . . (Silently or aloud individuals may share.)

L: Let us share our confessions of needs.

P: We need to be healed of our pain and sorrow.
We need to be touched with love and with the truth.
We need to trust our bodies.
We need to affirm our feelings, believe in our anger, trust in our loving kindness.
We need to break the locks we have placed on our hearts.
We are ready now to live without our shells.

AFFIRMATION OF FAITH

JULIA EMILY LOUISA PEEBLES

LEADER: We trust that beyond the absence:

WOMEN: there is a presence.

L: That beyond the pain:

W: there can be healing.

L: That beyond the brokenness:

W: there can be wholeness.

L: That beyond the hurting:

W: there may be forgiveness.

L: That beyond the silence:

W: there may be the word.

L: That through the word:

W: there may be understanding.

ALL: That through understanding: there is love.

A CELEBRATION OF SOLIDARITY

MARY PELLAUER

LEADER: In the name of God who created and is creating, who redeemed and is redeeming, who sanctified and is sanctifying, us and the whole world.

PEOPLE: Amen.

CONFESSION

L: We confess that by our thoughts, words, and deeds, we have turned away from life; we have limited ourselves to meager life; we have chosen many small deaths.

P: Forgive us, Lord.

L: We confess that we have offered our sisters and brothers stones when they asked for bread; that we have looked away from the needy; that we have given death instead of life.

P: Forgive us, Lord.

L: We confess that we have not lived in the Source of Life; we have not believed in the Word of Life; we have not had the Spirit of Life.

P: Forgive us, Lord.

L: Jesus said, "Courage, your faith has made you whole. Go in peace and be healed." Again in other healing stories, Jesus said, "Your sins are forgiven."

P: As our sin has been forgiven and we have been made whole, let us praise and celebrate that abundant life which was promised us, which we claim for our own and for the whole community of God's people.
(At this point litanies or songs of praise, liturgical dance, or offerings may be used.)

A LITANY OF THE WORD

Reading: Matthew 25:31–46.

RIGHT: I was hungry and you gave me bread.

LEFT: I was thirsty and you gave me drink.

R: I was a stranger and you welcomed me.

L: I was naked and you clothed me.

R: I was sick and you visited me.

L: I was in prison and you came to me.

R: I was raped and you stood by me.

L: I was beaten and you sheltered me.

R: I was harassed and you helped me act.

L: I was abused and you intervened.

R: I was in pain and you comforted me.

L: I was bleeding and you staunched my wound.

R: I was orphaned and you mothered me.

L: I was alone and you took my hand.

R: I was unworthy and you believed in me.

L: I was victimized and you empowered me.

R: I was confused and you brought insight.

L: I was silent and you listened to me.

R: I was seeking and you searched with me.

L: I was knocking and you opened the door.
    (A communion meal may be served at this time.)

PSALM 137: AN INTERPRETATION

GAIL BURRESS, AMELIE RATLIFF, AND LIZ SHELLBERG

READER 1: By the waters of Babylon . . .

READER 2: Babylon, land of forced exile, of powerlessness
           Babylon, being enslaved by another people
           There is no control.

READER 3: Babylon, living in powerlessness
           Terrorized in our homes and on the streets
           In the media and in education;
           the bedrooms, the newspapers, the cars, the shop-
           ping centers.
           Babylon, our work is for others and not for ourselves.
           There is no control.

R 1: There we sat down and wept, when we remembered Zion
      . . .

R 2: Weeping for our remembered home, our faith, our way of
      living.
      Weeping for the lost freedom of our people.

R 3: Weeping for the home we have never had.

Weeping because of our oppression,
Because of the violence against our bodies, our minds, and
our spirits.
Weeping for the hope of freedom for our kind.

R 1:   On the willows there we hung up our lyres.
For our captors there required of us songs,
And our tormentors, mirth,
Saying, "Sing us one of the songs of Zion!"

R 2:   The Babylonians would exploit the expressions of our faith,
our hymns, our prayers.
Our captors would rob us of our lullabies, the poetry, art,
and all the creativeness of our people,
The best of our thinking.
Our tormentors would have us dance and sing for them
rather than for Yahweh.
They would have us laugh.

R 3:   The Patriarchs would program the expressions of our being
and faith:
"God is Father, Son, and Holy Ghost . . ."
"All men are created equal . . ."
They have allowed us no songs, no prayers,
And we have sung their songs with full voice.
Our husbands, our fathers, our lovers, our brothers, uncles,
and cousins use our bodies for their pleasure and their
progeny.
They use our love and gentleness to oppress us,
They stifle our creativeness, the best of our thinking.
For the love and favors of our oppressors
And for lack of love for ourselves, we do not resist.

R 3:   Our oppressors put their feet on our necks by building
pedestals and whorehouses,
Insulting, beating, and raping us.
They ask if we enjoy it.

R 1:   On the willows there, we hung up our lyres.
For how can we sing the Lord's song in a foreign land?

R 2:   No! We cannot and will not go against our tradition, our
faith,

We cannot accept the injustices to our people and our children.
No! We cannot break our covenant with God.

R 3: No! We cannot and will not settle for traditional definitions of who we are and how we are to act.
We will not prostitute ourselves for money, for security, for the approval of our oppressors.
We cannot accept the injustices to ourselves, our sisters, and our children.
No! We cannot deny our faith and vision for the future.

R 1: How shall we sing the Lord's song in a foreign land?
If I forget you, O Jerusalem, let my right hand wither!

R 2: We must keep the covenant with Yahweh.
How can we remember our home, our faith, our way of living while in exile?
How will our children learn the ways of justice?

R 3: We must carry on the struggle of our sisters before us.
But how can we sing our own song:
    when we have no voice,
    when our voices are not heard,
    when we speak in the words of our captors,
    when we have no words of our own?
How will we and our children learn the ways of justice?

R 1: Let my tongue cleave to the roof of my mouth, if I do not remember you,
If I do not set Jerusalem above my highest joy!

R 2: Take away our tongues if we do not sing and proclaim
    the faith of our ancestors,
    the trust that we are not abandoned,
    the longing for our homes.
May we remain prisoners, if we relax in our captivity and acquiesce to our oppressors,
If we do not remember Jerusalem, our home, and Yahweh, our God, above all else,
May we perish in exile.

R 3: Take away our voices if we do not give voice
    to the truth of our past,

the reality of our present,
and the hope of our future.
May we remain victims, if we relax in our captivity and
acquiesce to our oppressors.
If we do not remember into the future the home we have
never had.
May we remain isolated in the homes of others.

HUNGER AND HOPE

BARBARA LUNDBLAD

Central to our new understandings of sexual assault and abuse
have been the stories told by victims. The images of this song
express in a new theological vein some of the meanings of telling
such new and old stories. It is dedicated by its author to "our
grandmothers in the flesh and in the faith." The title and refrain
are based on lines from May Sarton's poem, "Love", (from *Halfway
to Silence.*).

One morning when the sun was new
I watched a spider weaving
On my grandmother's porch so long ago;
Against the wind, the weaving,
Fragile threads between the rafters,
And I surely wondered how it could be so.

AND MY GRANDMOTHER TOLD ME
YOU HAVE TO KEEP ON SPINNING
TILL YOU FIND THE PLACE THAT HOLDS YOUR
STORY STRONG.
EV'RY WOMAN IS A WEAVER
SPINNING LIFE AGAINST DESTRUCTION,
IT IS HUNGER, YES, AND HOPE THAT MOVE US ON.
My stories were the spinning,
Fragile threads from deep inside me—
How I longed to spin them out and feel them hold.
"But that makes no sense," he told me,
Each professor, preacher, scholar,
And the web was broken, stories left untold. REFRAIN

One evening when the sun was old,
I dared to spin a thread out
To the edges of a circle without men,
I felt the thread hold tight
Across the room and close beside me,
And I knew I could start spinning once again. REFRAIN

O God, you keep on spinning
Threads of love out of aloneness
And you long to have them hold upon the earth;
O spin within me, through me,
Hold me close against the storming
For both you and I have stories yet to birth. REFRAIN

A SONG FOR RECOVERING WOMEN BASED ON PSALM 20,

DIANA VEZMAR

may yahweh answer you in time of trouble;
may the presence of sister sojourners protect you.

may you receive help from the spirit of wisdom,
and support from mother earth for your journey.
may your story be remembered,
   your pain be healed &
      your wounds be reverenced.
may your heart's desire be granted;
may your dreams be fulfilled and exceeded.
may we shout with joy for your recovery,
& celebrate your victory with song & dance.

may all your longings for persons, nature & nations be fulfilled.

now i know that yahweh shelters those in trouble
& prepares for their recovery
   by empowering them to choose that which is life-giving.

some boast of righteousness, some of salvation;
but we boast about yahweh's shelter & our sisters' presence.
the others may be saved,
but we shall stand, & stand firm.

yahweh, protect our sisters;
answer us when we call.

DEVOTIONS FOR THE SEXUALLY ABUSED

DANIEL M. HOEGER

Scripture: Psalm 22:1–2, 14–15: My God, my God, why have you abandoned me? I have cried desperately for help, but still it does not come. During the day I call to you, my God, but you do not answer, I call at night but get no rest . . . My strength is gone like water spilling on the ground. All my bones are out of joint; my heart is like melted wax. My throat is as dry as dust, and my tongue sticks to the roof of my mouth. You have left me for dead in the dust.

Meditation: Where is God when things go wrong? Where is God in an unjust world? Where is God when someone is sexually abused? Psalm 22 sings a bitter song of being abandoned by God. To ask such questions seems to many people to be almost sinful. "My God, my God, why have you forsaken me?" was also the question of Jesus hanging on the cross. It is a question that must be asked of God, for only God can be responsible for an answer. It is a painful song that God gives us the freedom to sing.

Prayer: God, this is your world. How can it be so terrifying? Are you evil or have you just abandoned us? Where were you during the rape? I ask these questions from a deeply wounded faith. I ache under my pain and ask that you not abandon me. Restore life and meaning to me. Amen.

Scripture: John 9:1–7: As Jesus was walking alone, he saw a man who had been born blind. His disciples asked him, "Teacher, whose sin caused him to be born blind? Was it his own or his parents' sin?" Jesus answered, "His blindness has nothing to do with his sins or his parents' sins. He is blind so that God's power might be seen at work in him. As long as it is day, we must do the work of him who sent me; night is coming when no one can work. While I am in the world, I am the light of the world." After he said this, Jesus spat on the ground and made some mud with the spittle; he rubbed the mud on the man's eyes and told him, "Go and wash your face in the Pool of Siloam." (This name means "sent.") So the man went, washed himself, and came away with his sight restored.

Meditation: Who sinned that I deserved to be sexually abused? Many times people avoid caring, helping, and questioning the world around us by saying, "She must have deserved what she got." When a victim can be found guilty of the crime that has been done against her or him, others are able to dismiss the reality of the injustice. Jesus did not fall into such an easy trap. He answered these questions by restoring the blind man's sight. When asked, "Why is it dark?" he answered by being light.

Prayer: God, you see the wrongs done to those who are oppressed. You do not need to avoid our suffering, for you have the power to make us survivors. As you healed the blind man, come now and heal us. Amen.

Scripture: Matthew 21: 12–13: Jesus went into the Temple and drove out all those who were buying and selling there. He overturned the tables of the moneychangers and the stools of those who sold pigeons, and said to them, "It is written in the Scriptures that God said, 'My Temple will be called a house of prayer' but you are making it a hide-out for thieves!"

Meditation: Anger is a gift from God. Often we are afraid of anger because it is a power that can be misused. But when it is used as a gift, it can be a source of strength for our lives. Righteous anger comes from a love of justice. When Jesus visited the temple in Jerusalem, he saw the injustice of those who corrupted the temple. His anger became action to restore the temple by kicking out the merchants and preaching the truth. When sexual abuse throws lives into confusion, anger can be a gift from God to empower us to restore our lives.

Prayer: God, if you are a god of love and mercy, then you must also feel anger when we are hurt by others. Let our anger become one with yours, and let them be a strength for truth and life. Amen.

Scripture: Ecclesiastes 8:11–14: Why do people commit crimes so readily? Because crime is not punished quickly enough. A sinner may commit a hundred crimes and still live. Oh yes, I know what they say: "If you obey God, everything will be all right, but it will not go well for the wicked. Their life is like a shadow and they will die young because they do not obey God." But this is nonsense. Look at what happens in the world: Sometimes the righteous get the punishment of the wicked, and the wicked get the reward of the righteous. I say it is useless.

Meditation: Our understanding of ourselves and our world can be so clean, shiny, and stable—then out of nowhere, something happens. Like a brick thrown through a window, it shatters our world. Then, where is the purpose? Where is the justice? Our dreams of life vanish. The author of Ecclesiastes understood that sometimes life seems meaningless. Do we need to settle for meaninglessness forever? True, when our illusions are gone, we can no longer afford to be fooled by this life. But we can also become seekers of a new, real, and meaningful life.

Prayer: God, sometimes the uselessness of this life is all too painfully clear. We know that Jesus spoke of a new life and a new kingdom of justice and peace. But comforting words are not enough. We also ask for truth and justice and healing. May your promises be true, may justice roll down like an everflowing stream. Amen.

Scripture: Psalm 69:1–3, 15: Save me, O God! The water is up to my neck; I am sinking in deep mud, and there is no solid ground. I am out in deep water, and the waves are about to drown me. I am worn out from calling for help, and my throat is aching. I have strained my eyes looking for your help . . . Don't let the flood come over me, don't let me drown in the depths or sink into the grave.

Meditation: Suffering can be the most tiring work that we will ever do. It strains our bodies, spirits, and minds. It is a burden that we ourselves must carry. But we do not need to carry it alone. We need to cry out for help. In our time of need we can be gracious receivers of healing.

Prayer: God, we can get so tired from just crying tears. We can even get so tired that it is almost too much even to continue crying for help. Watch over us and hear the sorrows of our hearts. Strengthen us and those around us as we carry our burdens. Grant us peace and rest, that we may continue to live. Amen.

A SERVICE OF HEALING FOR ONE WHO HAS BEEN SEXUALLY ABUSED

PATRICIA WILSON-KASTNER

When searching for a service of healing appropriate for one who has been sexually abused, I was not able to find anything that seemed suitable in either of the liturgical mainstays of the Episcopal tradition, the *Book of Common Prayer* or the *Book of Occasional Services.* Neither the service of reconciliation for the healing services provided touched the particular combinations of issues involved in sexual abuse and its effects.   I composed this service for the pastoral needs of a person who either has been recently abused or is presently coming to terms with the effects of past abuse. The service is intended to provide a structure for the expression of certain needs and processes in the person concerned and in the supportive community. The design of the service allows room— indeed expects—that much relevant to the individual situation will be expressed *ad libitum.* Like the pastoral rite of reconciliation, this service is to be used privately or with a small group of people in supportive relationships with the person who has been abused. Because each case of sexual abuse has its own peculiarities, and because each person who has been abused will be at a different stage in the process of healing, much individual variation will be necessary.

GREETING

LEADER: Grace and peace be with you, from God, through our Savior, Jesus Christ, in the power of the Holy Spirit.

PEOPLE: And also with you.

LEADER: O God, you have taught us that in turning to you we shall be saved, and that you will abundantly grant us your mercy. We ask you to enliven us with a sense of your grace, in order that we may find ourselves renewed in you, our Creator, Redeemer, and Sanctifier. Amen

LITURGY OF THE WORD

One or more of these suggested readings, or others, may be used. Readings from sources other than scripture may be used.

Isa. 52:1–2, 7–10
Ps. 27
Rom. 8:31–39
Luke 23:32–38

At this time a sermon may be preached; opportunity may be given for the person who has been sexually abused to reflect with the community on her or his experience; or silent reflection may take place.

PRAYERS FOR FORGIVENESS

L. N., do you forgive yourself for any part you fear you have played in this abusive relationship, for the doubts and anxieties that have plagued you, for the twisting of all relationships in your life that this abuse has worked in you?

N. I do, with God's help.

L. N., do you, aware of your worth and dignity as one created in God's image, forgive the person(s) who has (have) assaulted you for the pain of body and spirit caused you, for the betrayal of trust, and the damaging of your development as a mature person?

N. I do, with God's help.

L. Do you forgive us, the human and Christian community, for our silence and complicity as individuals and as a society, for allowing this abuse to have happened to you, and for our failures and inadequacies in reaching out to you and healing you when you needed us?

N. I do, with God's help.

L. Let us pray.

ALL. Ever-living and ever-gracious God, you care about the birds of the air and the flowers of the field, and even more about your children whom you have made in your image. We beg your forgiveness and the forgiveness of each other for this violation of your servant's body and spirit. Free us from the results of our hatred, suspicion, fear, and destructive deeds and feelings. Renew us in your Holy Spirit, that we may share in the life our Savior Jesus Christ has come to nurture in us. Amen.

L. The God of hope forgives us for failing each other. Because Christ has freed us, we have been anointed to liberate others. The Holy Spirit of love reigns in our hearts to renew our lives and strengthen our reconciliation.

PRAYERS FOR HEALING

(The community will gather around the person being prayed for with whatever gestures or actions seem appropriate and expressive to the persons concerned.)

L. Let us pray for N.

O God, grant her/him healing of self, to know with assurance that she/he is your child, made in your image, and worthy of your love and compassion.

O God, give her/him freedom from the crippling fear that prevents her/him from reaching out to receive your love and our support.

O God, restore in her/him trust in her/himself and in others, to enable her/him to know and feel you as a sure and constant refuge in in all pain and uncertainty, and us as ready agents of that consolation.

O God, renew in her/him the awareness of being your chosen vessel, a strong bearer of truth and healing to others, a power for compassion and change in bringing about your reign on earth.

(Out loud or in silence, others add appropriate prayers for the healing of this person.)

L. Ever-living and ever-gracious God, we pray in your Holy Spirit for the healing of body and spirit of this your servant, N. Restore her/his broken and distorted feelings, heal the past and present damage of her/his whole person. Renew and refresh her/him. Give wholeness to all that is incomplete or distorted. Teach her/him wisdom and compassion through this suffering. Let her/him know her/his own strength, and be freed to share in your grace with and through us. We ask this, o God, through Jesus Christ in the power of the Holy Spirit. Amen.

BLESSING AND DISMISSAL

L. *Our help is in the name of our God.*

P. Who made heaven and earth, and all who dwell in them.

L. Our strength is God, who made us and heals us.

P. We depend on God, in whose image we are made.

L. Go forth from here in peace, N. The healing and strengthening power of God's Spirit is active in you. The shadow of pain and fear will always walk with you, but it will diminish, as God's love grows and upholds you. We are going with you, in body and in spirit, to live and to labor with you, to struggle and rejoice with you. Living always with us and with you is the God who weeps and suffers with us, who knows your pain, fear, and humiliation, who has shared it on the cross, and who promises you and us the joy of a healing resurrection in which the power of sin and death is forever destroyed.

(If the leader is a bishop or priest, the following blessing, or one more specific to the situation, is added.)

May the blessing of the one and triune God, Creator, Redeemer, and Sanctifier, be with you all now and evermore.

(Rather than having a formal conclusion to the rite, it is suggested that all remain for prayer and a time together, which might well conclude with a common meal or some other tangible sharing of community support.)

PURIFICATION AND HEALING IN THE AMERICAN INDIAN TRADITION

LARRY MENS

Peace . . . comes within our souls when we realize our relationships, our oneness, with the universe and all its powers, and when we realize that at the center of the universe dwells the Creator, and that this center is really everywhere, it is within each of us.[1]

Ceremonies, rituals, and beliefs vary from one American Indian nation to another, often from one Native person to another within the same tribe. Some symbols and beliefs, however, are shared by almost all Native peoples. One of these is an understanding of the power of prayer within the sacred circle to purify, cleanse, heal, and renew. In this essay I wish to describe some of the rituals and symbols from my tradition which may be helpful to victims of sexual assault and abuse, and to offer one possible service of purification and healing.

SWEAT LODGE

Among many of the Plains Indians nations there is a ceremony called the Sweat Lodge, or Inipi in the Lakota Sioux language. This rite is for renewal or spiritual rebirth. In it all four elements —fire, earth, water, and air—contribute to the spiritual, emotional, psychic, and physical purification of the participants. It is used frequently for those in chemical dependency and physical abuse treatment as a way of letting go and letting God take control of one's life. It is also a ritual of connection and healing for women who have experienced physical and sexual abuse.

Within a small, dark, dome-shaped lodge of willow saplings and canvas or hides, there is a small pit filled with rocks already heated in a fire outside the lodge. Sage, cedar, and water are sprinkled over these rocks, causing them to give off steam and heat. Black Elk, a Lakota spiritual elder, explains that the lodge itself represents the universe, with the pit at its center as representative of the navel in which the Great Spirit lives with the power of the sacred fire. The willows represent all that grows from Mother Earth.

These too have a lesson to teach us, for in the fall their leaves die and return to the earth, but in the spring they come to life again. So too [we] die but live again in the real world of Wakan-Tanka, where there is nothing but the spirits of all things; and this true life we may know here on earth if we purify our bodies and minds, thus becoming closer to Wakan-Tanka who is all purity.[2]

The rocks represent the earth, and also the indestructible and everlasting nature of the creator. The water too reflects values for the people to learn from:

When we use water in the sweat lodge, we should think of Wakan-Tanka who is always flowing, giving power and life to everything; we should even be as water which is lower than all things, yet stronger even than the rocks.[3]

Thomas Goldtooth, a Navaho, explains the symbolism of this ritual in a similar way: Crawling on hands and knees into the sweat lodge is like "returning to the womb" as an ignorant and pitiful child. The sacred fire heats the rocks, which are "the ancient ones, the grandparents who have been here before us and will be here after us." The "living water," when poured over the heated rocks, becomes the "breath of life" that cleanses and makes new. After the prayerful ceremony, one leaves the sweat lodge, leaving behind one's sins and troubles, reentering the world as a new person.

THE CIRCLE

One of the symbols that most fully expresses the Native American understanding of the human relationship with the world and the creator is that of the cross within the circle. The elders share teachings about the circle, the four directions, and the center point. They talk of balance, making choices, and centering. These teachings can form a path for one's journey toward wholeness. Black Elk says of the circle:

You have noticed that everything an Indian does is in a circle, and that is because the Power of the World always works in circles, and everything tries to be round. In the old days when we were a strong and happy people, all our power came to us from the sacred hoop of the nation, and so long as the hoop was unbroken, the people flourished. The flowering tree was the living center of the hoop, and the circle of the four quarters nourished it. The east gave peace and light, the south gave warmth, the west gave rain, and the north with its cold and mighty wind gave strength and endurance. This knowledge came to us from the outer world with our religion. Everything the Power of the World does is done in a circle. The sky is round like a ball, and so are all the stars. The wind, in its greatest powers, whirls. Birds make their nests in circles, for theirs is the same religion as ours. The sun comes forth and goes down again in a circle. The moon does the same, and both are round. Even the seasons form a great circle in their changing, and often come back again to where they were. The life of a human is a circle from childhood to childhood; and so it is in everything where power moves. Our teepees were round like the nests of birds, and these were always set in a circle, the nation's hoop, a nest of many nests, where the Great Spirit meant for us to hatch our children.[4]

The circle below represents a model of holistic healing and empowerment, which can be helpful in developing balance and centering in one's life.

Black Elk refers to the teaching of the four directions. Again, these teachings varied from place to place. Sometimes animals, birds, or insects represented the directions—these too varied by clan and nation. Sometimes colors (#1) were used to represent each of the directions. The circle below has the Lakota colors. Sometimes seasons (#2) were ascribed to each direction. But while the teachings (#3) from the four directions varied by place, they often centered on the following understandings:

- East—the new day; the gift of another day, represented by the rising sun, used to walk the spiritual red road, recreation, rebirth
- South—the warmth of the summer sun causing the grasses to grow, the flowers to bloom, the berries to ripen, growth
- West—the darkness of the setting sun, night which sometimes represented the connection with the afterlife, reflection, and dreaming (a combination of left- and right-brain functions)
- North—the cold and mighty winter winds, endurance, and survival

So too we might understand the circle to represent dimensions of the whole person (#4), as with many contemporary therapists; the four basic elements of life (#8) or the stages of the life cycle (#9). Those who are Christian may recognize basic human capacities for

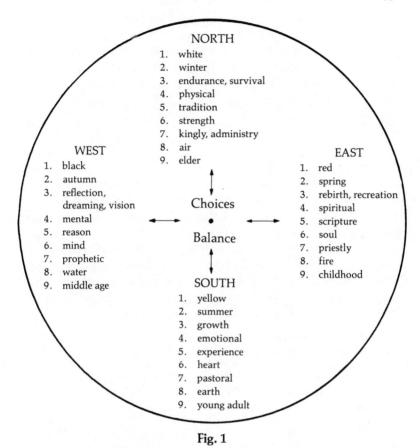

Fig. 1

leading a sacred life (#6) from Jesus' command, "Love the Lord your God with all your heart, with all your soul, with all your mind, and with all your strength" (Mark 12:20), or John Wesley's four cornerstones of faith (#5). Similarly, we may correlate the circle with four aspects of ministry (#7).

The understanding of Native peoples is that the human being stands at the middle of the circle. Every action, every work, is a prayer that affects the family, the clan, the nation, the two-leggeds, the four-leggeds, the wingeds, the water, the air, Mother Earth, and the Great Spirit. Everything is interconnected and interdependent—what goes around, comes around. Within that context, one is to strive for balance in one's walk on the sacred path of life. One can choose to learn the teachings of only one direction. That is okay; no one can judge another's spiritual path choice. But it is understood that wholeness for the universe is achieved when all things are in balance, that healing and renewal come only through centering.

VISION QUEST

Among many Plains Indians nations, there is another life-directing ritual that can be used for purification and recreation. It is called the vision quest. Among the Lakota, the ceremony is carried out in the form of a circle and a cross. A person in search of "vision," seeking wisdom and understanding, attempting to reach union with the Great Spirit (Wakan-Tanka), fasts and prays for one to four days. This is done under the direction of an elder and follows a prescribed ritual. Upon a hill in a sacred place, the person walks a path to each of the four directions and prays:

O Great Spirit, have pity on me, that my people may live!
O Great Spirit, be merciful to me, that my people may live![5]

The person returns to the center between prayers.

Of this ceremony, Black Elk says:

All day long, the "lamenter" sends a voice to the Great Spirit for aid and walks as described upon the sacred paths which form a cross. This form has much power in it, for whenever we return to the center, we know that it is as if we are returning to the Great Spirit who is the center of everything, and although we may think we are going away, so sooner or later we and all things must return.[6]

Through this ritual of prayer and fasting, cleansing, and refocusing, one returns from the hill with dreams and images of new directions and new life to share with the elder.

The teachings outlined above can be combined with other Native American understandings in a spiritual ceremony to cleanse, heal, make whole, and renew the participants who stand together in the sacred circle of prayer. This ritual can be adapted to various settings.

A LITURGY OF CLEANSING, HEALING, AND WHOLENESS

PRAYER OF INVOCATION

(Participants stand in a circle facing the center point. Hands may be joined in the circle, uplifted in prayer. They turn to each of the directions to pray the prayer of that direction.)

LEADER: Many and Great, O God, are your things, maker of earth and sky; grant unto us communion with you, you star-abiding one. Come unto us and dwell with us.[7]

PEOPLE: Come unto us and dwell with us.

L: (facing east) Hear, Spirit of the East, Great Spirit, source of light, place of the sun's rising, from whom the solar eagle flies through the crack of dawn calling us to prayer for a new beginning and a new life. Great Spirit, come as in the beginning, when at the dawning of the world you came, bringing light and illumination, insight, vision, and hope. Come with all the creatures of your direction, with all that gives light and renewal to our spiritual centers.

P: Come, and give to your children what we need.

L: (facing south) Hear, Spirit of the South, Great Spirit of new life and growth, from whose keeping the birds return as they came in the beginning to scatter the seeds of all plants. Spirit of warmth and nourishment and comfort, renew your creative act by making new our emotion-torn hearts.

P: Come, and give to your children what we need.

L: (facing west) Hear, Spirit of the West, Great Spirit of the sun's declining and setting, spirit of wisdom and old age, spirit of the people's past and knowledge they have gained, doorway to the departing, bring understanding and vision to our darkness.

P: Come, and give to your children what we need.

L: (facing north) Hear, Spirit of the North, Great Spirit of the strong winds and the cold, spirit of testing and ordeal, spirit of discipline and cleansing, spirit of healing and strength, come as in the beginning to empower each of us to once more have control over our own bodies, to bring balance and harmony to the world.

P: Come, and give to your children what we need.

L: (facing center) Hear, Father Sky, home of our brother the sun and our sister the moon and of all the wheeling stars, home of the clouds, where the strong thunder begins, home of the rain and snow and the cleansing winds, Great Spirit of the Sky,

P: Come, and give to your children what we need.

L: Hear, Mother Earth, dressed in the green of trees and grasses, decked with the beautiful flowers, through whose veins the waters run and from whose bounty food is given to all, gathering into your arms all creatures large and small,

P: Come, and give to each of us, your children, what we need. Amen.

RITUAL OF PURIFICATION AND RENEWAL

The Leader may speak words of explanation of this ceremony, such as these:

Sweetgrass, sage, and cedar are used by different Native people for cleansing and purification. Pipes are purified with sweetgrass before being used for prayer. Homes are cleansed each morning with prayer while smoke from the sage is brought into each room. Smoke from the cedar can be washed over a person to heal a spiritual, emotional, mental, or physical problem. The teaching is that the scent of sweetgrass, sage, or cedar as it rises on the winds is pleasing to the creator. Good spirits are attracted and bad spirits depart.

Many Indian people use water as part of the morning prayer ritual. The grandfathers and grandmothers share that in the old days, as the sun began to lighten the eastern sky, one journeyed alone to a nearby stream or lake. One washed one's body and let the breath of the creator, the winds, dry the water. While drying one stood, arms lifted to the sky, praying and singing, spirit pouring from the body into the sky to meet a greater spirit above, becoming one with the new light of the new day.

Flute music, or the winds outside, remind us that the song of dawn is also the song of the rainbow, which calls us to complete the circle of life in harmony.

Let us share this ceremony, combining these two traditions into one of cleansing and centering.

(Singly, each walks forward to the bowl of water, washing the physical body with it. Each moves to the burning sweetgrass, sage, or cedar, to cleanse the spiritual self with its healing smoke. Each washes the smoke over the entire body, concentrating on any area that might need special cleansing. As the community shares this ritual, prayers for all or songs of healing are appropriate.)

PRAYER FOR GOING FORTH

L: Great Spirit, Creator, behold us! You have placed a great Power where we always face, and from this direction many generations have come forth and have returned. There is a winged One at this direction who guards the sacred red path, from which the generations have come forth. The generation that is here today wishes to cleanse and purify itself, that it may live again!

P: We have burned the sweetgrass as an offering to you, O God, and the fragrance of this will spread throughout heaven and earth. It will make the four-leggeds, the wingeds, the star peoples of the heavens, and all things, as relatives. From you, O Grandmother Earth, who are lowly, and who supports us as does a mother, from you this fragrance will go forth. May its power be felt throughout the universe. May it purify the feet and hands of the two-leggeds, that we may walk forward upon the sacred earth, raising our heads to the creator! So be it!

ALL: Your spirits,
My spirit,
May they unite to make
One spirit in healing.[8]

APPENDIX

Organizations and Agencies

RELIGIOUS GROUPS

Center for the Prevention of Sexual and Domestic Violence
1914 North 34th Street, Suite 205
Seattle, WA 98103
206–634–1903

Commission on Women and the Church
The United Presbyterian Church in the USA
475 Riverside Drive
New York, NY 10025

The Office of Ministries with Women in Crisis
The United Methodist Church
475 Riverside Drive
New York, NY 10025

Many state or regional denominational offices, and some statewide
or regional ecumenical groups, sponsor task forces or committees
related to sexual violence, family violence, or both. There is unfortunately no simple way to locate or to list these on a nationwide
basis. Ask your own denominational leadership whether your religious community has established such a group and how you might
cooperate with them. Or take the initiative in creating one.

SHELTERS

There are presently more than five hundred women's shelters
across the nation, often organized into statewide coalitions. Frequently states or metropolitan areas maintain regional crisis numbers. For more help in locating a shelter near you, there is a
national listening of shelters: *National Shelter Directory*, from:

National Coalition against Domestic Violence
2401 Virginia Avenue North West, Suite 306
Washington, DC 20037
202–293–8860

CHILD SEXUAL ABUSE AND INCEST: PREVENTION AND TRAINING PROGRAMS

Child Assault Prevention Program
Women against Rape
P.O. Box 02084
Columbus, OH 43202
614-291-9751

Committee for Children
Seattle Institute for Child Advocacy
172 20th Avenue
Seattle, WA 98122
206-322-5050

Illusion Theater
The Touch Continuum
528 Hennepin Avenue South, #704
Minneapolis, MN 55403
612-339-4944

National Committee for the Prevention of Child Abuse
332 South Michigan Avenue, Suite 1250
Chicago, IL 60604-4357
312-663-3520

SEXUAL ASSAULT SERVICES

Following is a sample listing of sexual assault services from the fifty states. A more complete list of victim services can be obtained from:

The National Organization for Victim Assistance
717 D Street N.W.
Washington, DC 20004
202-393-NOVA

ALABAMA

Rape Response Program
3600 8th Avenue South
Birmingham, AL 35222
205-323-7273

ALASKA

Standing Together against Rape
111 East 13th Street
Anchorage, AK 99510
907–276–7273

ARIZONA

Center against Sexual Assault (CASA)
555 North 7th
Phoenix, AZ 85103

ARKANSAS

Rape Crisis, Inc.
P. O. Box 5181, Hillcrest Station
Little Rock, AR 72205
501–375–5181

CALIFORNIA

Bay Area Women against Rape
1515 Webster
Oakland, CA 94612
415–465–3890

COLORADO

Health and Hospitals Mental Health Program
Social Services Department
West 8th Avenue and Cherokee
Denver, CO 80204
303–893–7001

CONNECTICUT

Hartford YWCA Sexual Assault Crisis Service
135 Broad Street
Hartford, CT 06105
203–522–6666

DELAWARE

Rape Crisis Center
P. O. Box 1507
Wilmington, DE 19899
302-658-5011

FLORIDA

Rape Treatment Center
1611 Northwest 12th Avenue
Miami, FL 33136
305-325-6949

GEORGIA

Rape Crisis Center
Grady Memorial Hospital
80 Butler Street Southeast
Atlanta, GA 30335
404-588-4861

IDAHO

Rape Crisis Alliance
720 West Washington Street
Boise, ID 83702
208-345-7273

ILLINOIS

Chicago Women against Rape
Loop YWCA
37 South Wabash
Chicago, IL 60603
312-372-6600

INDIANA

Crisis Intervention Service
Community Hospital of Indianapolis
1500 North Ritter Avenue
Indianapolis, IN 46219
317-353-5947

IOWA

Story County Sexual Assault Center
P. O. Box 1150
ISU Station
Ames, Iowa 50010

KANSAS

Wichita Area Rape Center
1801 East 10th Street
Wichita, KS 67214
316-263-3002

KENTUCKY

Lexington Rape Crisis Center
P. O. Box 1603
Lexington, KY 40592
606-253-2511

LOUISIANA

YWCA Rape Crisis Service
601 South Jefferson Davis Parkway
New Orleans, LA 70801
504-483-8888

MAINE

Rape Crisis Center
193 Middle Street
Portland, ME 04101
207-774-3613

MARYLAND

Center for Victims of Sexual Assault
128 West Franklin Street
Baltimore, MD 21201
301-366-7273

MASSACHUSETTS

Rape Crisis Intervention Program
Beth Israel Hospital
330 Brookline Avenue
Boston, MA 02215
617-735-3337

MICHIGAN

Rape Counseling Center
4201 St. Antoine, Room 828
Detroit, MI 48201
313-224-4487

MINNESOTA

Sexual Violence Center
1222 West 31st Street
Minneapolis, MN 55408
612-824-5555

MISSISSIPPI

Gulf Coast Women's Center
P. O. Box 333
Biloxi, MS 39533
601-435-1968

MISSOURI

Rape Crisis Assistance
P. O. Box 1611
Springfield, MO 65805
417-866-1969

MONTANA

Billings Rape Task Force
1245 North 29th Street, Room 218
Billings, MT 59101
406-259-6506

NEBRASKA

Rape/Spouse Abuse Crisis Center
1133 H Street
Lincoln, NE 68508
402-475-7273

NEVADA

Community Action against Rape
749 Veterans Memorial Drive, Room 79
Las Vegas, NV 89101
702-735-7111

NEW HAMPSHIRE

Women's Crisis Line
72 Concord Street
Manchester, NH 03101
603-668-2299

NEW JERSEY

Sexual Assault Rape Analysis Unit
22 Franklin Street
Newark, NJ 07102
202-733-7273

NEW MEXICO

Rape Crisis Center
Box 2822
Santa Fe, NM 87501
505-982-4667

NEW YORK

Rape Crisis Program
St. Vincent's Hospital
153 West 11th Street
New York, NY 10011
212-790-8068

NORTH CAROLINA

Rape Crisis Center
401 East Whitiker Mill Road
Raleigh, NC 27650
919-755-6661

NORTH DAKOTA

Rape and Abuse Crisis Center
P. O. Box 1655
Fargo, ND 58107
701-293-7273

OHIO

Women Helping Women
216 East 9th Street
Cincinnati, OH 45202
513-381-5610

OKLAHOMA

Rape Crisis Center
YWCA
135 Northwest 19th Street
Oklahoma City, OK 73118
405-524-7273

OREGON

Rape Victim Advocate Project
804 Multnomah County Courthouse
Portland, OR 97204
503-248-5059

PENNSYLVANIA

Women Organized against Rape
1220 Sansom Street
Philadelphia, PA 19107
215-922-3434

RHODE ISLAND

Rape Crisis Center
235 Promenade Street, Room 202
Providence, RI 02908
401-941-2400

SOUTH CAROLINA

People against Rape
150 Meeting Street
Charleston, SC 29401
803-722-7273

SOUTH DAKOTA

Rape Education, Advocacy and Counseling Team (REACT)
Brookings Women's Center
802 11th Avenue
Brookings, SD 57006
605-688-4518

TENNESSEE

Rape Crisis Center
P. O. Box 2262
Knoxville, TN 37901
615-522-7273

TEXAS

Rape Crisis Center
P. O. Box 35728
Dallas, TX 75235
214-521-1020

UTAH

Women's Crisis Shelter
505 27th Street
Ogden, UT 84403
801-392-7273

VERMONT

Women's Rape Crisis Center
P. O. Box 92
Burlington, VT 05401

VIRGINIA

YWCA Women's Victim Advocacy Program
6 North 5th Street
Richmond, VA 23219
804-643-0888

WASHINGTON

Seattle Rape Relief
1825 South Jackson, #102
Seattle, WA 98144
206-632-7273

WEST VIRGINIA

Sexual Assault Information Center
1036 Quarrier Street, #317
Charleston, WV 25301
304-344-9834

WISCONSIN

Rape Crisis Center
312 East Wilson Street
Madison, WI 53703
608-251-7273

WYOMING

Western Wyoming Mental Health
115 West Snowking Avenue
P. O. Box 1868
Jackson, WY 83001
807-733-2046

Notes

CHAPTER 2. THE STATISTICS ABOUT SEXUAL VIOLENCE

1. As in S. Kirson Weinberg, *Incest Behavior* (Secaucus, NJ: Citadel Press, 1955).
2. Diana E. H. Russell, *Sexual Exploitation: Rape, Child Sexual Abuse, and Workplace Harassment*, vol. 155 of the *Sage Library of Social Research* (Beverly Hills, CA: Sage Publications, 1984), 31. Russell's work is extremely important in the field of contending statistics about rape. It is the first work done with a randomly generated sample of women rather than with volunteers or other particular populations. Therefore it is more likely to represent the population at large. Second, Russell's interviewers were specifically trained to be sensitive to the dynamics of sexual assault so that the people interviewed would not be silenced by callousness or misunderstanding of the interviewer. Third, Russell's workers were chosen to be representative of the racial and ethnic minority composition of the sample population so that racism would be less likely to skew results. See also fn. 5 below.
3. Recent revisions in the law codes often include many more areas of possible damage and abuse than the earlier laws. Progressive legal codes use the language of intrafamilial sexual abuse rather than incest so that stepparents or live-in sexual partners of a parent may be charged. Furthermore, in some states sexual exploitation by counselors and therapists is now included in the criminal sexual conduct laws. See the article by Jeanette Milgrom and Gary Schoener in part three below.
4. Allan Griswold Johnson, "On the Prevalence of Rape in the United States," *Signs* 6 (Autumn 1980): 145.
5. This research and many other findings are reported in Diana E. H. Russell, *Rape in Marriage* (New York: Macmillan, 1982) 87–116.
6. A. Nicholas Groth and H. Jean Birnbaum, *Men Who Rape: The Psychology of the Offender* (New York: Plenum Press, 1979), 222–23. See also Russell, *Sexual Exploitation*, 101–102.
7. This evidence is reviewed and summarized by Judith Lewis Herman, *Father-Daughter Incest* (Cambridge, MA: Harvard University Press, 1982).
8. Diana E. H. Russell, "The Incidence and Prevalence of Intrafamilial and Extrafamilial Sexual Abuse of Female Children," *Child Abuse and Neglect* 7 (1983): 133–46.
9. Karin C. Meiselman, *Incest: A Psychological Study of Causes and Effects with Treatment Recommendations* (San Francisco: Jossey-Bass, 1978), 67, 165. Note that in this study (with a much smaller sample than Russell's), no disclosure occurred in 72 percent of the cases; in 17 percent, after disclosure or discovery the case reached at least the preliminary stages of trial; in 11 percent, nothing happened even though reporting did occur (177).
10. Groth, *Men Who Rape*, 101–3; Nicholas Groth, "The Incest Offender," in

Handbook of Clinical Intervention in Child Sexual Abuse, ed. Suzanne M. Sgroi (Lexington, MA: Lexington Books, 1982), 226.

11. Russell, *Sexual Exploitation,* 88–99.
12. See the evidence surveyed in Catharine A. MacKinnon, *Sexual Harassment of Working Women* (New Haven: Yale University Press, 1979), 26–27.
13. Merit Systems Protection Board, *Sexual Harassment in the Federal Workplace: Is It a Problem?* (Washington, D.C.: Office of Merit Systems Review and Studies, U.S. Government Printing Office, 1981).
14. Billie Wright Dziech and Linda Weiner, *The Lecherous Professor: Sexual Harassment on Campus* (Boston: Beacon Press, 1984), 15.

CHAPTER 4. RECOGNIZING THE SYMPTOMS AND CONSEQUENCES OF SEXUAL ASSAULT AND ABUSE

1. Ann Wolbert Burgess and Lynda Lytle Holmstrom, *Rape: Crisis and Recovery* (Bowie, MD: Prentice-Hall, 1978).

CHAPTER 5. ELDER ABUSE: THE VIEW FROM THE CHANCEL

1. Research that led to the development of this chapter was funded by a grant from the Minneapolis Foundation. See Jane A. Boyajian, Barbara Chester, and Nancy Biele, *Strategies for Preventing and Responding to Elder Abuse: A Report to the Minneapolis Foundation,* available from the Sexual Violence Center, 1222 W. 31st St., Minneapolis, MN 55408.
2. House of Representatives Select Committee on Aging, *Elder Abuse: A National Disgrace—Introduction and Executive Summary,* Washington, D.C.: United States Government Printing Office, (June 1985), 1.
3. Helen O'Malley, *Elder Abuse in Massachusetts: A Survey of Professionals and Paraprofessionals* (Boston: Legal Research & Services for the Elderly, 1979).
4. Donna J. Shell, *Protection of the Elderly: A Study of Elder Abuse,* (Winnipeg: Manitoba Council on Aging and the Manitoba Association on Gerontology, 1982) 39.
5. Quoted by Carol R. Watkins, *Victims, Aggressors, and the Family Secret* (St. Paul, MN: Minnesota Department of Public Welfare, 1982), 39. The Attorney General's Task Force on Family Violence (William L. Hart, Chair) notes similar findings in its September 1984 *Final Report* (Washington, D.C.: U.S. Government Printing Office, 1984).
6. Problems of method often hamper studies of crime victimization among the elderly. For example, the studies on sexual abuse by Diana E. H. Russell, which we praise often in this volume, were conducted with heads of households, ignoring the elder who might be living in a dependent situation.
7. A fuller discussion of quality of life issues and implications for the practice of formal and informal care providers is found in Jane A. Boyajian, "Living with the Grey: Ethical Issues and Aging," in *Ethics and Aging,* ed. J. Thornton and E. Winkler (Vancouver: University of British Columbia Press, 1987).
8. E. E. Lau and J. I. Kosberg, "Abuse of the Elderly by Informal Care Providers," *Aging* 299–300 (Sept.-Oct., 1979): 10–15.
9. Shell, *Protection of the Elderly,* 39.

10. William L. Hart, *Report of the Attorney General's Task Force on Family Violence* (Washington, D.C.: Office of the Attorney General, 1984), iii.
11. For further discussion, see Boyajian, Chester, and Biele, *Strategies for Preventing and Responding to Elder Abuse*, 17–21.
12. Watkins, *Victims*, 40–41.
13. See, for instance, Dorothy J. Hicks and Denise M. Moon, "Sexual Assault of the Older Woman," in *Victims of Sexual Aggression: Treatment of Children, Women, and Men*, ed. Irving R. Stuart and Joanne G. Greer (New York: Van Nostrand Reinhold, 1985), 180–96.
14. From the Missouri Department of Social Services, Division of Aging, *Indicators of Abuse, Neglect, and Exploitation of the Elderly* (1981).

CHAPTER 8. A COMMENTARY ON RELIGIOUS ISSUES IN FAMILY VIOLENCE

1. Chaim Stern, ed. *Gates of Repentance: High Holy Days Prayer Book* (New York: Central Conference of American Rabbis, 1978), 67.
2. Moses Maimonides, "On Forbidden Relations," "Yad Ishut" XIV–2, *Mishneh Torah*, (New Haven: Yale University Press, Yale Judaica Series), 87.
3. Maimonides was a Jewish philosopher (1135–1204) whose *Mishneh Torah* became a standard work of Jewish law and a major source for all subsequent codification of Jewish law.
4. Maimonides, "Yad Ishut" XIV–8, 89.
5. Maurice Lamm, *Jewish Way in Love and Marriage* (New York: Harper & Row, 1982), 157.
6. Rabbi Solomon Ganzfried, ed., *Code of Jewish Law* (*Kitzur Shulchan Aruch*), trans. Hyman E. Golden (New York: Hebrew Publishing Co., 1961).

CHAPTER 9. A THEOLOGICAL PERSPECTIVE ON SEXUAL ASSAULT

1. Quoted in Anne E. Jordheim, "Helping Victims of Rape," *The Lutheran* (Oct. 1, 1980), 8.
2. Quoted in Susan Brownmiller, *Against Our Wills: Men, Women, and Rape* (New York: Simon & Schuster, 1975), 400.
3. Ann Wolbert Burgess and Lynda Lytle Holmstrom, *Rape: Victims of Crisis* (Bowie, MD: Robert J. Brady, 1974), 3.
4. Quoted in Diana E. H. Russell, *The Politics of Rape: The Victim's Perspective* (New York: Stein & Day, 1975), 18–19.
5. Ibid., 19.
6. Ibid., 48. Poignantly, this woman continued, "And I was also very sure that God was watching the whole thing and shaking his head and saying what a horrible person I was for allowing myself to get raped."
7. Nancy Gager and Cathleen Schurr, *Sexual Assault: Confronting Rape in America* (New York: Grosset & Dunlap, 1976), 85.
8. Russell, *Politics of Rape*, 94, 77.
9. Mary Douglas, *Purity and Danger: An Analysis of Concepts of Pollution and Taboo* (London: Routledge & Kegan Paul, 1970), 12, 48.
10. Gager and Schurr, *Sexual Assault*, 106–107.

11. Burgess and Holmstrom, *Rape: Victims of Crisis,* 45–46.
12. Russell, *Politics of Rape,* 47, 135, 91.
13. Sandra Butler, *Conspiracy of Silence: The Trauma of Incest* (New York: Bantam Books, 1979), 33.
14. Erik Erikson, *Childhood and Society,* 2d ed. (New York: W. W. Norton, 1963), 250.
15. Quoted in Butler, *Conspiracy of Silence,* 162–163, 166.
16. Ann Wolbert Burgess and Lynda Lytle Holmstrom, "Recovery from Rape and Prior Life Stress," *Research in Nursing and Health* 1 (1978): 170.
17. Adrienne Rich, "Natural Resources," in *The Dream of a Common Language: Poems, 1974–1977* (New York: W. W. Norton, 1978).

CHAPTER 11. STANDING BY VICTIMS OF SEXUAL VIOLENCE: PASTORAL ISSUES

1. Because most victims are women, I here use the feminine pronoun. While acknowledging that men too are sexually assaulted, I wish here to bring emphatically to the reader's attention the (often unseen) victim.
2. Apparently some of us still reflect this view. See for instance, Kenneth G. Smith and Floy M. Smith, *Learning to be a Woman* (Intervarsity Press, 1978). This workbook for women is intended to reinforce our "proper" role in family, church, and society. Thus 1 Cor. 7:1–6 is interpreted as a lesson to women on frigidity.
3. *The Book of Common Prayer* (1928 version) illustrates what our hymnbooks and liturgies convey. The prayer "For All Poor, Homeless, and Neglected Folk" in the family prayer section reads: "O God . . . Mightily befriend innocent sufferers, and sanctify to them the endurance of their wrongs."
4. For further discussion, see London Rape Crisis Centre, *Sexual Violence: The Reality for Women* (London: The Women's Press Handbook Series, 1984), 88ff.
5. It may be excruciatingly painful and frightening, for instance, to return daily to the parking garage at work where one was assaulted. See especially "The Power of Consciousness: A Collage," Part Four of Susan Griffin's *Rape: The Power of Consciousness* (San Francisco: Harper & Row, 1979).
6. Diana E. H. Russell, *The Secret Trauma: Incest in the Lives of Girls and Women* (New York: Basic Books, 1986), 219.
7. Sissela Bok, *Secrets: On the Ethics of Concealment and Revelation* (New York: Vintage Books, 1983), 79–81. See also the excellent discussion on the ethical concepts of listening to and telling secrets, 81–85.
8. Martha Wolfenstein, *Disaster* (Glencoe, IL: The Free Press, 1957).
9. Jean Baker Miller, *Toward a New Psychology of Women* (Boston: Beacon Press, 1976), Chapter One, "Domination-Subordination."
10. Carol Gilligan, *In a Different Voice* (Cambridge, MA: Harvard University Press, 1982), 149.
11. Susan Brownmiller, *Femininity* (New York: Simon & Schuster, 1984), presents a powerful analysis of the ways girl children learn femininity/dependence.
12. Griffin, *Rape: The Power of Consciousness,* 10.
13. Donna Schaper, "Imbalance of Power," *Sojourners* 10 (November 28, 1981), 27.
14. Bernard Loomer, "Two Kinds of Power," *Criterion,* (Winter 1976), 29.

CHAPTER 13. SHARING THE CRISIS OF RAPE: COUNSELING THE MATES AND FAMILIES OF VICTIMS

1. D. Silverman, "First Do No More Harm: Female Rape Victims and the Male Counselor," *American Journal of Orthopsychiatry* 47 (1977): 91–96.
2. Ann Wolbert Burgess and Lynda Lytle Holmstrom, "Rape Trauma Syndrome," *American Journal of Psychiatry* 131 (1974): 981–86.
3. Menachem Amir, *Patterns of Forcible Rape* (Chicago: University of Chicago Press, 1971).
4. E. Bassuk, et al., "Organizing a Rape Crisis Program in a General Hospital," *Journal of the American Medical Women's Association* 3 (1975): 486–90.
5. Susan Brownmiller, *Against Our Wills: Men, Women, and Rape* (New York: Simon & Schuster, 1975).
6. S. Sutherland and D. Scherl, "Patterns of Response Among Victims of Rape," *American Journal of Orthopsychiatry* 40 (1970): 503–11.
7. E. Lindemann, "Symptomatology and Management of Acute Grief," *American Journal of Psychiatry* 101 (1944): 141–56.
8. M. Notman and C. Nadelson, "The Rape Victim: Psychodynamic Considerations," *American Journal of Psychiatry* 133 (1976): 408–12.
9. Sutherland and Scherl, "Patterns of Response."
10. Ibid.
11. Burgess and Holmstrom, *Rape: Victims of Crisis* (Bowie, MD: Robert J. Brady, 1974); L. Schultz, ed., *Rape Victimology* (Springfield, IL: Charles C. Thomas, 1975).
12. Burgess and Holmstrom, "Coping Behavior of the Rape Victim," *American Journal of Psychiatry* 133 (1976): 413–18.
13. D. Winnicott, *The Maturational Processes and the Facilitating Environment* (New York: International University Press, 1965), 47.
14. R. Lazarus, *Psychological Stress and the Coping Process* (New York: McGraw-Hill, 1966).

CHAPTER 15. SEXUAL HARASSMENT: VICTIM RESPONSES

1. J. Chapman and G. C. Chapman, "Sexual Harassment of Women in Employment Parts One-Three," *Response: Journal of the Center for Women Policy Studies,* (Part One, Mar.-Apr. 1984: 3–13; Part Two, May-June 1984: 3–13; Part Three, Fall 1984: 8–11.) See also Merit Systems Protection Board, *Sexual Harassment in the Federal Workplace: Is It a Problem?* (Washington, D.C.: Office of Merit Systems Review and Studies, U.S. Government Printing Office, 1981); Diana E. H. Russell, *Sexual Exploitation: Rape, Child Sexual Abuse, and Workplace Harassment,* vol. 155 of the *Sage Library of Social Research* (Beverly Hills, CA: Sage Publications, 1984).
2. Lin Farley, *Sexual Shakedown: The Sexual Harassment of Women on the Job* (New York: Warner, 1978).
3. Shakti Gawain, *Creative Visualization* (New York: Bantam Books, 1979); Melita Denning and Osborne Phillips, *Practical Guide to Creative Visualization* (St. Paul, MN: Llewellyn Publications, 1985).

CHAPTER 16. BEYOND BELIEF: THE RELUCTANT DISCOVERY OF INCEST

1. Suzanne Sgroi, "Introduction: A National Needs Assessment for Protecting Child Victims of Sexual Assault," in *Sexual Assault of Children and Adolescents,* ed. A. W. Burgess, A. N. Groth, L. L. Holmstrom, and S. M. Sgroi (Lexington, MA: Lexington Books, 1978), xv.
2. Louise Armstrong, "The Cradle of Sexual Politics: Incest," in *Women's Sexual Experience: Exploring the Dark Continent,* ed. M. Kirkpatrick (New York: Plenum Press, 1982).
3. The use of the feminine pronoun does not assume that victims of sexual abuse are necessarily female. Emerging evidence indicates that boys are at least as likely to be sexually exploited as girls, and that they are even more frequently trapped in silence. Boys, like girls, are most often victimized by trusted men. Unlike girls, boys are more likely to be victimized by someone outside the immediate family. In many cases, the use of a feminine pronoun can be considered generic for boys as well as girls.
4. This figure is a rough but conservative estimate derived from David Finkelhor's date (1980), assuming approximately 10 percent of women are survivors of child sexual abuse contact with an adult male relative, and assuming an adult female population of fifty million.
5. J. Landis, "Experiences of 500 Children with Adult Sexual Deviants," *Psychiatric Quarterly Supplement* 30 (1956): 91–109; J. Gagnon, "Female Child Victims of Sex Offenses," *Social Problems* 13 (1965): 180; D. Finkelhor, *Sexually Victimized Children* (New York: The Free Press, 1979), 53.
6. Finkelhor, *Sexually Victimized Children.*
7. Michael Rothenberg, "Is There an Unconscious National Conspiracy Against Children in the United States?" *Clinical Pediatrics* 19 (1980): 10–24.
8. Finkelhor, *Sexually Victimized Children;* Ann Wolbert Burgess and Lynda Lytle Holmstrom, "Sexual Trauma of Children and Adolescents: Pressure, Sex, and Secrecy," *Nursing Clinics of North America* 10 (1975): 551–63.
9. Leonard Shengold, "Child Abuse and Deprivation: Soul Murder," *Journal of the American Psychoanalytic Association* 27 (1979): 539.
10. S. Ferenczi, "Confusion of Tongues between Adults and the Child," in *Final Contributions to the Problems and Methods of Psychoanalysis* (1933; reprint, New York: Basic Books, 1955), 163.
11. Barbara Myers, "Incest: If You Think the Word is Ugly, Take a Look at the Effects," in *Sexual Abuse of Children: Selected Readings,* ed. K. MacFarlane, B. Jones, and L. Jenstrom (Washington D.C.: National Center on Child Abuse and Neglect, Department of Health and Human Services, U.S. Government Printing Office, 1981), 100.
12. Gagnon, "Female Child Victims," and Finkelhor, *Sexually Victimized Children.*
13. Suzanne Sgroi, "Sexual Molestation of Children: The Last Frontier in Child Abuse," *Children Today* 4 (1975): 20.
14. Sigmund Freud, "The Aetiology of Hysteria," in *Collected Papers,* vol. 1 (1896; reprint, London: Hogarth Press, 1953).
15. M. Bonaparte, A. Freud, and E. Kris, eds., *The Origins of Psychoanalysis: Letters to Wilhelm Fliess, Drafts, and Notes: 1877–1902* (New York: Basic Books, 1954), 79–80, quoted in Florence Rush, "The Freudian Coverup," *Chrysalis* 1 (1977): 34–35.

16. Bonaparte, et al., *Origins of Psychoanalysis*, 215–17, quoted in Rush, "Freudian Coverup," 37.
17. Sigmund Freud, *The Complete Introductory Lectures of Psychoanalysis* (1933; reprint, New York: Norton, 1966), 584.
18. Joseph Peters, "Children Who Are Victims of Sexual Assault and the Psychology of Offenders," *American Journal of Psychiatry* 30 (1976): 401, 402, 407–8, 421.
19. D. Finkelhor, "Risk Factors in the Sexual Victimization of Children," *Child Abuse and Neglect* 4 (1980): 265–73.
20. R. Summit and J. Kryso, "Sexual Abuse of Children: A Clinical Spectrum," *American Journal of Orthopsychiatry* 48 (1978): 237–51.
21. R. Summit, "Sexual Child Abuse, the Psychotherapist, and the Team Concept," in *Dealing with Child Sexual Abuse*, ed. H. Donovan and R. J. Beran (Chicago: National Committee for Prevention of Child Abuse, 1978), 2:19–33.
22. H. Giaretto, "Humanistic Treatment of Father-Daughter Incest," in *Child Abuse and Neglect: The Family and the Community*, ed. R. E. Helfer and C. H. Kempe (Cambridge, MA: Ballinger, 1976), 143–57; H. Giaretto and A. Giaretto, "Coordinated Community Treatment of Incest," in *Sexual Assault of Children and Adolescents*, ed. Burgess, et al. (Lexington, MA.: D.C. Heath & Co, 1980), 231–40.
23. Giaretto, "Humanistic Treatment," 155.
24. Giaretto and Giaretto, "Coordinated Community Treatment."
25. L. Berliner and D. Stevens, "Special Techniques for Child Witnesses," in *The Sexual Victimology of Youth*, ed. L. G. Shultz (Springfield, IL: Charles C. Thomas, 1979).
26. Sgroi, "Introduction," xx–xxi.

CHAPTER 17. CONFIDENTIALITY AND MANDATORY REPORTING: A CLERGY DILEMMA?

1. Sissela Bok, "The Limits of Confidentiality," *The Hastings Center Report* (February 1983), 24–25.
2. Summary of notes provided by Seth Dawson, Prosecuting Attorney of Snohomish County, May 1984.
3. Bok, "Limits of Confidentiality," 26.
4. Ibid., 30.

CHAPTER 18. RESPONDING TO CLIENTS WHO HAVE BEEN SEXUALLY EXPLOITED BY COUNSELORS, THERAPISTS, AND CLERGY

1. As of 1986 sexual exploitation by a counselor or therapist is a criminal offence is Minnesota and Wisconsin. Thus in Minnesota, where we work, an offending counselor may be charged with criminal sexual conduct in the third or fourth degree. If found guilty, the counselor may be sentenced to a jail term up to five or ten years and/or fines up to $10,000 or $20,000. Claiming that sexual contact is part of the client's treatment program is termed a "therapeutic deception" in these laws. Consent of the client is not a defense. Since counse-

lors across the nation are becoming increasingly aware of this abuse, in the future we expect to see it become a criminal offence in other states also.
2. The "Client Bill of Rights" is adapted from a similar document written at the Sexual Violence Center in Hennepin County, Minnesota.

CHAPTER 19. WHAT CAN THE CHURCH DO?

1. Excerpted and adapted from Peggy Halsey, *Abuse in the Family: Breaking the Church's Silence* (New York: United Methodist Church Office of Women in Crisis, 1984), 7–9.

CHAPTER 20. RESOURCES FOR RITUAL AND RECUPERATION

1. Joseph Epes Brown, *The Sacred Pipe* (Norman, OK: University of Oklahoma Press, 1953), 115.
2. Brown, *The Sacred Pipe*, 31–32.
3. Brown, *The Sacred Pipe*, 31.
4. John Neihardt, *Black Elk Speaks* (New York: William Morrow, 1932; reprint, Lincoln, NE.: University of Nebraska Press, Bison Books, 1961), 198–200.
5. Brown, *The Sacred Pipe*, 57.
6. Brown, *The Sacred Pipe*, 59.
7. Originally from the Dakota Hymnal; may be found in the *United Methodist Hymnal* (Nashville: Methodist Publishing House, 1964), 40.
8. A prayer by Ojibwe medicine women when gathering plants. From Basil Johnston, *Ojibwe Heritage* (Toronto, Ont.: McClelland & Stewart, 1976), 82.

Selected Bibliography by Subject

RAPE

Amir, Menachem. *Patterns of Forcible Rape.* Chicago: University of Chicago Press, 1971.

Bart, Pauline, and Patricia H. O'Brien. *Stopping Rape: Successful Survival Strategies.* New York: Pergamon Press, 1985

Beneke, Timothy. *Men on Rape: What They Have to Say About Sexual Violence.* New York: St. Martin's Press, 1982.

Brownmiller, Susan. *Against Our Wills: Men, Women, and Rape.* New York: Simon & Schuster, 1975.

Burgess, Ann Wolbert, and Lynda Lytle Holmstrom. *Rape: Crisis and Recovery.* Bowie, MD: Robert J. Brady, 1974; rev. ed., Englewood Cliffs, NJ: Prentice-Hall, 1978.

———. "Recovery from Rape and Prior Life Stress." *Research in Nursing and Health* 1 (1978): 165–174.

Clark, Lorenne, and Debra Lewis. *Rape: The Price of Coercive Sexuality.* Toronto: The Woman's Press, 1977.

Connell, Noreen, and Cassandra Wilson, eds. *Rape: The First Sourcebook for Women.* New York: New American Library, 1974.

Gager, Nancy, and Cathleen Schurr. *Sexual Assault: Confronting Rape in America.* New York: Grosset & Dunlap, 1976.

Griffin, Susan. *Rape: The Power of Consciousness.* San Francisco: Harper & Row, 1979.

Groth, A. Nicholas, with Jean Birnbaum. *Men Who Rape: The Psychology of the Offender.* New York: Plenum Press, 1979.

Katz, Judy H. *No Fairy Godmothers, No Magic Wands: The Healing Process after Rape.* Saratoga, CA.: R & E Publishers, 1984.

Kirkpatrick, Martha, ed. *Women's Sexual Experience: Explorations of the Dark Continent.* New York: Plenum Press, 1982.

Ledray, Linda. *Recovering from Rape.* New York: Henry Holt & Co., 1986.

Russell, Diana E. H. *The Politics of Rape: The Victim's Perspective.* New York: Stein & Day, 1975.

———. *Sexual Exploitation: Rape, Child Sexual Abuse, and Workplace Harassment.* Vol. 155 of *Sage Library of Social Research.* Beverly Hills, CA: Sage Publications, 1984.

———. *The Secret Trauma: Incest in the Lives of Girls and Women.* New York: Basic Books, 1986.

Snitow, Ann, Christine Stansell, and Sharon Thompson, eds. *Powers of Desire: The Politics of Sexuality.* New York: Monthly Review Press, 1983.

Vance, Carol, ed. *Pleasure and Danger: Exploring Female Sexuality.* Boston: Routledge & Kegan Paul, 1984.

Wilson, Carolyn F., comp. *Violence Against Women: An Annotated Bibliography.* Boston: G. K. Hall, 1981.

DOMESTIC VIOLENCE

Clarke, Rita-Lou. *Pastoral Care of Battered Women.* Philadelphia: Westminster, 1986.

Dobash, R. Emerson, and Russell Dobash. *Violence Against Wives.* New York: The Free Press, 1979.

Fortune, Marie, and Denise Hormann. *Family Violence: A Workshop Manual for Rural Communities.* Seattle: Center for the Prevention of Sexual and Domestic Violence, 1980.

Halsey, Peggy. *Abuse in the Family: Breaking the Church's Silence.* New York: United Methodist Church Office of Women in Crisis, 1984.

Martin, Del. *Battered Wives.* San Francisco: Glide Publications, 1976.

NiCarthy, Ginny. *Getting Free: A Handbook for Women in Abusive Relationships.* Seattle: The Seal Press, 1982.

NiCarthy, Ginny, Karen Merriam, and Sandra Coffman, *Talking It Out: A Guide to Groups for Abused Women.* Seattle: The Seal Press, 1984.

Russell, Diana E. H. *Rape in Marriage.* New York: Macmillan, 1982.

Stacey, William A. and Anson Shupe. *The Family Secret: Domestic Violence in America.* Boston: Beacon Press, 1983.

Watkins, Carol R. *Victims, Aggressors, and the Family Secret.* St. Paul, MN: Minnesota Department of Public Welfare, 1982.

Working Together to Prevent Sexual and Domestic Violence. Newsletter of the Center for the Prevention of Sexual and Domestic Violence, 1914 North 34th Street, Suite 205, Seattle, WA 98103.

CHILD ABUSE

Allen, Charlotte Vale. *Daddy's Girl.* New York: Berkeley Books, 1982.

Angelou, Maya. *I Know Why the Caged Bird Sings.* New York: Bantam Books, 1970.

Bass, Ellen, and Louise Thornton, eds. *I Never Told Anyone: Writings by Women Survivors of Child Sexual Abuse.* New York: Harper & Row, 1983.

Burgess, Ann Wolbert, A. Nicholas Groth, Lynda Lytle Holmstrom, and Suzanne M. Sgroi, eds. *Sexual Assault of Children and Adolescents.* Lexington, MA: Lexington Books, 1978.

Butler, Sandra. *Conspiracy of Silence: The Trauma of Incest.* New York: Bantam, 1979.

Daugherty, Lynn B. *Why Me? Help for Victims of Child Sexual Abuse (Even If They Are Adults Now).* Racine, WI: Mother Courage Press, 1984.

Finkelhor, David. *Sexually Victimized Children.* New York: The Free Press, 1979.

Fortune, Marie M. *Sexual Abuse Prevention: A Study for Teenagers.* New York: United Church Press, 1984.

Forward, Susan, and Craig Buck. *Betrayal of Innocence: Incest and Its Devastation.* New York: Penguin Books, 1978.

Helfer, R. E., and C. H. Kempe, eds. *Child Abuse and Neglect: The Family and the Community.* Cambridge, MA: Ballinger, 1976.

Herman, Judith Lewis. *Father-Daughter Incest.* Cambridge, MA: Harvard University Press, 1981.

Kempe, C. H. and Ray E. Helfer, *The Battered Child.* Chicago: University of Chicago Press, 3rd. ed., 1980.

Janssen, Martha. *Silent Scream: I Am a Victim of Incest.* Philadelphia: Fortress Press, 1983.

Jones, B., and L. Jenstrom, eds. *Sexual Abuse of Children: Selected Readings.* Washington, D.C.: National Center on Child Abuse and Neglect, Department of Health and Human Services, U.S. Government Printing Office, 1981.

McNaron, Toni, and Yarrow Morgan, eds. *Voices in the Night: Women Speaking About Incest.* Minneapolis: Cleis Press, 1982.

Meiselman, Karin C. *Incest: A Psychological Study of Causes and Effects with Treatment Recommendations.* San Francisco: Jossey-Bass, 1978.

Plummer, Carol A. *Preventing Sexual Abuse: Activities and Strategies For Those Working with Children and Adolescents.* Holmes Beach, FL.: Learning Publications, 1984.

Rush, Florence. *The Best Kept Secret: Sexual Abuse of Children.* New York: McGraw-Hill, 1980.

Russell, Diana E. H. "The Incidence and Prevalence of Intrafamilial and Extrafamilial Sexual Abuse of Female Children." *Child Abuse and Neglect* 7 (1983): 133–46.

———. *The Secret Trauma: Incest in the Lives of Girls and Women.* New York: Basic Books, 1986.

———. *Sexual Exploitation: Rape, Child Sexual Abuse, and Workplace Harassment.* Vol. 155 of *Sage Library of Social Research.* Beverly Hills, CA: Sage Publications, 1984.

Sanford, Linda Tschirhart. *The Silent Children.* New York: McGraw-Hill, 1980.

Sgroi, Suzanne M., ed. *Handbook of Clinical Intervention in Child Sexual Abuse.* Lexington, MA: Lexington Books, 1982.

———. "Sexual Molestation of Children: The Last Frontier in Child Abuse." *Children Today* 4 (1975): 18–21, 44.

Shengold, Leonard. "Child Abuse and Deprivation: Soul Murder." *Journal of the American Psychoanalytic Association* 27 (1979): 533–59.

Sweet, Phyllis E. *Something Happened to Me.* Racine, WI: Mother Courage Press, 1981.

FILMS

Child Molestation: When to Say No. Glendale, CA: AIMS Instructional Media Services, 1977.

Incest: The Victim Nobody Believes. Sausalito, CA: J. Gary Mitchell Film Company, 1976.

No Easy Answers (for high school students). Available from MTI, 180 Wilmot Rd., Deerfield, IL 60015. Phone: 800–323–5343.

Shatter the Silence. Los Angeles: S-L Film Productions, 1979.

Touch (for gradeschool children). Available from MTI, 180 Wilmot Road, Deerfield, IL 60015. Phone: 800–323–5343.

Who Do You Tell? Available from MTI Teleprograms, 180 Wilmot Rd., Deerfield IL 60015 Phone: 800–323–5343.

ELDER ABUSE

Benedict, Helen. "The Older Victim" in Helen Benedict, *Recovery: How to Survive Sexual Assault.* Garden City, NY: Doubleday, 1985.

Block, Marilyn and Jan D. Sinnot. *The Battered Elder Syndrome: An Exploratory Study.* College Park, MD.: University of Maryland Center on Aging, 1979.

Boyajian, Jane A. "Living with the Grey: Ethical Issues and Aging." In *Ethics and Aging,* ed. J. Thornton and E. Winkler. Vancouver: University of British Columbia Press, 1987.

Boyajian, Jane A., Barbara Chester, and Nancy Biele. *Strategies for Preventing and Responding to Elder Abuse: A Report to the Minneapolis Foundation.* Available from the Sexual Violence Center, 1222 West 31st Street, Minneapolis, MN 55408.

Davis, Linda J. & Elaine M. Brody. *Rape and Older Women: A Guide to Prevention and Protection.* U.S. Department of Health, Education & Welfare Publication no. (ADM) 78–734. Washington, D.C.: U.S. Government Printing Office.

House of Representatives Select Committee on Aging. *Elder Abuse: A National Disgrace: Introduction and Executive Summary.* Washington, D.C.: U.S. Government Printing Office. 1985.

Lau, E. E., and J. I. Kosberg. "Abuse of the Elderly by Informal Care Providers." *Aging* (Sept.-Oct., 1979), 10–15.

O'Malley, Helen. *Elder Abuse in Massachusetts: A Survey of Professionals and Paraprofessionals.* Boston: Legal Research and Services for the Elderly, 1979.

Shell, Donna J. *Protection of the Elderly: A Study of Elder Abuse.* Winnipeg: Manitoba Council on Aging and the Manitoba Association on Gerontology, 1982.

Watkins, Carol R. *Victims, Aggressors, and the Family Secret.* St. Paul, MN: Minnesota Department of Public Welfare, 1982.

SEXUAL HARASSMENT

Chapman, J., and G. C. Chapman. "Sexual Harassment of Women in Employment:" *Response: Parts One-Three; Journal of the Center for Women Policy Studies* (2000 P. Street N.W., Suite 508, Washington, D.C., 20036). Part one, Mar.-Apr. 1984: 3–13. Part two, May-June 1984: 3–13. Part three, Fall 1984: 8–11.

Dziech, Billy, and Linda Wiener. *The Lecherous Professor: Sexual Harassment on Campus.* Boston: Beacon Press, 1984.

Farley, Lin. *Sexual Shakedown: The Sexual Harassment of Women on the Job.* New York: Warner, 1978.

MacKinnon, Catharine. *Sexual Harassment of Working Women.* New Haven: Yale University Press, 1979.

Merit Systems Protection Board. *Sexual Harassment in the Federal Workplace: Is It a Problem?* Washington, D.C. Office of Merit Systems Review and Studies, U.S. Government Printing Office, 1981.

Russell, Diana E. H. *Sexual Exploitation: Rape, Child Sexual Abuse, and Workplace Harassment.* Vol. 155 of *Sage Library of Social Research.* Beverly Hills, CA: Sage Publications, 1984.

COUNSELING AND PASTORAL CARE

Bellinger, Dottie, ed. and comp. *Sexual Assault, a Statewide Problem: A Procedural Manual for Law Enforcement, Medical, Human Services, and Legal Personnel.* Available from Minnesota Program for Victims of Sexual Assault, Department of Corrections, Minnesota State Documents, 117 University Avenue, St. Paul, MN 55155.

Bentley, Steven. "The Pastoral Challenge of an Abusive Situation." *Journal of Religion and Health* 23 (Winter 1984): 283–289.

Bowker, Lee H. "Battered Women and the Clergy: An Evaluation." *Journal of Pastoral Care* 36 (1982): 226–234.

Burgess, Ann Wolbert, and Lynda Lytle Holmstrom. "Rape Trauma Syndrome." *American Journal of Psychiatry* 131 (1974): 981–86.

Bussert, Joy. *Battered Women: From a Theology of Suffering to an Ethic of Empowerment.* New York: Division for Mission in North America, Lutheran Church in America, 1986.

Fortune, Marie. *Sexual Violence, the Unmentionable Sin: An Ethical and Pastoral Perspective.* New York: Pilgrim Press, 1983.

Meiselman, Karin C. *Incest: A Psychological Study of Causes and Effects with Treatment Recommendations.* San Francisco: Jossey-Bass, 1978.

Pellauer, Mary. "Counselling Victims of Family Violence." *Lutheran Partners* 2 (July-August 1986): 17–24.

———, ed. *Sexual Assault: A Training Manual for Advocates and Counselors.* Available from Minnesota Program for Victims of Sexual Assault, Department of Corrections, 450 Syndicate Avenue, St. Paul, MN 55104.

Sgroi, Suzanne M., ed. *Handbook of Clinical Intervention in Child Sexual Abuse*
Lexington, MA: Lexington Books, 1982.

Silverman, D. "First Do No More Harm: Female Rape Victims and the
Male Counselor." *American Journal of Orthopsychiatry* 47 (1977): 91–
96.

Stuart, Irving R., and Joanne G. Greer, eds. *Victims of Sexual Aggression:
Treatment of Children, Women, and Men.* New York: Van Nostrand
Reinhold, 1985.

Thistlethwaite, Susan Brooks. "Battered Women and the Bible: From
Subjection to Liberation." *Christianity and Crisis* (Nov. 16, 1981),
308–314.

Whiston, Sheila K. "Counseling Sexual Assault Victims: A Loss Model."
The Personnel and Guidance Journal Feb. 1981, 363–66.

THEOLOGY, SPIRITUALITY, AND LITURGY

Allen, Paula Gunn. *The Sacred Hoop: Recovering the Feminine in American
Indian Tradition.* Boston: Beacon Press, 1986.

Andolsen, Barbara Hilkert, Christine E. Gudorf, and Mary D. Pellauer,
eds. *Women's Consciousness, Women's Conscience: A Reader in Feminist
Ethics.* Minneapolis: Winston Press, 1985.

Brownmiller, Susan. *Against Our Wills: Men, Women, and Rape.* New York:
Simon & Schuster, 1975.

Bussert, Joy. *Battered Women: From a Theology of Suffering to an Ethic of Empowerment.* New York: Division for Mission in North America, Lutheran
Church in America, 1986.

Christ, Carol, and Judith Plaskow, eds. *Womanspirit Rising.* New York:
Harper & Row, 1979.

Clark, Linda, Marian Ronan, and Eleanor Walker. *Image-Breaking, Image-
Building: A Handbook for Creative Worship with Women of Christian Tradition.* New York: Pilgrim Press, 1981.

Daly, Mary. *Beyond God The Father: Toward a Philosophy of Women's Liberation.*
Boston: Beacon Press, 1973.

———. *Gyn/Ecology: The Meta-Ethics of Radical Feminism.* Boston: Beacon
Press, 1978.

Delacost, Frederique, and Felice Newman, eds. *Fight Back: Feminist Resistance to Male Violence.* Minneapolis: Cleis Press, 1981.

Douglas, Mary. *Purity and Danger: An Analysis of Concepts of Pollution and
Taboo.* London: Routledge & Kegan Paul, 1970.

Eaton, Evelyn. *The Shaman and the Medicine Wheel.* Wheeler, IL: Theosophi-
cal Publishing House, 1982.

Fiorenza, Elisabeth Schüssler. *In Memory of Her: A Feminist Theological Reconstruction of Christian Origins.* New York: Crossroad, 1983.

Fortune, Marie. *Sexual Violence, the Unmentionable Sin: An Ethical and Pastoral
Perspective.* New York: Pilgrim Press, 1983.

Gilligan, Carol. *In a Different Voice: Psychological Theory and Women's Development.* Cambridge, MA.: Harvard University Press, 1982.

Harrison, Beverly Wildung, with Carol Robb. *Making the Connections: Essays in Feminist Social Ethics.* Boston: Beacon Press, 1985.

Harrison, Beverly Wildung. *Our Right to Choose: Toward a New Ethic of Abortion.* Boston: Beacon Press, 1983.

Herman, Judith Lewis. *Father-Daughter Incest.* Cambridge, MA: Harvard University Press, 1981.

Iglehart, Hallie. *WomanSpirit: A Guide to Women's Wisdom.* San Francisco: Harper & Row, 1983.

Jordheim, Anna E. "Helping Victims of Rape." *The Lutheran* (Oct. 1, 1980), 8–9.

Mariechild, Diane. *Mother Wit: A Feminist Guide to Psychic Development.* Trumansburg, NY: The Crossing Press, 1981.

Mudflower Collective, The, (Katie G. Cannon, Beverly W. Harrison, Carter Heyward, Ada Maria Isasi-Diaz, Bess B. Johnson, Mary D. Pellauer, Nancy D. Richardson). *God's Fierce Whimsey: Christian Feminism and Theological Education.* New York: Pilgrim Press, 1985.

Ochs, Carol. *Women and Spirituality.* Totowa, NJ: Rowman & Allenheld, 1983.

Ruether, Rosemary Radford. *Sexism and God-Talk: Toward a Feminist Theology.* Boston: Beacon Press, 1983.

———. *Womanguides: Readings Toward a Feminist Theology.* Boston: Beacon Press, 1985.

———. *Women-Church: Theology and Practice.* San Francisco: Harper & Row, 1986.

Schechter, Susan. *Women and Male Violence: The Visions and Struggles of the Battered Women's Movement.* Boston: South End Press, 1982.

Shaffer, Carolyn R. "Spiritual Techniques for Re-Powering Survivors of Sexual Assault." In *The Politics of Women's Spirituality,* ed. Charlene Spretnak. Garden City, NY: Doubleday, Anchor Books, 1982.

Soelle, Dorothy. *Suffering.* Philadelphia: Fortress Press, 1975.

Spretnak, Charlene, ed. *The Politics of Women's Spirituality.* Garden City, NY: Doubleday, 1982.

Starhawk. *The Spiral Dance: A Rebirth of the Ancient Religion of the Great Goddess.* San Francisco: Harper and Row, 1979.

Thistlethwaite, Susan Brooks. "Battered Women and the Bible: From Subjection to Liberation." *Christianity and Crisis* (Nov. 16, 1981): 308–313.

Trible, Phyllis. *God and the Rhetoric of Sexuality.* Philadelphia: Fortress Press, 1978.

———. *Texts of Terror: Literary-Feminist Readings of Biblical Narratives.* Philadelphia: Fortress Press, 1984.

Wilson, Carolyn F., comp. *Violence Against Women: An Annotated Bibliography.* Boston: G. K. Hall, 1981.

About the Contributors

The Rev. Jane Boyajian, D. Min., is presently director of the Northwest Institute of Ethics and the Life Sciences. She has taught ethics at several theological seminaries and worked as a consultant in ethics. Major projects include curriculum development for the State of Washington and the State of Minnesota in the field of adult protective services and abuse. She writes widely on subjects of concern in ethics, bioethics and ministry; recent books include *Ethics in the Practice of Ministry.*

Gail Burress, Amelie Ratliff and Liz Schellberg were participants in the 1978 Seminary Quarter at Grailville, Loveland, Ohio, when they wrote "Psalm 137: An Interpretation."

Barbara Chester, Ph.D., previously served as executive director of the Sexual Violence Center, Minneapolis, MN. Her doctoral work in the field of psychology and genetics focused on criminal justice issues. She has taught and served widely in the field of sexual and domestic violence. She is presently the executive director of the Minnesota Center for Torture Victims, Minneapolis, MN.

The Rev. Marie Fortune has pioneered in bringing sexual and physical abuse issues to the attention of religious communities. She is executive director of the Center for the Prevention of Sexual and Domestic Violence, Seattle, WA. She has written widely on religion and abuse, including *Sexual Violence, The Unmentionable Sin: An Ethical and Pastoral Perspective.*

Ellen Goodman is a widely read syndicated columnist. Her latest book is *Keeping in Touch.*

Peggy Halsey is executive director of the Office of Ministries with Women in Crisis, Board of Global Missions of the United Methodist Church.

Daniel M. Hoeger is a graduate of Luther-Northwestern Theological Seminary and presently serves as a lay missionary in Japan.

Martha Janssen is a mother, writer, poet, and author of *The Silent Scream.* She lives in the Midwest and is very active in the Lutheran Church.

The Rev. Barbara Lundblad is a Lutheran parish pastor in New York City, a graduate of Yale Divinity School, and a songwriter and creative liturgist.

The Rev. Larry Mens is assistant director, Division of Indian Work of the Greater Minneapolis Council of Churches, and director of the Minneapolis Native American ministries of the United Methodist Church.

Jeanette Hofstee Milgrom, M. S. W., and *Gary Schoener,* licensed psychologist, have pioneered in the treatment of victims of sexual exploitation by counselors and therapists, including clergy. Since 1974 the Walk-In Counseling Center, Minneapolis, MN, where Gary is the executive director and Jeanette the director of consultation and training, has seen about six hundred clients of this abuse. They have been involved in consumer education, professional education, consultation to other organizations, and legislation regarding sexual exploitation by counselors.

Mary Pellauer, Ph.D., in 1976 taught the first seminary course ever on violence against women at McCormick Seminary in Chicago. She previously served as assistant professor of women in ministry at Union Theological Seminary in New York. Presently she is a paraprofessional sexual assault counselor and a freelance writer and speaker.

Chris Servaty, M.A., is a licensed psychologist on the staff of the Sexual Violence Center, Hennepin County, MN. She has been doing long-term therapy with victims of sexual assault and sexual abuse since 1981. She has also done therapy and conducted therapy groups with adolescents and mentally handicapped victims.

Ntozake Shange is a widely read black feminist poet. Among her many works are *For Colored Girls Who Have Considered Suicide When the Rainbow is Enuf* and *Nappy Edges.*

Daniel Silverman, M.D., is director of outpatient psychiatry services at Beth Israel Hospital, Boston, MA, and associate professor of psychiatry at Harvard University Medical School. He teaches and writes widely in the field of crisis intervention.

Roland Summit, M.D., is assistant clinical professor at the Community Consultation Service of Harborview Medical Center, Torrance, CA, and adjunct professor of psychiatry at U.C.L.A. He has pioneered in treatment programs for child victims of abuse.

The Rev. Diana Vezmar is director of Recovering Women Ministries, Minneapolis, MN, a mission project of the Presbytery of the Twin Cities area, providing counseling, worship, and spirituality groups for women in recovery from physical, sexual, chemical, and/or religious abuse.

The Rev. Cooper Wiggen is a pastor in the United Methodist Church and a member of the board of directors of the Sexual Violence Center, Hennepin County, MN.

The Rev. Patricia Wilson-Kastner, Ph.D., is a member of Trinity Church in Manhattan. She is professor of preaching at General Theological Seminary, New York, a priest in the Episcopal church, and the author of many articles and several books about church history and theology, including *Faith, Feminism and the Christ.*